Canada's 'Wars of Religion'

Richard Brown

Published by Authoring History

© Richard Brown, 2020

ISBN: 9798567499542

For Carol

Whose very presence makes writing so much easier

Contents

Acknowledgements

For those of us who spend our lives researching and writing (I was going to use the word 'choose' but then I have never felt I had a choice), there are somewhat contradictory feelings in doing what we do. On the one hand, there is an intense joy in doing the research and writing about things hopefully from a different perspective to others. On the other, there is a sadness in knowing that we will never complete our project and that ultimately what we do will always be tentative, a chimera and pallid reflection of reality. History is a hard task-master and a fickle mistress.

For all the changes that have occurred in education over the last decades, there remains no substitute for being in the classroom working with students and watching the spark of understanding develop into the flame of argument and analysis. In a world of change and chaos, it is the one constant and it is something of which throughout my career I have never tired. As always, I must acknowledge the contribution made by my students. Teaching history was a challenging experience for them and me: they challenged each other's views with often incisive argument and challenged me as well, something that all teachers relish as it gives us the opportunity of testing our ideas and modifying or even rejecting them when they are found wanting. For those of us who remember when teaching was once rather more than getting students through examinations or reaching often specious targets, the mutual enjoyment of discovering the past and understanding its histories is something I still savour.

Researching and writing about Canadian history is not something that was planned. I originally trained as a medieval historian though teaching in schools of necessity meant that my focus lay with modern and contemporary history. It was while researching the first volume of my *Rebellion Trilogy* that I took my first tentative steps into the histories of Canada. My interest was stimulated by this and the consideration of resistance and rebellion in Canada continued in the two subsequent volumes. There is always a risk in a historian of one nationality writing about the history of another. It is difficult enough to empathise with the past of one's own ancestors, let alone those in different communities. It was a risk I am glad that I took.

Preface

What historians eventually publish inevitably represents a small part of the research that they have undertaken. While researching the *Rebellions Trilogy* and the two volumes of *Rebellion in Canada, 1837-1885*, I drafted a series of papers on Canadian history that contributed to the published work.[1] This was part of the process of honing drafts of the books into a form that combined a narrative of the key events, their causation and consequences with a critique of that narrative by examining linkage and remembrance. The result was *'A Peaceable Kingdom': Essays on Nineteenth Century Canada* published in 2013 and hopefully a second volume of essays in 2023.

There is a widespread acceptance of the central role of rebellion in 1837-1838, 1866, 1869-1870 and 1885 in Canada's national history.[2] These populist uprisings, especially those of 1837 and 1838 provided justification for the development of responsible government or a critique of its application for particular ethnic groups. The issue was one of constitutional change and continuity across the 1837-1838 divide, and of progress towards Confederation in 1867. The rebellions were rarely seen outside this Whiggish view of constitutional progress and this was reflected in the different ways in which Canadians learned about the history of their country. For French-Canadians in Quebec, their history was traditionally taught to inspire loyalty to their homeland.[3] They pointed to the survival of their national language and

---

[1] Brown, Richard, *Three Rebellions: Canada 1837-1838, South Wales 1839 and Australia 1854*, (Clio Publishing), 2010, *Famine, Fenians and Freedom, 1840-1882*, (Clio Publishing), 2011, and *Resistance and Rebellion in the British Empire, 1600-1980*, (Clio Publishing), 2013. These were later extended as second editions: *Three Rebellions: Canada, South Wales and Australia*, (Authoring History), 2016, *Famine, Fenians and Freedom, 1830-1882*, (Authoring History), 2017, and *Disrupting the British World, 1600-1980*, (Authoring History), 2017.

[2] Berger, Carl, *The Writing of Canadian History: Aspects of English-Canadian Historical Writing since 1900*, (Oxford University Press), 1976, 2nd ed., (Toronto University Press), 1986, and Wright, Donald, *The Professionalization of History in English Canada*, (Toronto University Press), 2005, are important complementary studies.

[3] Cook, Ramsay, *Canada and the French-Canadian Question*, (Macmillan of Canada), 1966, considers the cultural significance of French-Canadian historiography; see also his *Watching Quebec: Selected Essays*, (McGill-Queen's University Press), 2005, pp. 1-16, 36-55, 98-115. Bouvier, Félix, *L'Histoire Nationale a l'École Québécoise Regards Sur Deux Siécle*, (Septentrion), 2012, Sarra-Bournet, Michel, and Bouvier, Félix, (eds.),

identity that had, elsewhere in North America, been submerged by the dominant English-speaking culture. It was their linguistic and cultural unity when faced with this cultural onslaught that allowed them to maintain their 'French' space and its continuance depends on maintaining this unity. This view is deeply rooted in the notion of a 'solemn pact' dating from the British Conquest of 1760 that established the terms on which the inhabitants of the former New France and their descendants were to live as a community even if they were obliged to share their homeland with the British. Its pervasive nature was especially evident in the aftermath of union in 1840 when French-Canadians were threatened by the assimilation project of Lord Durham. The historiographical consequence of this was that British and French-Canadians learned different and incompatible histories of Canada in which one group's history portrayed the other as an adversary. This lack of accepted history made it more difficult for the two groups to gel as a community.[4]

There is also a sense in which Canadian history has been used and abused, something highlighted by Donald Creighton in 1965.[5] He suggested that history could be 'used' for political purposes and that purging it of anything that smacked of the country's British heritage had led to two things. First, given the importance of Canada's British heritage, it created a sense of historical vacuum. Secondly, those who wanted to make radical changes to Canada's constitution sought to abuse history by twisting it into a 'myth' to justify their political stance. 'History', Creighton warned:

> ...must be defended against attempts to abuse it in the cause of change; we should be constantly on our guard against theories which either dismiss the past or give it a drastically new interpretation...A nation that repudiates or distorts its past runs a grave danger of forfeiting its future.[6]

L'Enseignement de l'histoire au début du XXIe siècle au Québec, (Septentrion), 2017, especially pp. 9-22, 44-52, summarises the current position of school history in Quebec.

[4] Black, Jeremy, *The Curse of History*, (Social Affairs Unit), 2008, pp. 205-206.

[5] Creighton, Donald, 'Confederation: The Use and Abuse of History', first delivered at Trent University, 4 November 1965, published in *Journal of Canadian Studies*, Vol. 1, (1), (1966) and reprinted in Creighton, Donald, *Towards the Discovery of Canada: Selected Essays*, (Macmillan), 1972, pp. 65-83.

[6] Creighton, Donald, 'The Use and Abuse of History', in ibid, Creighton, Donald, *Towards the Discovery of Canada: Selected Essays*, p. 83.

Creighton popularised a modernised version of the Canadian tradition of conservatism characterised by loyalty to traditional values, national unity and resistance to American domination. This view of Canada's history resulted in some aspects of Canada's past being included in its story, while others were excluded, ignored, or simply forgotten and this closed off avenues of enquiry that called it into question. It enabled those who favoured a centralised state to side-line the separatist aspirations of French-Canadians and the significance of their rebellions in 1837 and 1838. There was little place in this perspective for the principle of provincial rights. Mackenzie and his supporters could be caricatured not simply as disloyal to the British tradition but as pro-American, a position reinforced by the annexationists in the late 1840s. Theirs was a radically subversive view of the past that had no place in a country inexorably moving towards Confederation.[7]

These essays seek to unpick the notion of the 'peaceable kingdom' in the light of the religious and cultural violence that permeated Canada between 1800 and 1885. Far from having little impact on the development of Canada from a colonial state to a continental dominion, violence played a seminal influence in stimulating political and constitutional development. The British government's response to the rebellions in Upper and Lower Canada in 1837 and 1838 was to establish a union of the two provinces in 1841 and rule by a 'responsible' government from 1848 that proved sufficiently resilient in facing down the Tory reactions to the Rebellion Losses legislation. The Fenian invasions in 1866 impacted on the Confederation debates, though to what extent is unclear, but the fear of further Fenian incursion—that occurred in 1870 and 1871—reinforced the argument that domestic security could only be achieved through a closer constitutional federalism. The resistance in Manitoba in 1869 and 1870 reflected the hesitant nature of the new Confederation especially its failure to take account of minority interests while the North-West rebellion in 1885 demonstrated its unwillingness to negotiate for a second time and the growing confidence of its political and military position.

---

[7] Romney, Paul, *Getting it Wrong: How Canadians Forgot Their Past and Imperilled Confederation*, (Toronto University Press), 1999, was written, in part, with this in mind; an iconoclastic and provocative study.

1 A Peaceable Kingdom

Physically considered, British America is a noble territory, grand in its natural features, rich in its varied resources. Politically, it is a loosely united aggregate of petty states, separated by barriers of race, local interest, distance and insufficient means of communication. As naturalists, we hold its natural features as fixing its future destiny, and indicating its present interests, and regard its local subdivisions as arbitrary and artificial...nothing more enlarges men's minds than the belief that they form units, however small, in a great nationality. Nothing more dwarfs them than exclusive devotion to the interests of class, a coterie, or a limited nationality.[1]

The Atlantic world was buffeted by often violent political disturbances in the decades around 1850. Throughout Europe and North America, people took to the streets, to protest injustices and pursue their own political objectives and, as a result, were inclined to confront change and injustice, whether cultural, economic, religious or political, collectively.[2] Yet, while American life has been characterised by continuous and often intense violence, Canada has been portrayed at the 'peaceable kingdom', a self-image that retains a remarkable popular appeal.[3]

One of Canada's sustaining myths is that it is a 'peaceable kingdom', and that even when Canadian armed forces are dispatched on missions abroad, they will be recognised as spreading goodwill. The ideal was comedian Robin Williams' satire of the unarmed British bobby, chasing a thief, who yells, 'Stop! And if you don't stop, I'll shout STOP! again.' The notion of Canada as a peaceable kingdom originated in the writings of Northrop Frye, perhaps the greatest Canadian literary critic for whom 'a Canadian is an American who rejects the Revolution'. He described a painting of that title by Edward Hicks in 1830 depicting Indians, Quakers and lions, bears, oxen, lambs, and dogs all reconciled with one another and with the forces of

---

[1] Dawson, Sir J. W., 'Review', *Canadian Naturalist and Geologist*, Vol. 3, (1858), pp. 392-393.

[2] See, Scott, W., 'Nineteenth-Century Collective Violence: Towards a North American Context', *Labour/Le Travail*, Vol. 39, (1997), pp. 13-38, provides a detailed analysis of North American historiography of collective violence. See also, Scott, Nick, 'The Social Dynamics of Canadian Protest Participation', in Hammond-Callaghan, Marie, and Hayday, Matthew, (eds.), *Mobilizations, Protests & Engagements: Canadian Perspectives on Social Movements*, (Fernwood Publ.), 2008, pp. 35-61.

[3] Torrance, Judy M., *Public Violence in Canada, 1867-1982*, (McGill-Queen's University Press), 1986, pp. 100-106, contains a useful discussion of the 'peaceable kingdom' ideal.

nature, as a 'haunting vision of serenity.' To him, this portrayed the most frequently recurring theme in Canadian literature. Frye argued that:

> ...if we had to characterize a distinctive emphasis in that tradition, we might call it a quest for the peaceable kingdom.[4]

This position was also adopted by William Kilbourn who argued that many of 'The subtle but profound ways in which Canada differs from the United States', such as greater Canadian respect for the law and toleration of other groups, coalesce around the idea of Canada as a peaceable kingdom.[5]

'Canada is an unmilitary community,' wrote C. P. Stacey, Canada's pre-eminent military historian. 'Warlike her people have often been forced to be, military they have never been.'[6] There is a

---

[4] Frye, Northrop, 'Conclusion to a Literary History of Canada (1965)', in *The Bush Garden: Essays on the Canadian Imagination*, (Anansi), 1971, p. 249.

[5] Kilbourn, William, *Canada: A Guide to the Peaceable Kingdom*, (Macmillan of Canada), 1970, p. xii

[6] Stacey, C. P., *Six Years of War: The Army in Canada, Britain and the Pacific*, (Queen's Printer), 1953, p. 3. Several years before Prime Minister

view that, unlike almost every other democracy, Canadians have not had to fight for their freedom. The rebellions in Lower and Upper Canada in 1837 and 1838 and Louis Riel's Red River 'Resistance' of 1869-1870 and the North-West Rebellion of 1885 are portrayed as little more than military skirmishes while describing the four-day action at Batoche as a 'battle' is seen as a serious overdramatisation. Similarly, the Quebec conscription riots of 1917, the Winnipeg General Strike of 1919 and unemployment marches of the 1930s, as well as the October Crisis of 1970 that led the government to invoke the War Measures Act and mobilise more than 10,000 troops, were merely policing actions that spun out of control. Canadians have only gone to war seriously when its allies on foreign continents were threatened and then did so with great energy and distinction.

The notion of the 'peaceable kingdom' is based on the idea that violence did not contribute to the development of Canada as a nation state and where there were outbreaks of violence, they had been failures. This can, in part, be explained by Canadian rejection of other societies' violent models for political change. The French Revolution, for instance, had little impact on the development of French Canada and few French-Canadians, even in the 1830s, saw themselves as republicans. British Canada had been created by and for Loyalists who has specifically rejected the colonial revolutionary solution of the 1770s. Canadians, it is argued, have an instinctive acceptance of established institutions and when the state expanded west from the 1850s it was accompanied by the institutions of government limiting the effects of the 'anarchic' frontier.

What Canadians fear is not what government does, but of the lawless vacuum if government collapsed or did not exist. The consequence of this is that Canadians are said to be particularly law-abiding, deferential to authority and toleration is celebrated as a national quality. Canadians also have an almost Hobbesian view of human nature with little faith in man's ability to grapple with destiny and mould it to a desired course. Violence is unnecessary for most Canadians because they have accepted the institutional restraints necessary to constrain it. National survival depends not on the legitimate use of violence but on the pursuit of peace in national and foreign affairs.

W. L. Mackenzie King had stated: 'We are fighting to defend democratic and Christian ideals [and] we have transformed one of the least military people on earth into a nation organised for modern war', *Hutchinson's Pictorial History of the War*, no. 1, Series 13, July-December, 1941, p. 199.

For all its faults, this country has remained blessedly free of those deadly clashes of rival ideologies, dreams, and purities with which almost every other corner of the earth is still plagued today. To say otherwise, to state in portentous tones that our recent history too has been terrible, is about as useful as proclaiming that Canada is the worst country in the world except for the others.[7]

The significance of the notion of the 'peaceable kingdom' lies in providing a focus for national sentiments and in delineating the fundamental difference between Canadians and Americans. The United States placed its faith in the role of the individual unrestricted by oppressive government as the means of achieving personal and national advancement while in Canada it was collective governmental authority that was regarded as essential to protect individuals and groups from the selfish actions of others as well as managing economic growth. It was the contrast between the liberal individualism of 'life, liberty and the pursuit of happiness' and the conservatism of 'peace, order and good government'.

For Canadians, violence was the visible expression of Hobbesian man in the state of nature threatening national unity and identity. Violence, however, was not ignored by contemporaries and Canadian governments were prompt in dealing with it and in their strong actions against the violent, often vilified as traitors, selfish levellers, or foreigners, had widespread popular support. Though not on the scale of the American Civil War, Canada was far from a 'peaceable kingdom'. Between 1800 and 1885, there is abundant evidence of political, social, religious and ethnic violence and, contrary to the defenders of Canadian mythology, people waged their battles in British North America with a fervour matching that of their southern neighbours.[8]

Much of the traditional historical narrative of Canada has focused on the road to responsible government, social and political reforms and the more or less 'peaceful' course of Canadian history as a means of constructing a pan-Canadian sense of nationalism. Conciliation rather than conflict lies at the heart of this narrative. Historians such as George Wrong, Adam Shortt, and Donald Creighton emphasised Canada's nationalistic progress and celebrated

---

[7] Kilbourn, W., 'The Peaceable Kingdom Still', in Graubard, Stephen R., (ed.), *In Search of Canada*, (Transaction Publishers) 1989, p. 28

[8] Chambers, Lori, 'Exposing the Myth of the Peaceable Kingdom: Trends and Themes in Recent Canadian Legal History', *Acadiensis*, Vol. 41, (1), (2012), pp. 247-256.

its unique contributions to North American history.[9] In the mainstream of Canadian historical writings, the phenomenon of collective violence seemed somehow out of place in the landscape of the past. Within this Whiggish grand narrative, uprisings, rebellions and violent struggles had little place and those who did rebel were seen as aberrations, opposed to progress and modernisation and were relegated to its margins.[10] The administrative and political powers that made up the British North American colonisation project saw acts of violence as justification for greater control and for more extensive centralised government. Although never without its critics especially in French-Canadian historiography, this imperialist, 'Canada First' continentalist view of history dominated English-Canadian thinking well into the second half of the twentieth century.

The overarching consensual narrative with a single story was challenged and became a subject of derision and divisiveness once the gauntlets of class, gender, race and ethnicity were thrown down by the New Social History leading to what Michael Bliss termed 'the sundering of Canadian History'.[11] Developments in historical thinking were paralleled by a shift away from the guiding conservative principle that Canada's ideological glue should be its British orientation. The Quiet Revolution and revived immigration saw the federal government, especially under Lester Pearson and Pierre Trudeau, reverse attempts to suppress the ethnic self-identification that many Canadians preferred. Established narratives were challenged as historians recognised the diversity of cultural interstices especially in the realm of ideas and that historical analysis was about worlds within worlds, about diversities of experiences and about contrasting and conflicting narratives.[12] In these narratives, psychological as well as

[9] McClelland and Stewart's multi-volume *Canadian Centennial Series* designed to celebrate the emergence of the Canadian nation-state is its most outstanding example. See also, Johnson, J. K., 'Gerald Craig's *Upper Canada: The Formative Years* and the Writing of Upper Canadian History', *Ontario History,* Vol. 90, (1998), pp. 117-134.
[10] Fallis Jr., L., 'The Idea of Progress in the Province: A Study in the History of Ideas', in Morton, W. L., (ed.), *The Shield of Achilles: Aspects of Canada in the Victorian Age,* (McClelland & Stewart), 1968, p. 176. See also, Lower, A. R. M., 'Nationalism and the Canadian Historian', *Canadian Historical Review* (hereafter *CHR*), Vol. 66, (1985), pp. 541-549.
[11] Bliss, Michael, 'Privatizing the Mind: The Sundering of Canadian History, the Sundering of Canada', *Journal of Canadian Studies*, Vol. 26, (4), (1991-92), pp. 5-17.
[12] On the evolution of Canadian historiography and the historical profession see, Berger, Carl, *The Writing of Canadian History*, second edition,

physical violence took on a heightened and more nuanced role in shaping the nation-building project in the nineteenth century that challenged the populist adage of 'peace, order and good government'. It is within this historiographical framework that the rebellions between 1837 and 1885 are now considered.

Allan Greer is critical of those historians who have tried to force the narrative of the rebellion of 1837 into a narrative of resisting progress and modernisation, arguing that many felt 'what was so deplorable about the rebels of 1837, was not only their violence, but also their republicanism, their failure to appreciate the wonders of the British constitution.'[13] He argues that the rebellions of Upper and Lower Canada were primarily a grassroots response to injustices and inequalities with the system of governance by the largely British elite and were important markers of social unrest and desire for responsible government. Greer claims that the rebellions were seen as violence caused by troublemakers and in the case of the rebellion of Lower Canada, it is easy to see how the peculiar forms of violence and public protest like the charivari could be re-appropriated as a reckless populist resistance to progress and modernisation.[14] Economic change, especially if rapid and tensions between different economic agendas were significant reasons behind collective violence. This was evident in the rebellions in Upper and Lower Canada in 1837 where there were increasingly irreconcilable tensions between localised, traditionalist and agrarian values and continentalist, modernist, commercial priorities associated primarily, though not exclusively with the British mercantile elite. The Rebellions failed to separate the Canadas from their imperial masters and fell short of altering inherent inequalities in the colonial power structure.

The Patriote party was eventually defeated by imperial forces, but the struggle was greater than the Governor of Lower Canada had expected and threat of violence and popular resistance reinforced the notion that the Canadian state was well-versed in using punitive force to put down rebellions. The increasing concentration of power in state agencies, especially after 1840, accentuated the diminution of individual rights. During the Confederation debates, Joseph-Xavier

(University of Toronto Press), 1986, and Wright, Donald, *The Professionalization of History in English Canada*, (University of Toronto Press), 2005.

[13] Greer, Allan, '1837-38: Rebellion Reconsidered', *CHR*, Vol. 76, (1), (1995), p. 2.

[14] Greer, Allan, 'From Folklore to Revolution: Charivaris and the Lower Canadian Rebellion of 1837', *Social History*, Vol. 15, (1), (1990), p. 36.

Perrault of Richelieu remarked, hinting at the Lower Canadian uprising:

> Our past recalled to us the constant struggle which we had to keep up in order to resist the aggression and the exclusiveness of the English element of Canada. It was only through heroic resistance...that we succeeded in obtaining the political rights.[15]

For Perrault, violent opposition to English Canadian statehood was necessary to obtaining rights and recognition.

Similar struggles for cultural recognition and opposition to the state-building project of Canada took place all over British North America, such as the struggle between Protestants and Catholics in Saint John, New Brunswick less than a decade after the Lower Canadian Rebellion. Religious belief served as the basis for both self and community identification; for the Catholic and Protestant immigrants to North America it comprised the most conspicuous piece of 'cultural baggage' that they transported to the New World. Zealous Protestants, defending their religion against 'encroachment', combated Irish immigrants who clung tenaciously to Catholicism in a hostile atmosphere. Tensions were further heightened by revivalist and aggressively evangelical sects such as Methodists and Baptists who prospered in the frontier regions of Canada. Religious conflict and violence for which there was a long tradition in Britain and Ireland, were an important element in riots across all of the colonies and in the rebellions in the Canadas, the Fenian incursions and in the North-West.

Between 1845 and 1850, violent nativist protests and riots erupted between Catholics and Protestants in Saint John, New Brunswick as the Orange Order defended Protestantism against the urban encroachment of Irish Catholics. Their response, as was typical among North American nativists, was an essentially conservative attempt to maintain social, religious, and economic hegemony. According to Saint John's *Loyalist and Conservative Advocate*:

> The facts were these: several thousands of immigrants were annually landing upon our shores: they were nearly all Catholics, nearly all ignorant and bigoted, nearly all paupers, many of them depraved...What have we to expect but murder, rapine, and anarchy? Let us ask, then, should not Protestants unite? Should they not organize?[16]

---

[15] Waite, P. B., *The Confederation Debates in the Province of Canada 1865*, (McClelland and Stewart), 1963, p. 128.

[16] *Loyalist and Conservative Advocate*, 13 August 1847.

The Protestant response was not simply mindless violence against 'the other' but a reaction to what were seen as Catholic disregard of Protestantism and British institutions.[17] Much of Canada's 'identity' in terms of statehood was predicated upon British models of governance and bureaucracy and during the Orange riots, Canadian identity was co-opted by the white English-Protestant to the exclusion of others. Susanna Moodie remarked in her sketch of Grosse Île of a 'fresh cargo of lively savages from the Emerald Isle':

> The vicious, uneducated barbarians who form the surplus of over-populous European countries, are far behind the wild man in delicacy of feeling or natural courtesy. The people who covered the island appeared perfectly destitute of shame, or even of a sense of common decency...[18]

For Moodie and many other English Protestants, the Irish represented a challenge to the perceived and to some degree, very real hegemony of the British models viewed as 'Canadian'.

From 1837, clashes between the Orange Order and Irish Catholics, especially on St. Patrick's Day and on 12 July were frequent and often deadly. During the riots 'dozens of combatants' were 'hurt seriously enough to warrant medical attention.'[19] Some blamed the bloodshed on the police's inability to prevent disturbances on the failure to convict those involved. Violence acted as a deterrent to prosecutors, who would frequently find themselves in courthouses surrounded by angry supporters of those on trial. The largest riot occurred in 1849 where at least a dozen were killed but few were charged. However, the 1849 riot was a turning point and although minor skirmishes still occurred, improved economic conditions from 1850 saw the emergence of a double standard, as authorities found that the 'social control' of Orangeism was preferable to mob rule by the lower-class Irish Catholics.[20]

Events such as the uprising at Trois-Rivières, popularly known as the candlesnuffer's war, were seen by 'contemporary authorities who interpreted opposition to school laws as a regressive attempt to snuff

---

[17] See, Scott, 'The Orange Order and Social Violence in Mid-Nineteenth Century Saint John', *Acadiensis*, Vol. 13, (1), (1983), p. 72. See also See, Scott, *Riots in New Brunswick: Orange Nativism and Social Violence in the 1840s*, (University of Toronto Press), 1993.

[18] Moodie, Susanna, *Roughing It in the Bush: or, Forest Life in Canada*, (George P. Putnam), 1852, p. 11.

[19] Ibid, see, Scott, 'The Orange Order and Social Violence in Mid-Nineteenth Century Saint John', p. 83.

[20] Ibid, p. 90.

out the light of learning.'[21] Violence as a powerful symbol of opposition to progressive changes, reared its head in 1850 as a group of government tax assessors began assessing the small town of St. Gregoire le Grand for new school taxes:

> Hardly had they begun when they were confronted by a mob of three hundred angry men who ordered them to stop, tore up and burned their assessment books, and warned them not to carry out the government's work.[22]

As more assessors and eventually police and militia were called in to aid the process of assessment, 'la guerre des eteignoirs' broke out at Trois-Rivières. Barns and schoolhouses were burnt, officials publicly harassed and intimidated and people refused to pay taxes in what many began to see as a 'larger movement, a disparate, violent opposition to authority and to modernization which tore British North American society.'[23] However, such opinions are based on the assumption that the hegemony of colonial control in British North America was an even, inevitable and just movement. The Trois-Rivières incidents were downplayed as trifling matters caused by an uneducated working class or similarly, blamed on immigrants, bent on blocking the path to what liberals and Victorian-minded 'progressives' saw as a necessary progression towards education.

The objection of many of those involved in the events at Trois-Rivières in 1850 was having property taxes imposed upon them by the governing elite. This was deeply resented by French-Canadians particularly, as Cross pointedly argues of the governing elites: 'they had not yet seen the pressing necessity to tax themselves to pay for the police forces and compulsory schools which would establish their hegemony for decades to come.' The participants in uprisings at Trois-Rivières were not opposing modernization, rather they were challenging the authority of colonial powers and modern government that was 'intent on establishing order and new values' and 'had to break down rival justice systems' here the rival justice system being the local level participants in social uprisings.[24]

---

[21] Nelson, Wendie, 'Rage against the Dying of the Light: Interpreting the Guerre des Éteignoirs' *Canadian Historical Review*, Vol. 81, (4), (2000), pp. 551-589, at p. 552.

[22] Cross, Michael, 'The Laws are Like Cobwebs: Popular Resistance to Authority in Mid-Nineteenth Century British North America', in Waite, Peter, Oxner, Sandra, and Barnes, Thomas, (eds.), *Law in a Colonial Society The Nova Scotia Experience*, (Carswell Co.), 1984, p. 103.

[23] Ibid, p. 104.

[24] Ibid, p. 106.

Decades of crop failures, devastating illnesses and a changing economy contributed to the maelstrom of tension that led to Louis Riel's Red River Resistance, Irene Spry argues that much intermingling and cooperation still occurred prior to and during the Red River Resistance and that it was newcomers from Ontario:

> ...were eagerly sowing racial and religious conflict, banding together to fan the flames of discord between different groups in the Red River Settlement. These émigrés from Ontario, all of them Orangemen, looked as if their one dream was in life was to make war on the Hudson's Bay Company, the Catholic Church and anyone who spoke French...[25]

The violence that arose out of the uprising at Red River was popularly passed off for many racial reasons but was ultimately a direct challenge to the legitimacy of Canada's national project. Sir John A. Macdonald passed the Manitoba Act in 1870 promising many improvements to the Red River Métis and offered Riel amnesty if he left Manitoba for five years. Riel accepted but in 1885 returned, to assist the struggling Métis who felt that much of what was promised in the Manitoba Act had not come to fruition. Unfortunately for Riel, the Métis were ill-equipped and unable to fend of Macdonald's newly established North-West Mounted Police. Louis Riel and his supporters resisted what they saw as an imperial threat to their culturally distinct settlement and land ownership.

In popular conception, the rebellion marked a watershed between two ages: the primitive west sparsely occupied by fur traders and Native peoples and a west domesticated, ordered and developed by settlers and North-West Mounted Police, by merchants and industrialists. This is what George Stanley in his study published in 1936 called the 'inevitable disorganization which is produced among primitive people when they are suddenly brought into contact with a more complex civilization.'[26] Neither the First Nations nor the Métis were able to withstand the impact of the 'superior civilization' or adjust to the 'new order'. The actions of the First Nations in this 'whiggish' drama required little explanation, as at the time there was an unspoken understanding of them as natural warriors but as morally weak, impressionable, and easily led into deviance. The Métis were described as the lead rebels, convincing the First Nations to join them

---

[25] Spry, Irene, 'The Métis and Mixed Bloods of Rupert's Land Before 1870', in Peterson, Jacqueline, and Brown, Jennifer S. H., (eds.), *The New Peoples: Being and Becoming Métis in North America*, (University of Manitoba Press), 1985, p. 95.

[26] Stanley, G. F. G., *The Birth of Western Canada: A History of the Riel Rebellions*, (University of Toronto Press,) 1936, p. 198.

in their struggle. The Métis and First Nations were necessarily cast as the antagonists in their challenge to government authority and their threat to the advancement of the Dominion of Canada. This remains an important marker in Canadian history of popular resistance to colonisation and in turn, the state's use of violence and immigration against those with previous claims on land it sought.

Fear of violence led politicians and policymakers throughout the nineteenth century to make 'progressive' changes but also relied upon the creation of the North-West Mounted Police and a burgeoning host of intricate laws. Following the candle-snuffers' war, the state could still be challenged by the force of community and violent opposition to the state's law could still be exercised with realistic hopes of success. It would be a gradual process of decades before the cobwebs of the law became sufficiently intricate and resilient to choke out the struggling tradition of popular resistance. Inhabitants found various ways of 'domesticating' officials who appeared in theory to be the agents of an external power. In Lower Canada, for instance, each militia captain was presented with a 'maypole', a tall tree trunk decorated with flags and banners and planted in the ground in front of his house, in an elaborate ceremony that implied popular ratification of the governor's choice. In the autumn of 1837, many maypoles became 'liberty poles' and, to mark the transformation, a sign reading 'elected by the people' was attached to a captain's mast.

Expressions of communal violence that challenged the hegemony of the Canadian nation-state were used as justification for the further colonisation and pacification of British North America. With uprisings like those in Red River, John A. Macdonald had little trouble convincing citizens to foot the enormous bill of building the Canadian Pacific Railway and forming the North-West Mounted Police. That Canada's 'founding fathers' were concerned about violence, both at home and abroad, can be found in calls for organising an efficient defence against every hostile pressure, 'from whatever source it may come.' Evidence of arguments for a stronger, homogenous Canadian colonisation project were also made in the Confederation debates, as John A. Macdonald called for a project that would bring dissidents into line and improve relations with England:

> I believe that if one thing more than another has raised British North America...in the estimation of the people and Government of England, it is that by this scheme there was offered to the Mother Country a means by which these colonies should cease to be a source of embarrassment, and become, in fact, a source of strength. This feeling pervades the public mind of England. Every writer and speaker of note in the United Kingdom...says a new era of colonial existence has been inaugurated, and that if these colonies, feeble while

disunited, were a source of weakness, they will, by forming this friendly alliance [Confederation], become a strong support for England.[27]

Macdonald put much emphasis on England as the model against which Canada's success or failure should be compared and pursued a nation-making policy that would see the West populated by English-speaking European immigrants and form the hegemonic central power that would become Canada.

If the state sought to enhance its authority and establish political stability, religion especially in its populist form acted as a source of conflict and instability. In each of the rebellions there was an underlying tension between Roman Catholicism and Protestantism that, in many respects represented Canada's 'wars of religion'. Although there were clear doctrinal differences between Catholicism and Protestantism and within Protestantism itself, the issue was less one of belief than of the nationalist identity that came from having particular beliefs and of the social, political and cultural expressions of those identities.

---

[27] Ibid, Waite P. B., *The Confederation Debates in the Province of Canada 1865*, p. 130.

2 Canada's 'Wars of Religion'

Conflict within and between communities is perennially occasioned by a combination of three things: need, greed, and ideas. Land and natural resources play a central role in this aggression. As population grows, land and natural resources can quickly become exhausted. Unless resources can be imported, then societies may have little alternative but to take what they need from neighbouring communities if necessary, by force. This applies especially where one community has natural resources other communities lack or where restrictions on the supply of resources from outside is seen as a threat to community security. Imperial aspirations, which may or may not be linked to need but are generally an expression of greed, also play an important role in the use of force to obtain land and resources. The more land a community controls the greater its political power or influence over neighbouring communities. For conflict caused by need or greed, direct action tends to be beyond the frontiers of the community; indeed, its prime motivation is to expand those frontiers.

By contrast, conflict caused by ideas has an internal as well as an external dimension. Within communities, this involves the imposition of a particular set of ideas on the community by force when all else fails. Externally, a community may seek to impose those ideas on neighbouring communities again, if necessary, by force. The problem with ideas lies in their ethereal nature. People may well outwardly conform to the orthodox values of a community for fear of the possible consequences of not doing so while subscribing to an antithetical set of values. Communities can only go so far in enforcing conformity. Religious belief has long played a seminal role in determining relations within and between communities and 'wars of religion' remain a central feature of modern conflict. Unlike seeing land and natural resources where the issue was material, there can be no equivocation between those who maintain one religious dogma and those who hold to an alternative. Some communities may avoid conflict if they have espoused a principle of toleration where all faiths are welcomed and, if they remain within the law, free to worship as they will. But even if this is the case, religious belief creates fissures within communities that have proved difficult to close.

Since the Reformation, there has been a broad division in Europe between the Roman Catholic south and the Protestant north.[1]

---

[1] Wolffe, John, (ed.), *Protestant-Catholic Conflict from the Reformation to the 21st Century: The Dynamics of Religious Difference*, (Palgrave Macmillan), 2013, pp. 1-45.

The principle 'cuius regio, eius religio' established in 1555 meant that the religion of the ruler became the religion in his dominions and where the ruler converted to a different religion either his or her people had to convert or the ruler was forced from the throne. This occurred between 1553 and 1558 when Mary I of England sought to reimpose Roman Catholicism as the state religion but died without an heir to carry on her mission, while in 1654 in Protestant Sweden and in 1688 in Protestant Britain Queen Christina and James II, who had converted to Roman Catholicism, went into exile. With Europe divided into Protestant and Catholic blocs, the century after 1555 was punctuated by religious conflict culminating in the Thirty Years War (1618-1648). Whether this century of communal bloodletting led to anything other than an uneasy compromise is questionable, but it established an atmosphere of mutual suspicion and fear that persists in some communities.

Britain and Ireland did not escape this European devastation. The Civil Wars between 1642 and 1651 were as much over religion as they were political principles. England, Scotland, and Wales were regarded as Protestant countries, Ireland was a different matter. Despite bloody rebellions in 1641 and 1798, failed nationalist risings in 1848, 1867 and 1916, sectarian conflict and religious repression, Ireland remained stubbornly Catholic. The Catholic majority lost its political power, a position given legislative expression in the various Penal Laws but the minority Protestant ascendancy failed to anglicise Ireland. Throughout the eighteenth, nineteenth and twentieth centuries, sectarian divisions played a major role in determining the political evolution of the country. This was important for Canada since the religious divisions of Ireland migrated across the Atlantic and Irish sectarianism was replicated in the colonies adding to the tensions already evident between French-Canadians and British settlers. From the 1820s, these erupted into sectarian conflict between Catholics and Protestants and within the Protestant community between Anglicans and Dissent. Religious belief became a badge of loyalty, racial identity, and political allegiance.

Canadian identity is essentially local and regional in nature and this applies to its religious belief and adherence.[2] Canadians had more

[2] Handy, Robert T., *A History of the Churches in the United States and Canada*, (Oxford University Press), 1976, pp. 116-135, 228-261, 344-376, Noll, Mark A., *A History of Christianity in the United States and Canada*, (Eerdmans Publishing Company), 1992, 2019, Chapter 5, Choquette, Robert, *Canada's Religions: An Historical Introduction*, (University of Ottawa Press), 2002, pp. 95-116, 137-205, 206-284, and Christie, Nancy, and

in common with each other than they did with Americans who lived to the south of their communities. There may have been a broad spectrum of religious belief among Protestants on either side of the border but the Canadian approach tended to be less radical and fundamentalist than in the United States. The centrality of religion to the dynamics of development and identity of French-speaking communities was evident from the beginnings of British rule. In English Canada, by contrast, the economy and the role of the state as an agent of social change took a dominant position until the late-nineteenth century. Religion, though an important way of expressing popular political culture, was regarded as one of several ways of identifying individual identity. Before the introduction of elected municipal councils and school councils, religious denominations were the only institutions of local self-government. This, across all communities, encouraged an ethos of voluntarism that was willing to accept state support for roads and schools but was far less responsive to central governments calls for local taxation to finance this support. The problem, as Northrup Frye commented, was that it led to a 'garrison mentality'.[3]

The British North American colonies may have had different economic, social and demographic dimensions but they had similar political structures. They were under the authority of the Colonial Office in London led by a Colonial Secretary, generally a member of the British Cabinet. He appointed the Lieutenant-Governors who were responsible for the good governance of each colony. In Upper and Lower Canada, legislative and executive functions were divided between appointed councils, which held most of the power, and an elected assembly that sought great democratic authority. Apart from money bills, any legislation brought forward by the assemblies required the approval of the appointed councils and was often vetoed by the British government, the ultimate authority for approving new law. Across Upper and Lower Canada, Nova Scotia and New Brunswick, centres of patronage and privilege lay with council members and their political networks—variously called the Family

---

Gauvreau, Michael, *Christian Churches and Their Peoples, 1840-1965: A Social History of Religion in Canada*, (University of Toronto Press), 2010, pp. 3-59, provide a succinct discussion of Canada and its major religious developments to the 1840s. See also, Noll, Mark A., 'Religion in Canada, 1759-1815', in Stein, Stephen J., (ed.), *The Cambridge History of Religions in America*, 3 Vols. (Cambridge University Press), 2012, Vol. 1, pp. 610-633, and Van Die, Marguerite, 'Religion and Law in British North America, 1800-1867', in ibid, Vol. 2, pp. 46-65.
[3] Frye, Northrup, *The Bush Garden: Essays on the Canadian Imagination*, (Anasi), 1971, pp. 226, 231, 236.

Compact, the Château Clique and the System--that sought to replicate the moral, hierarchical and oligarchic order of eighteenth and early-nineteenth century Britain.[4]

Christian morality, enforced through the local magistracy and often grounded in executing vigorously 'all Laws against Blasphemy, Profaneness, Adultery...and to take due care for the Punishment of these and every other Vice and Immorality', placed the Established Church at the heart of governance as a bulwark against social threats such as religious enthusiasm, republicanism and disloyalty.[5] By 1802, legislation in support of religious establishment was in place in every British North American colony: Nova Scotia in 1754, New Brunswick 1786, Upper and Lower Canada in 1791 and Prince Edward Island 1802. The Church of England (after 1800 the United Church of England and Ireland), as the established church, received government funding and privileges designed to ensure religious homogeneity across the English-speaking colonies. Colonial bishops such as Charles and John Inglis in Nova Scotia, Jacob Mountain[6] in Quebec and John Strachan[7] in Upper Canada promoted the religious establishment as the religion of order especially through their role in founding exclusive institutions to educate the colonial leadership and resident clergy of the future.

---

[4] Wallace, W. Stewart, *Family Compact: A Chronicle of the Rebellion in Upper Canada*, (Glasgow, Brook & Co.), 1922; Ewart, Alison, and Jarvis, Julia, 'The Personnel of the Family Compact, 1791-1841', *CHR*, Vol. 7, (1926), pp. 195-272; Patterson, G. H., 'Early Compact Groups in the Politics of York', in Keane, David, and Read, Colin, (eds.), *Old Ontario: Essays in Honour of J. M. S. Careless*, (Dundurn Press), 1990, pp. 174-191, and Earl, David W. L., (ed.), *The Family Compact: Aristocracy or Oligarchy?*, (The Copp Clark Publishing Company), 1967, provide the best general introduction.

[5] Murray, David, *Colonial Justice: Justice, Morality and Crime in the Niagara District, 1791-1849*, (Osgoode Society), 2002, pp. 77-78.

[6] Millman, T. R., *Jacob Mountain, first lord bishop of Quebec; a study in church and state, 1793-1825*, (University of Toronto Press), 1947, and Millman, Thomas, 'Jacob Mountain', *Dictionary of Canadian Biography*, (hereafter *DCB*), Vol. 6, pp. 523-529, are good biographies of this irascible figure.

[7] Biographical studies include: Bethune, A. N., *Memoir of the Right Reverend John Strachan, D.D., LL.D., first bishop of Toronto*, (Henry Rowsell), 1870; Robertson, B., *The fighting bishop: John Strachan, the first bishop of Toronto, and other essays in his times*, (Graphic), 1926, pp. 11-68; Boorman, Sylvia, *John Toronto: a biography of Bishop Strachan*, (Clarke, Irwin), 1969, and Craig, G. M., 'John Strachan', *DCB*, Vol. 9, pp. 751-766.

Of the various problems facing a religious establishment in a colonial setting, how to fund its undertakings proved a major difficulty. The colonial church did not have the financial resources of the church in Britain. It had no historic endowments to underpin expansion and no legal right to church rates and tithes to fund daily parochial needs. This meant that the church was heavily reliant on state aid. In the Maritimes, this came largely from the farming of glebe lands and the annual parliamentary grants to the Society for the Propagation of the Gospel (SPG) for church buildings, schools and the salaries of clergy and teachers. In Lower and Upper Canada, the SPG was also a major source of funding but the Constitutional Act 1791 set aside one-seventh of the Crown Lands for the 'Maintenance and Support of a Protestant Clergy' providing for the building of parsonages or rectories in every township and parish. None of these provisions was sufficient and 'the Clergy Reserves' proved a contentious issue as the growing population of the Canadian colonies became more culturally and religiously diverse.[8] Reliance on state aid proved unsatisfactory especially from the 1830s when the reforming Whig government in London began to reduce the annual SPG grants in its quest for economy and efficiency. This marked a shift from London supporting colonial institutions to transferring responsibility for funding across those institutions to the colonies themselves and was not confined to Canada.

Between 1815 and 1840, half a million people left Britain for Canada resulting in dissenting Protestants far outnumbering Anglicans. The position of the Church of England was far from supreme in Upper Canada. In 1819, there were only 10 Anglican clergymen and 2 Anglican chaplains in the province while there were 6 Presbyterian ministers and 6 Catholic priests plus an unspecified number of itinerant Methodists.[9] Dissenters deeply resented the monopolistic claims and privileges of the established church, tensions that became a gnawing source of discontent and political activism, part of a more general attack on the colonial oligarchies.[10] In 1828, Methodists in

---

[8] Wilson, Alan, *The Clergy Reserves of Upper Canada: A Canadian Mortmain*, (University of Toronto Press), 1968.

[9] *The Christian Recorder*, Vol. 1 (1), (1819), pp. 13-16. See also, Strachan, John, *Canada church establishment: copy of a letter addressed to R. J. Wilmot Horton, Esq. by the Rev. Dr. Strachan, archdeacon of York, Upper Canada, dated 16th May, 1827, respecting the state of the church in that province*, (London: s.n.), 1827.

[10] French, Goldwin, *Politics & Parsons: The Role of the Wesleyan Methodists in Upper Canada and the Maritimes from 1780 to 1855*,

Upper Canada succeeded in gaining the legal right to hold church property and three years later to perform marriages. The critical question in the1830s and 1840s for dissenting churches was whether they should accept state aid or not. Only Baptists were consistent in their support for the separation of church and state. The Church of Scotland insisted on parity with the Church of England on the basis of their establishment status in Scotland although its Secessionist members after the 'Great Disruption' in 1843 were voluntarists. Free Church Presbyterians, established in Canada in 1844, were not officially voluntarists but held ambivalent views about the inclination of the establishment to undermine its spiritual autonomy. Wesleyan Methodists were, as in Britain, supportive of the Anglican establishment accepting state aid for its Indian missions in 1832. Methodist Episcopals led by Egerton Ryerson[11] were strongly opposed though they did enter an abortive union with the Wesleyans between 1833 and 1840 that was made permanent in 1847.

Much as in Britain in the late 1820s, Anglican exclusivity was under attack. For instance, its claims to exclusive funding for higher education forced other denominations to establish their own institutions. By 1845, there were ten colleges, four in Upper Canada and six in the Maritimes, a reflection of the failure to establish a moral order based on a religious establishment. By the 1830s, the Clergy Reserves began to generate some income and increasingly the needs of a commercialised market economy led to the Reserves becoming a source of religious division, In 1841, the Clergy Reserves Act allocated the proceeds of land sales on a sliding scale to the Church of England, Church of Scotland, Wesleyan Methodists and the Roman Catholic Church. This lasted until 1854 when a moderate Conservative administration abolished the reserves with the proceeds allocated to the municipalities.[12] Voluntarists were angered when provision was made for the financial rights of existing clergy claimants through allotments to their respective denominations. The 65 per cent

---

(Ryerson Press), 1962, and the more general Semple, Neil, *The Lord's Dominion: The History of Canadian Methodism*, (McGill-Queen's University Press), 1996, pp. 71-99, remain central on this issue.

[11] Ryerson, Egerton, *The Story of My Life*, (W. Briggs), 1883, is a useful, if slanted autobiography. Sissons, C. B., *Egerton Ryerson: His Life and Letters*, 2 Vols. (Clarke Irwin), 1937, remains the standard biography. Gidney, R. D., 'Egerton Ryerson', *DCB*, Vol. 11, pp. 783-795, takes account of more recent work.

[12] Ibid, Wilson, Alan, *The Clergy Reserves of Upper Canada*, pp. 197-222, examines the debates on Clergy Reserves from 1848 to 1854. Moir, John S., 'The Settlement of the Clergy Reserves, 1840-1855', *CHR*, Vol. 37, (1956), pp. 46-62, also remains useful.

allotment to the Church of England provided sufficient endowment to support its clergy into the next century. Although Nova Scotia was to only colony to pass legislation disestablishing the Anglican Church, in practice by the mid-1850s, all the colonies had disestablished the Church. At the end of 1854, *La Minerve*, could congratulate Canada on

> ...her rapid march of progress...reciprocity of trade with the United States, the secularisation of the Anglican Clergy Reserves and reform of seigneurial tenure open a new era in our country.[13]

This was completed in 1859 when a Liberal government passed legislation secularising King's College, Fredericton renaming it the University of New Brunswick.

The Anglican Church may have sought to replicate the British pattern of a single dominant church that enjoyed a privileged relationship with the state but it failed. By the censuses of early 1840s, the population of Upper Canada was divided into four equally vibrant religious denominations: Anglicans (22 per cent), Methodists (17 per cent), Presbyterians (19 per cent) and Roman Catholics (13 per cent) with 17 per cent claiming 'no religion', not members of the institutional churches recognised by census takers. Roman Catholics made up 82 per cent of the population of Lower Canada but Protestants made up the bulk of the English-speaking population. This pattern of religious pluralism and competition in which religious allegiance was divided into a small number of larger institutional churches was replicated in the Maritime Provinces. This set Canada apart from the United States where religious identities were more fragmented. Canadian religious identities remained fluid and flexible and the authority of the institutional churches and the state were consequently weaker.

The fear in the Anglican Church was that disestablishment and the new system of voluntarism would lead to a fragmentation of Protestant Christianity into individualistic and populist expressions of religion as had been the case with the separation of church and state in the United States. In practice, disestablishment did not lead to a radical dislocation in Canada between the old and the new and, in fact, there was considerable continuity between the pre-1850s and post-1860s churches. The Anglican Church reconstructed itself into a Victorian denomination that stressed practical piety and active lay involvement and sought religious continuity through Sunday Schools and family worship, common to all Protestant denominations. Although the five main Protestant evangelical denominations—

---

[13] *La Minerve*, 17 November 1854.

Wesleyans and smaller Methodist groups, Presbyterians, Baptists, Congregationalists and 'low church' Anglicans—jealously guarded their distinctive traditions, their common aim was the creation of a Christian society through the medium of the 'moral crusade'.[14] They cooperated in a variety of areas including Sunday Schools, philanthropic work, Sabbatarianism and the temperance movement.

The growing political influence of Canadian evangelicals was particularly evident in their work on temperance and Prohibition. Temperance societies were first formed in the Maritimes and in Montreal in the 1820s and, influenced by American groups such as the Sons of Temperance, abstinence and temperance groups evolved from their largely middle-class origins into a more populist movement that saw Prohibition as a form of communal regeneration supported through legislative action. The message of moral improvement soon spread from Montreal into Canada West and the Eastern Townships of Quebec. A government committee in Canada West published in 1849 linked intemperance and crime and led to stricter for tavern keepers, punishment for drunkenness and moved licensing from central government to town and township councils. In 1855, a Prohibition Bill passed the legislature by a large majority but was ruled out of order by the Speaker, a controversial decision that was met with outrage from abstainers. Nine years later, the Dunkin Act was passed that enabled localities to vote to eliminate bars in their area. The hope was that this would lead to a more general Prohibition across Canada West. The process was enshrined in the Canada Temperance Act of 1878 that gave local governments the right to hold votes to ban the sale of alcohol. One side-effect was to give prohibitionists political experience through organising local and referendum campaigns. Prohibitionists secured a major victory in 1900 when Prince Edward Island outlawed the retail sale of alcohol throughout the province.[15]

Evangelical Protestants were active participants in the commercialising economies and political structures of the colonies seeking to ensure that the new order upheld the values of a Christian

---

[14] Little, John I., *Borderland Religion: The Emergence of an English-Canadian Identity*, (University of Toronto Press), 2006, a detailed local study. Little, John I., 'The Catholic Church and the French-Canadian Colonization of the Eastern Townships, 1821-1851', *Revue de l'université d'Ottawa*, Vol. 52, (1982), pp. 142-165, and Little, John L., *Nationalism, Capitalism, and Colonization in Nineteenth-Century Quebec: the Upper St Francis District*, (McGill-Queen's University Press), 1989,pp. 81-92.

[15] Noel, Janet, *Canada Dry: Temperance Crusades before Confederation*, (University of Toronto Press), 1995, Warsh, Cheryl K., *Drink in Canada: Historical Essays*, (Mcgill-Queens University Press), 1993, pp. 43-69, 92-114, 257-259.

society. As the economy grew more complex, communication by train, canals and steamboats and postal services posed questions over the place of Sunday within the community that could not be addressed simply by church discipline or public prosecution. What some saw as the public violation of Sundays led to a Sabbatarian movement especially in the Free Church that was strongly committed to holding the state to its divinely appointed duties. In Canada West, the Sabbath Alliance was formed in 1852 and succeeded in the Sunday closure of saloons and eight years later, after a concerted campaign, the Post Office voluntarily abandoned Sunday working. Unlike in Britain, moral crusading evangelicals were not at the periphery of cultural and political power but increasingly reflected a 'civic religion', a broad consensus of moral and religious beliefs that formed a functional alternative to a formal established church.

In Canada, Roman Catholics were never a marginal group. The Roman Catholic dominance of Quebec and a significant influx of Scottish Highland and Irish Roman Catholics after 1800 meant that their sheer numbers guaranteed religious rights. The British conquest of Canada in 1760, considered by some as a holy war against papist tyranny, threatened a complete reversal of the religious history of New France.[16] Both the population of the thirteen colonies and of New France saw the battle on the Plains of Abraham in a religious context. In a decisive series of decisions, Britain broke the notion of the Protestant Supremacy view allowing French-Canadians to retain their Catholicism and the Catholic Church to function freely. It was assumed that French-Canadians would become anglicised over time and that Protestant immigration would change the demographic dynamics of the colony. There was a long period of adjustment by the French Catholic colony under the new largely Protestant colonial administration. The threat of revolution in the Thirteen Colonies led the British government to make further concessions to French-Canadians in the 1774 Quebec Act. The policy of anglicisation was reversed and the rights of the Catholic Church and, by inference, those of the *seigneurs* would be enforceable, a remarkable commitment by a Protestant state to sustain the Catholic majority's religion. Invitations by the American Continental Congress for French-Canadians to join the rebellion met with no success, but there was also little active support for the war from *habitants* who were content to watch their old enemies fighting each other.

---

[16] Fay, Terence J., *A History of Canadian Catholics*, (McGill-Queen's University Press), 2002, pp. 29-47, and Lemieux, Lucien, *Histoire du catholicisme québécois, Les XVIIIe et XIXe siècle, Vol. 1, Les années difficiles, (1760-1839)*, (Boreal), 1989, discuss Catholicism to the rebellions.

No other sect has persecuted Catholics as the Bostonians' has. None has insulted priests, desecrated churches and the relics of saints as it has, none has attacked the confidence of Catholics in the protection of the Saints and the Holy Mother of God with more horrible blasphemies than it has.[17]

For most French-Canadians, the republican 'liberators' turned out to be the same old enemies: stabling horses in Catholic churches and pillaging supplies from *habitant* farms.[18] They still put their community interests and heritage first but began to follow their seigneurial and clerical élites in concluding that they were better off with the British. The Catholic clergy condemned any supporters of the American 'rebels' under pain of excommunication. The Quebec Act at least guaranteed their own special rights and character under British rule, guarantees that Americans certainly would not have given. Thus, for different reasons, neither community in Quebec took the American path of revolution. They stayed within the British Empire above all, to avoid being swallowed up in the United States, another emerging empire. The Constitutional Act 1791 extended the rights obtained in 1774 and gave Roman Catholic men the right to vote for and sit in the Assembly in Upper and Lower Canada. This was less the case in the older British colonies where anti-Catholicism resulted in more piecemeal concessions. For instance, in Nova Scotia, the legal right of Roman Catholics to hold land was given in 1783, to open Catholic schools three years later and finally Catholic enfranchisement in 1789, something not granted in New Brunswick until 1810. The English Test Acts, which required office-holders to gave a Protestant oath of loyalty, were not removed in Nova Scotia until 1823 and in New Brunswick in 1830, two years after they were repealed in Britain.[19]

Although snti-Catholicism had been a feature of Canadian society since the Conquest and was reinforced by immigrant intervention from Britain, it proved far more contentious after 1841 more so with Confederation in 1867. The growing anxiety about

---

[17] 'Mandement de Mgr Briand', June 1776, *Mandements, lettres pastorales, et circulaires des évéques de Montreal*, 18 Vols. (Quebec), 1887-, Vol. 2, p. 275.

[18] Brown, G. K., 'The Impact of the Colonial Anti-Catholic Tradition and the Canadian Campaign, 1775-1776', *Journal of Church & State*, Vol. 35, (3), (1993), pp. 559-575.

[19] Miller, J. R., 'Anti-Catholicism in Canada. From the British Conquest to the Great War', in Murphy, T., and Stortz, G., (eds.), *Creed and Culture: The Place of English-Speaking Catholics in Canadian Society, 1750-1930*, (McGill-Queen's University Press), 1993, pp. 23-45.

'Popery' came from various sources such as the Orange Order, the Wesleyan Methodist Missionary Society, the Tractarian movement, the influx of Irish Catholics in the 1840s, the growing power of nativist movement in the United States and the 'papal aggression' of 1850. For evangelicals, Roman Catholicism was seen as the antithesis of their moral order with Roman Catholics seen as under the control of their priests and confessional and indoctrinated their children in church-controlled schools. The attempt by evangelical missionaries to convert Catholics proved limited even in areas with more unstable populations and French Roman Catholic identity remained strong.

In the century between Conquest and Confederation, Roman Catholics built their own distinctive moral order in French-Canadian Quebec and bolstered their identity in Anglo-Protestant communities such as Toronto and St. John's, New Brunswick. The Catholic population of the diocese of Quebec doubled from 70,000 to 140,000 in the thirty years after 1760 and would more than double again reaching 400,000 by 1820. This was not the priest-ridden society of older Protestant historiography but one in which clergy and bishops integrated the Church into popular culture and strengthened its public presence. Fear of republicanism and revolution fostered cooperation between the Church and the colonial state. The Roman Catholic Church remained loyal to the British Crown during the War of 1812. Joseph-Octave Plessis, bishop since 1806 galvanised the entire apparatus of the Church to support the British cause. He then adroitly used his influence with the British to reform the administration of the Catholic Church throughout Canada and in 1818 was made a member of the Legislative Council with the title of 'Bishop of the Roman Catholic Church of Quebec'.[20] The process of dividing the Quebec diocese up took several decades. In 1817, Nova Scotia was separated while after 1819, Rome made Quebec a metropolitan see with two suffragan bishops for Upper Canada in 1826 and Prince Edward Island and New Brunswick three years later. The major threat to the Church's leadership of French-Canadians came not from the colonial authorities but from the increasingly nationalist French-Canadian bourgeoisie that proclaimed itself the sole defender of the rights of French Canada against British oppression.

The Roman Catholic Church enjoyed a moral monopoly in Francophone Quebec though until after the rebellions in 1837 and 1838, this was constrained by the reformist liberalism of those seeking radical political change. It supported local conservatism and was generally hostile to capitalism, industry and cities, liberalism and republicanism and other aspects of the Protestant colonial state. The

---

[20] Lambert, James, 'Joseph-Octave Plessis', *DCB*, Vol. 6, pp. 586-599.

Catholic Church gave Quebec a uniform religious character while French ultramontanist Roman Catholicism adopted a fiercely defensive attitude towards the influences of Britishness and Protestantism after 1841 and gave Quebec a strong sense of mission and destiny. The Catholic hierarchy led the fight to safeguard Quebec's national consciousness. Protestantism was seen, not only as a threat to the religious character of Quebec but also to its national identity. It has been said that to be French and Catholic is normal, to be English and Protestant is permissible, but to be French and a Protestant is heresy. In the words of one nineteenth century bishop the providential mission:

> ...entrusted to French-Canadians is basically religious in nature: it is, namely to convert the unfortunate infidel population to Catholicism, and to expand the Kingdom of God by developing a predominantly Catholic nationality.[21]

Tensions between Protestants and Catholics was particularly evident on the question of public education. The attempt to replace the wide diversity of local and denominational schools with one public school system founded on religious differences. The view in Protestant and Catholic Canada was that education was the job of the state and but they disagreed over whether the formation of its citizens was to be based on non-sectarian principles. For Catholics, 'non-sectarian Christianity' was a contradiction in terms and was really Protestant religion in disguise. The result was the development of separate schools for Catholics in Canada West with public funding from 1841 onwards. In Canada East, Protestants acquired similar rights. Attempts at similar educational reform in Nova Scotia and New Brunswick encountered strong resistance but Roman Catholics were a weaker force and were unable to obtain minority funding though in practice their schools still receiving some public monies.[22] As a result, the educational system strengthened the francophone concept of a distinct society within Canada. It shaped the morals, religious

---

[21] Laflèche, Mgr L.-F.-R., *Quelques Considérations sur les rapports de la societé civile avec la religion et la famille*, (Eusebe Senecal), 1866, pp. 457-458, Bell, David V. J., *The Roots of Disunity: A study of Canadian Political Culture*, (Oxford University Press), 1992, p. 95.

[22] Greer, A., and Radforth, I., (eds.), *Colonial Leviathan: State Formation in Mid-Nineteenth Century*, (University of Toronto Press), 1992, and Curtis, Bruce, *The Politics of Population: State Formation, Statistics, and the Census of Canada, 1840-1875*, (University of Toronto Press), 2002, and *Ruling by Schooling Quebec: Conquest to Liberal Governmentality--A Historical Sociology*, (University of Toronto Press), 2012.

convictions and the cultural outlook of a large part of Quebec's population.[23]

The union of the two Canadas in 1841 and the vacuum left by the discredited revolutionary leaders coincided with a devotional and institutional revolution within the Roman Catholic Church. The elements of French-Canadian identity—language, religion and law—that had been part of the political struggle for greater democratic rights in the Assembly were now adopted by the Church as central to its socially conservative moral order. Its ultramontane piety came from Rome to counter revolutionary and anti-clerical forces in Europe. Under successive bishops of Montreal—Joseph-Octave Plessis, Jean-Jacques Lartigue and Ignace Bourget—Catholicism became more distinctively 'Roman' with lay participation founded on the rosary, confessional, sacraments, religious retreats and devotional fraternities. Worship was elaborate; Sundays and feast days engrained in individual and communal life. Meeting the needs caused by migration, urbanisation and economic change saw the Church, through its control of education, increase the number of priests and religious orders. Roman Catholicism became the persistent public religion in Quebec while a similar ultramontane identity took shape among Catholics beyond Quebec.

In the 1840s and 1850s, Catholic and Protestant churches had to adjust to the administrative reforms caused by the shift from a pre-industrial agrarian economy to one dominated by capitalist, industrial relations. Both shifted their stance tow economic change and industrial innovation. Their respective clergies had a direct interest in the economic development of their respective communities and they lobbied for roads, bridges, railways and canals and other public amenities necessary for an industrialising society, used their accumulated capital in railway and commercial speculation as well as taking part in municipal councils and school boards. The ultramontane Catholic culture with its focus on internal discipline, social welfare and the public role of religion had much in commons with the Protestant moral order. Both religions called for active lay participation in creating a godly society and in instilling proper social behaviour such as temperance and thrift. But both religions were socially conservative willing, in the case of Catholics, to use the threat of excommunication to silence dissent while Protestants were equally intolerant of ideas considered harmful to their beliefs. The sanctity of

---

[23] Guindon, Roger, *Coexistence Difficile: La dualité linguistique a l'Université d'Ottawa, Volume 1: 1848-1898*, 4 Vols. (University of Ottawa Press), 1989, provides a detailed discussion of the centrality of language to university education.

marriage, male authority and a patriarchal view of the family was indicated in the Civil Code of Lower Canada in 1866 and the reform of property laws in other colonies. The interests of women and children were subordinate to those of the family as an economic unit. Catholics and Protestants shared a religious and moral economy that saw the family 'as a sacred institution whose welfare was of eternal import'[24] and fuelled their separate efforts to create a Christian order.

North America's Jewish population originated in 1760 when a group of British and American Jewish traders accompanied the British army to Quebec and Montreal.[25] Numbers were sufficient by 1778 for a small synagogue to be built in Montreal followed by the purchase of a cemetery but they were reliant on New York for religious leadership until 1840. The relative size of the Jewish population remained small and it constituted less that 0.03 per cent of the total Canadian population in 1871 but they had moved into many areas from the Maritimes to Vancouver. As British subjects, they had no statutory limits to freedom of movement, occupation and the right to own real estate. They played important roles as philanthropists, creditors and financiers and shared the economic and political attitudes of the Protestant elites who dominated commerce and political institutions.

However, they did not have the same civil rights they had enjoyed in the United States. For instance, when Ezekiel Hart was elected to the Assembly in 1807 and again in 1809, he was prevented from being sworn in and taking his seat.[26] Persistent campaign by Hart's younger relatives to remove the offensive 'on the true faith of a Christian' from the oath ended in 1831 when Jews were given full civil rights, over two decades before the same rights were given in Britain in 1858. Although they identified with English rather than French Canada, their religious observance was weakened in a society that conducted business on the Jewish Sabbath and holy days and that classified their children as Protestants in the school system. Despite this and their economic integration, their religion resulted in Jews remaining

---

[24] Van Die, Marguerite, 'Religion and Law in British North America, 1800-1867', in ibid, Stein, Stephen J., (ed.), *The Cambridge History of Religions in America*, Vol. 2, p. 61.
[25] Tulchinsky, Gerald, *Canada's Jews: A People's Journey*, (University of Toronto Press), 2008, pp. 13-91, Davies, Alun, (ed.), *Anti-Semitism in Canada: History and Interpretation*, (Wilfrid Laurier University Press), 1998, pp. 11-37.
[26] Vaugeois, Denis, *Les premiers Juifs d'Amérique (1760-1860): L'extraordinaire histoire de la famille Hart*, (Septentrion), 2011, pp. 137-161, for the Hart affair.

outsiders. Anti-Jewish sentiments were certainly present across pre-Confederation Canada, but the Jewish question was not central politically or religiously.

British North America's black population faced a different ambiguity in their status as colonists under British rule.[27] Central to their lives was the question of their emancipation from slavery. This was achieved in Upper Canada in 1793 but had to wait until the abolition of slavery in the other British colonies in 1834. By 1860, aided by the Fugitive Slave Act passed in the United States, the number of people of African descent numbered about 21,000. They generally established their own churches since these met their social needs and were not readily integrated into white society. The education of black children in Nova Scotia after 1800, for instance, had been in the hands of the Church of England working through the SPG and charity groups with minimal provincial help. This proved to be a major issue after 1841 with the introduction of the publicly funded common schools in the Maritimes and central Canada. Despite most blacks paying taxes to the common schools and sharing a Protestant identity with white children, they encountered regular resistance to racially integrated schools from local white populations. The intensity of prejudice forced them into calling for separate institutions and in 1850 in Canada West, the Separate School Act allowed any group of five black families to ask public school trustees to establish a school for them.[28] Whatever their legal position, Egerton Ryerson, the superintendent of schools accepted that in the moral order of mid-nineteenth century Canada, 'the prejudices and feelings of the people are stronger than the law.'[29]

These ambiguities had acute implications for Canada's native peoples. European settlement in the Maritimes began in the seventeenth century and by 1812 Indians had lost most of their land through encroachment and dispossession.[30] In Upper Canada, where they were valued as military allies, Indian lands were under the protection of colonial government until the end of the War of 1812 brought more cordial relations with the United States. Their military support was no longer needed and the dramatic influx of British

---

[27] Winks, Robin W., *The Blacks in Canada: A History*, 2nd ed., (McGill-Queen's University Press), 1997, pp. 96-113, 142-232.

[28] Ibid, Winks, Robin W., *The Blacks in Canada: A History*, pp. 337-389.

[29] Ibid, Winks, Robin W., *The Blacks in Canada: A History*, p. 369.

[30] *Indian* has been used because of the precision of the name. It was, and continues to be, used by government officials, Indigenous peoples and historians when discussing the school system. Historically, Indigenous peoples in Canada were referred to as Indians rather than by the languages that distinguishes First Nations, Inuit and Métis peoples.

immigrants from the 1820s meant that they were now seen as a social and economic problem. Through treaties and small annuities as compensation, vast tracts of their land were transferred to the new settlers between 1820 and 1840. Parallel to this there was a shift away from diplomatic relations between colonial military authorities and native Canadians in Upper and Lower Canada to their gradual 'civilising' and cultural assimilation under civilian administration. Upper Canada's dwindling native population no longer relied on annual gifts but were moved from economically prosperous lands to marginal lands on Indian reserves where they could be exposed to Christianisation, schooling and instruction in farming.[31]

The framework for this approach had already been laid by the missionary activities of different churches. During the 1820s and 1830s, this enabled missionaries, Indian leaders and government to work together. By the 1840s, this partnership had largely broken down as churches became more bureaucratic in nature and less responsive to native needs. A similar process occurred in government and the Bagot inquiry gave a grim picture of Indian life in its report in 1844 and its recommendations governed Indian affairs beyond 1867. It called an extension of the schools—first established in 1828--for native children run by the various Christian denominations reinforcing the close relationship between religion and the state.[32] These schools were intended to be self-funding and to give a practical education with equal time spent on manual work and study. Their aim was the assimilation of Indian children into the dominant culture but there was little consultation with Indian leaders. A system of residential schools persisted in Canada West after 1867 and they were transplanted to the North West territories acquired from the Hudson Bay Company in 1869.[33] Over 130 residential schools were located across Canada except in Newfoundland, Prince Edward Island and New Brunswick, and the last school only closed in 1996. Indigenous children—some 150,000 in total—were taken, often forcibly, from their homes by the Royal Canadian Mounted Police and isolated from the influence of

---

[31] Grant, John W., *Moon of Wintertime: Missionaries and the Indians of Canada in Encounter since 1534*, (University of Toronto Press), 1984, pp. 91-95.

[32] The Mohawk Institute Residential School in Brantford, Upper Canada was established in 1828 as a day school for boys of the Six Nations of the Grand River reserve and became a residential school for boys in 1831 and for girls three years later.

[33] *Canada's Residential Schools: The History, Part 1, Origins to 1939: The Final Report of the Truth and Reconciliation Commission of Canada*, Volume I, (McGill-Queens University Press), 2016.

their homes, families, traditions and cultures in the schools. There was a 40-60 per cent mortality rate in Indian residential schools. Almost all suffered from severe physical, emotional and sexual abuse.[34]

In the two myths of Anglo-Saxonism in English Canada and in the western provinces and the mystique of the French Canadian nation in Quebec saw an historical friction between the major ethnic and cultural communities that make up the 'Canadian mosaic'. Myths and friction have always carried their own dangers especially a climate of mutual suspicion that could degenerate into various types of disagreement. Religious conflicts in nineteenth century Canada lacked the bloody intensity of the wars in Europe but they were, nonetheless, 'wars' where people took sides and fought against each other through words as well as physical violence. The characteristic features of the internecine conflict in sixteenth and seventeenth century Europe were equally present in nineteenth century Canada. From the 1820s, there was a war of words within the Protestant and Catholic communities and between Catholics and Protestants occasioned by conflict over missionary activities, evangelicalism and the relationship between church and state. On occasions and especially with the influx of Orange and Catholic Irish immigrants and the emergence of the nativist movement in the 1850s, the war of words erupted into intense sectarian violence. The discourse of a dejected Ireland was evident in the contemporary press from the 1820s that increasingly commented on matters such as the persecution of Catholics and the sorry fate of 'la malheureuse Irlande' continued to haunt French-Canadians:

> In Ireland my friends, the Catholics have been reduced to the worst misery, take care; if they had been as firm as us the Irish would be free today but they are slaves! What a lesson![35]

Finally, the rebellions in Canada in 1837-1838, the Fenian incursions in 1866, 1870 and 1871 and the Métis resistance to Protestant Canadian expansionism in 1869-1870 and 1885 were grounded in conflict between Roman Catholics and Protestants whose differences in dogma took violent forms over their relationship to the colonial and federal states.

---

[34] The six volumes of the Truth and Reconciliation Commission published in 2015, seven years after the Commission was established, is the essential historical analysis of the appalling impact of residential schools.
[35] *La Minerve*, 6 November 1827.

3 Words as 'wars of religion'

The Protestant narrative that developed in the United States by 1830 stated that the Reformation had begun a process whereby freely saved Christians founded colonies in the New World and subsequently fought a revolution for the spiritual and political freedoms of that land. This version of American history was the logical conclusions of a similar British narrative. In that account, the United Kingdom was seen as inherently Protestant despite the presence of several million Catholics, and as having already achieved perfection in spiritual and political freedoms. These values, British immigrants, whether from the United States or Britain, brought to British North America. In Upper Canada, for instance, Loyalism rather than independence was the logical result of post-revolutionary events as many disposed loyal American colonists emigrated from the newly independent Republic. Despite this divergence in how the United States and Upper Canada constructed their histories, anti-Catholicism was common in both places in part because of religious bigotry, but also because it was widely understood that the triumph of Protestantism was central to the success of the nation and the colony. It was in this context that the 'war of words' between the different religious groups took place.

Legally established under the Crown by the Quebec Act of 1774 and the Constitutional Act of 1791, the Roman Catholic Church enjoyed a moral monopoly in Francophone Quebec. It supported local conservatism and was generally hostile to capitalism and industry, though this should not be over-emphasised and liberalism and other aspects of the Protestant colonial state. The Catholic Church gave Quebec a uniform and traditional religious character and French Canada remained a stronghold of clericalism. Ultramontanist Roman Catholicism adopted a fiercely defensive attitude towards the influences of Britishness and Protestantism after 1840 and gave Quebec a strong sense of mission and destiny. The Catholic hierarchy led the fight to defend Quebec's national consciousness. Protestantism was seen, not only as a threat to the Catholic hegemony in Quebec but also to its national identity. It has been said that to be French and Catholic is normal, to be English and Protestant is permissible, but to be French and Protestant is heresy.

In 1806, *Le French Canadian* was established by Pierre Bédard in Quebec with its motto: '*Notre foi, notre langue, nos institutions*'. These became the three pillars of survival for French-Canadians and had increased resonance in the aftermath of Durham's *Report* in defining the distinctiveness of French Canada. The focus was placed upon what Michel Brunet called 'Messianism', 'agriculturalism' and 'anti-statism'.[1] From 1841, leadership was progressively assumed by the Roman Catholic Church and religion was increasingly stressed to distinguish the French-Canadian people from their 'Protestant' environment. The Church emphasised the duty of French-Canadians to spread their religion and the conservative rural values associated with it. It also preached distrust of a state that was dominated by a majority alien in culture and religion. It was therefore better to rely on the Church to provide services normally associated with the State: charity, health, welfare and education. The Church was regarded as the guardian not just of the faith of the people but also of the nation. Within a few decades, it supplied the French-Canadians with a transcendental vision of their new situation.[2] Its definition of the French-Canadian nation explicitly refuted that of the Patriotes with its strong liberal and emancipating ideology. As emphasised by a clerical ideologist in the 1840s:

> ...it is not borders, nor even laws or political administrations which make a nationality; it is a religion, a language, a national character.[3]

The entanglement of Catholicism with nationalism later evolved into a close relationship between the Catholic faith and the French language according to which the latter was the best means to keep alive the former and was condensed into the motto 'the language, guardian of the faith'.[4]

---

[1] Brunet, Michel, *La Présence Anglaise et les French Canadians: Études sur l'histoire et la pensée des deux Canadas*, (Beauchemin), 1964, pp. 113-166.

[2] Eid, N. F., *Le clergé et le pouvoir politique au Québec: une analyse de l'idéologie ultramontaine au milieu du 19ᵉ siècle*, (Hurtubise), 1978, Ferretti, L., *Brève histoire de l'Église catholique au Québec*, (Boréal), 1999, Hardy, R., *Contrôle social et mutation de la culture religieuse au Québec, 1830-1930*, (Boréal), 1999, and Voisine, N., *Histoire du catholicisme québécois: Les XVIII et XIXe siècles, Vol. 2: Réveil et consolidation (1840-1898)*, (Boréal), 1991, provide context.

[3] Cit, Dumont, F., *Genèse de la société québécoise*, (Boréal), 1993, p. 227, and Lamonde, Y., *Histoire sociale des idées au Québec, 1760-1896*, (Fides), 2001, p. 286.

[4] Sylvain, Philippe, 'Libéralisme et Ultramontanisme au Canada français: affrontement idéologique et doctrinal (1840-1865)', in Morton, W. L., (ed.), *Le Bouclier d'Achille: regards sur le Canada de l'Ère victorienne*, (McClelland & Stewart), 1968, pp.111-138, 220-255. Garneau, Jean-Philippe, 'Gérer la différence dans le Québec britannique : l'exemple de la langue', in Derocher, Lorraine, Gélinas, Claude, Lebel-Grenier, Sébastien, et Noël, Pierre C., *L'État canadien et la diversité culturelle et religieuse, 1800-1914*, (Presses de l'Université du Québec), 2009, pp. 21-48.

Central to the 'war of words' within Catholicism and between Catholicism and the Protestant state was the provision of schooling.[5] For the Catholic Church, education was essential for clergy, professionals and officials but it resisted compulsory education when this made subsistence farming more difficult. Education should be thoroughly Catholic and designed not to develop critical thinking but for assimilating Catholic traditions. After 1760, the education of *habitants* had been left in the hands of the Church at the parochial level and was largely ignored by the colonial state. Levels of *habitant* literacy remained stubbornly low and this prompted the colonial government into action.[6] The system of education remained decentralised but in 1801, legislation allowed the Governor to appoint a Board of Trustees for a Royal Institute to administer a new system of education and also commissioners in parishes or townships that wished to set up a Royal Institute school. Commissioners supervised the construction, financing and maintenance of schools while the colonial government paid for teachers. Although the legislation originated in a proposal from the Anglican bishop Jacob Mountain, there was little initial opposition to the Royal Institute schools from Catholics. They were not imposed on French-Canadian parishes and the Board of Trustees allowed considerable local autonomy so parishes could appoint French-speaking Roman Catholic teachers.[7]

Despite this, by the 1810s, the Catholic hierarchy under Plessis was concerned that these schools were part of an assimilationist plan by Anglicans. Its opposition limited their development and between 1801 and 1824 only between 13 and 17 French-Canadian localities established these schools. Although resistance by the Roman Catholic Church was a major factor, there were other reasons for the limited impact of Royal Institute schools. There was an unwillingness of parents to contribute to costs and deteriorating relations between the

[5] Audet, Louis-Philippe, *Le système scolaire de la province de Québec*, 6 Vols. (Presses Universitaires Laval), 1950-1956 and *Histoire de l'enseignement au Québec, 1608-1971*, 2 Vols. (Holt, Rinehart and Winston), 1971, though traditional in character remain important studies of elementary schooling.
[6] Greer, Allan, 'The Pattern of Literacy in Québec, 1745-1899', *Histoire sociale/Social History*, Vol. 11, (1978), pp. 295-335.
[7] MacLeod, Roderick, and Pitanen, Mary Anne, *Meeting of the People: School Boards and Protestant Communities in Quebec, 1801-1998*, (McGill-Queen's University Press), 2004, pp. 20-49.

Legislative Assembly and colonial government over government funding.[8]

A different strategy was necessary and in 1824, the government introduced legislation providing for elementary education directly controlled by the parish *fabriques* (church council roughly equivalent to church vestries in Anglican communities) with the support of both the Church and the nationalist Parti Canadien. It allowed the parish priest and the *fabriques* to use a quarter of the parish's annual revenue to finance schools. This legislation did not replace Royal Institute schools but established a parallel system more in keeping with French-Canadian needs and wants. Although the *fabriques* system had considerable potential, it made as little impact on the education of French-Canadians as the Royal Institute schools. Parish revenues were generally inadequate to maintain a school and priests appear to have preferred spending money on enriching the fabric of their churches rather than on educating their parishioners. In addition, there was growing alienation between the Church and the more radical and reorganised Parti Patriote that took a more liberal nationalist view and wanted to snatch education from the grasp of the Church.

This growing ideological and political split was exacerbated in 1829 with the passage of the Assembly School Act that gave deputies rather than local priests control over the elementary school system.[9] This legislation, renewed in 1832, created a third system of education, the Écoles de Syndic that the colonial state was prepared to finance. It wanted a system of public education to reduce levels of illiteracy but the clergy saw it as lay interference in what they thought should be a Catholic education. The anglophone middle-class exerted pressure in London to establish a free and public system of education conscious of its importance in producing a skilled workforce. The plan called for primary and secondary schools in each parish or canton and the introduction of a university in Quebec. The Church feared that

---

[8] Curtis, Bruce, *Ruling by Schooling Quebec: Conquest to Liberal Governmentality—an Historical Sociology*, (University of Toronto Press), 2012, demonstrates that although attempts to govern Quebec by educating its population consumed huge amounts of public money, they had little impact on rural ignorance: while near-universal literacy reigned in New England by the 1820s, at best one in three French-speaking *habitants* in Quebec could sign his name during the insurrectionary decade of the 1830s.
[9] Ibid, Lemieux, Lucien, *Histoire du catholicisme québécois, Les XVIIIe et XIXe siècle, Vol. 1, Les années difficiles, (1760-1839)*, pp. 191-197. Dessureault, Christian, and Hudon, Christine, 'Conflits sociaux et élites locales au Bas-Canada: Le clergé, les notables, la paysannerie et le contrôle de la fabrique', *CHR*, Vol. 80, (1999), pp. 413-439, shows clearly the contested nature of education.

schooling would occur in ways that were contrary to Catholic faith and morality and that the centralising nature of the legislation would further limit its control.[10] However, attempts by parish clergy to put pressure on *habitants* by, for instance, refusing the sacrament to those who sent their children to Assembly schools had a negative effect, a reflection of the growing resentment by *habitants* of the ways priests spent *fabriques* revenues and their simmering anticlericalism. The hegemony of parish clergy was being challenged by rural liberal professionals and merchants who were increasing critical of the Church's attitudes to education and who sought control through the democratic nature of the *fabriques*. This, however, had the effect of hardening the attitude of the Church hierarchy to the Assembly's School legislation.

When the Assembly attempted to amend the legislation in 1836, it was rejected by the Legislative Council on the grounds that the new bill was too costly and would extend the control of deputies over the existing system in unacceptable ways. This rejection was the result of the effective lobbying by bishop Lartigue that met with a sympathetic hearing in the Council and increasingly bitter disputes between the Patriote deputies and the nominated Council members. The rejection of the School Bill left Lower Canada without an official school system, something lamented by contemporaries. *La Minerve* stated:

> Today, a vital law for this colony expires...The Legislative Council in its rage and folly has closed 1665 elementary schools...[11]

In 1839, Durham's *Report* was equally critical of Assembly schools because he maintained that they promoted patronage and abuse and that Patriote deputies had used them for their own political advantage. However in rural areas, Assembly schools led to rising levels of literacy and had the widespread support of *habitants*.[12] Despite calls for the reestablishment of the Écoles de Syndic, in 1838 Arthur Buller proposed a new non-sectarian system of education for the United Canada where anglophones and francophones would be educated together, Dufour suggests, 'in order to develop harmony and mutual understanding and, in the long term, the anglicising of French-

---

[10] Dufour, Andrée, *'Tous à l'école', État, communautés rurales et scolarisation au Québec de 1826 à 1859*, (HMH, Cahiers du Québec, Collection Psychopédagogie), 1996, p. 36.

[11] *La Minerve*, 1 May 1836.

[12] Ibid, Dufour, Andrée, *'Tous à l'école', État, communautés rurales et scolarisation au Québec de 1826 à 1859*, p. 93.

Canadians.'[13] Curtis, however, argues that Buller was opposed to clerical control over schooling but that his proposals were not aimed at assimilation of French-Canadians but for creating a 'new', if undefined, nationality that synthesised British and French-Canadian traditions within a non-sectarian state.[14] To avoid colonial government assuming the expenses of running this system of education, it would be funded by a school tax paid by parents and landowners. This provoked widespread opposition from both Protestant and Catholic clergy who saw this as an attempt to take education into the hands of the state.[15] The anglophone desire for French-Canadian assimilation was always a vain political hope and because of opposition from the clergy, Buller's call for a single public system was not implemented.[16] The Catholic Church's campaign for control of the French-Canadian education system in Lower Canada during the 1840s proved an important feature in its revival as the institutional basis for revived French-Canadian nationalism that was conservative rather than liberal in focus.[17]

The development of public education after 1840 was closely linked to changes in local administration introduced by Lord Sydenham during his brief stint in Canada in 1840 and 1841. Institutions that had previously been under the control of local bodies and newly established institutions were increasingly centralised. Municipal and school legislation created a local structure of governance in Lower Canada where none had existed before and this was regulated by a centralised state. In 1840, the Municipal Ordinance established a two-tier system of district councils and municipal corporations in Lower Canada. These developments were criticised by Lower Canadian members of the new Assembly largely because the new councils were firmly under executive control and there was also considerable resentment among *habitants* at their taxing powers. This

---

[13] Ibid, Dufour, Andrée, *'Tous à l'école', État, communautés rurales et scolarisation au Québec de 1826 à 1859*, p. 97.

[14] Curtis, Bruce, 'Irish Schools for Canada: Arthur Buller to the Bishop of Québec, 1838', *Historical Studies in Education/Revue d'histoire de l'éducation*, Vol. 13, (1), (2001), pp. 49-58, at p. 50.

[15] Ibid, Dufour, Andrée, *'Tous à l'école', État, communautés rurales et scolarisation au Québec de 1826 à 1859*, p. 99.

[16] Curtis, Bruce, 'The State of Tutelage in Lower Canada, 1835-1851', *History of Education Quarterly*, Vol. 37, (1), (1997), pp. 25-43 considers the question of 'liberalism' and 'conservatism' in education reforms.

[17] Lajeunesse, Marcel, 'L'évêque Bourget et l'instruction publique au Bas-Canada, 1841-1846', *Revue d'histoire de l'Amérique française*, Vol. 23, (1969), pp. 35-52, is important of the Catholic reaction to Buller's proposals and the 1841 legislation.

situation was exacerbated by Sydenham's belief that a comprehensive public education system was as important as municipal government. The result was an often intense 'war of words' over the form that this public education system should take lasting from 1841 until 1846.

In 1841, a Common Schools Act was applied to both Upper and Lower Canada and briefly remained in force in the upper province until replaced in 1843. After this the two parts of the United Province developed distinct systems of education. The control of schools, previously vested in the Assembly, now lay with the office of the Superintendent of Education. The original legislation established one superintendent but in 1842 Governor Sir Charles Bagot appointed an Assistant Superintendent for each province and Jean-Baptiste Meilleur was appointed for Lower Canada.[18] Meilleur's appointment relieved French-Canadian fears of absorption into the secular British school system and ensured that Lower and Upper Canada would develop different education systems. Under his dynamic leadership and with the Church's support, elementary education for all was introduced despite the hostility of those who wanted to retain their local autonomy. The legislation introduced, with several modifications to satisfy opposition to Buller's proposals, floundered. Initially few schools were founded and local opposition often prevented their construction and financing.[19] The cooperation of district councils was essential if the new system was to succeed and this was not forthcoming. Meilleur made clear in 1843 that the reason why local taxation was not introduced was suspicion that the monies collected would be used for other than local purposes.

Despite opposition to the 1841 legislation, schools did gradually increase in number during the first half of the 1840s largely because parents and the Church were willing to provide funding on a voluntary basis. The Schools Act for Canada East in 1845 established French-Canadian schools in Catholic parishes with similarly religious-based schools for the Protestant minority.[20] This set the pattern for the development of schooling in Canada East as the 1843 Schools Act had done for Canada West. The question of funding was addressed a year later by the 1846 Act 'to make better provision for Education in Lower Canada'. The most significant feature of this Act was the return to compulsory school taxes: in addition to annual school taxes, parents

[18] Ibid, Voisine, N., *Histoire du catholicisme québécois: Les XVIII et XIXe siècles, Vol. 2: Réveil et consolidation (1840-1898)*, p. 29. Lortie, L., 'Jean-Baptiste Meilleur', *DCB*, Vol. 10, pp. 504-509.
[19] Ibid, Dufour, Andrée, *'Tous à l'école', État, communautés rurales et scolarisation au Québec de 1826 à 1859*, p. 101.
[20] Ibid, pp. 272, 291, 413, 441.

of children between 5 and 16 had to pay a monthly tax whether their children attended school or not and this was symptomatic of a more centralised approach to education. The Church gained a little ground through this legislation as it allowed Roman Catholic clergy to act as visitors to the schools. However, there was widespread opposition to the compulsory nature of school taxes with Catholics objecting to paying taxes that might fund Protestant schools and vice versa. This opposition took the form of withdrawing children from school, refusing to elect local officials and putting pressure on the Church to make the tax voluntary.[21]

The legislation in 1841, 1845 and 1846 represented a compromise between the clergy who wanted church-controlled schools and those who sought common non-sectarian public schools. For Montreal and Quebec, there would be two kinds of schools, officially 'common' or public, one run by a Catholic and the other by a Protestant council of six members named by the municipal authorities. Elsewhere, there was one set of common schools runs by elected school boards, but in each township, the minority denomination, generally the Protestants, would set up a separate 'dissentient' school if the majority of its members so wished. This lay the foundations for a dual denominational school system. Although priests were often elected to school boards in the 1840s and 1850s, it was not until after Confederation that the Catholic Church finally achieved control over Catholic schooling when the Constitution Act of 1867 placed denominational boards beyond the reach of provincial legislators. In 1869, legislation resolved the problematic and explosive nature of funding education by establishing the denominational principle with regard to property-based school taxes: taxes from Protestants went to Protestant boards and from Catholics to Catholic boards. The abolition of the Ministry of Public Instruction in 1875 finally established the principle of clerical domination. With bishops holding half the seats on the Catholic Committee of the Council of Public Education, they had a working majority in meetings giving them the authority to fend off any attempts by Liberal Quebec governments to reassert state influence over education.[22] The 'war of words' over public schooling was resolved by a pragmatic solution with Catholic schools where French-Canadian Catholics were in the majority but with provision for the educational rights of the minority Protestants constitutionally safeguarded.

---

[21] Ibid, Dufour, Andrée, 'Tous à l'école', État, communautés rurales et scolarisation au Québec de 1826 à 1859, pp. 110-111.

[22] Audet, Louis-Phillipe, Histoire du Conseil de l'Instruction publique de la province de Québec, 1856-1964, (Léméac), 1964.

The Manitoba Act of 1870 established a dual system of Protestant and Catholic schools. Although seen as a religious issue, there was also a question of the language of education since most Roman Catholics were francophones and Protestants anglophones. The Manitoba Act responded to these issues by giving the province the power to pass laws relation to education and also by giving constitutional protection to denominational school rights that existed '...by Law or practice in the Province at the Union'. What this meant in practice and the extent of the constitutional rights it promised was not defined and subsequently became a matter of considerable legal debate.

What may have been a reasonable solution quickly unravelled. During the 1870s and 1880 the proportion of Catholics in the province fell because of Anglo-Protestant settlement and the equal rights to denominational schooling no longer reflected the linguistic composition of the province. Ontarian settlers were also emboldened by the defeat of the Métis rebellion in 1885 in pushing their assimilist agenda. D'Alton McCarthy formed the Equal Rights Association in 1889 calling for fairer representation in the province instead of privileges for the diminishing French population. On 5 August 1889, he delivered a speech at Portage la Prairie in which he railed against French-Canadian 'nationalists' who were aggressively asserting their right to remain a 'distinct race' in Canada. Attorney-General Joseph Martin also spoke at the meeting asserting: 'he was an Englishman and he believed this was an English country. French was a most beautiful language, but to him it was beautiful at home, to him it was a foreign language; and (he) maintained we should speak the language of the country'. This is traditionally interpreted as the beginning of the Manitoba Schools' Question although J. R. Miller suggests that the origins of the Question lay in the prior erosion of the province's cultural duality.[23]

In March 1890, Manitoba's Liberal government under Thomas Greenway introduced the Manitoba Public Schools Act abolishing public funding of Catholic and Protestant schools and establishing a system of non-sectarian public schools funded from provincial taxation.[24] Separate legislation was also introduced that made English the only official language in the province, a precedent followed by the

---

[23] Miller, J. R., 'D'Alton McCarthy, Equal Rights and the Origins of the Manitoba School Question', *CHR*, Vol. 54, (4), (1973), pp. 369-392.
[24] Clark, Lovell, (ed.), *The Manitoba School Question: majority rule or minority rights?*, (Copp Clark Publishing), 1968, includes key documents.

neighbouring North-West Territories two years later.[25] This inaugurated a period of intense Catholic political and religious opposition.[26]

On 7 April 1890, Archbishop Alexandre Taché, as President of the Catholic section of the Board of Education, called on the federal government to disallow the two educational acts. This was followed on 12 May by a letter from Louis-François Laflèche, bishop of Trois-Rivières, Quebec, to Joseph-Adolphe Chapleau, Secretary of State of Canada, requesting that the federal government disallow the unjust laws enacted by the Manitoban government but his request was rejected on 23 May. A National Congress of French Catholics of Manitoba was convened in St. Boniface on 4 June. Delegates from each of the parishes of Manitoba were to be sent adding their weight to the wave of protest sweeping Catholic Manitoba over the school laws. This was followed, probably in August, by a petition from the Roman Catholic clergy and laity of 4,267 signatures calling on the federal government to hear their appeal against legislation that was prejudicial to the rights and privileges of denominational schools.[27]

The debate soon spread beyond Manitoba, whose Catholics received support from other Catholic communities. In March 1891, the archbishops and bishops of the ecclesiastical provinces of Quebec, Montreal and Ottawa signed jointly a Pastoral Letter on the subject of the Manitoba schools supporting Mgr. Taché in his struggle. While on 24 March a petition signed by all but one of the Roman Catholic bishops and archbishops in Canada was given to the Secretary of State requesting that the Canadian government 'afford a remedy to the pernicious legislation above mentioned (the two educational bills), and that in the most efficacious and just way.'[28] There was also intense activity by the Protestant Protective Association, an anti-Catholic organisation of American origins with as many as 100,000 members in its various chapters across Canada. It attacked Catholics and French-

---

[25] Aunger, Edmund A., 'Justifying the End of Official Bilingualism: Canada's North-West Assembly and the Dual Language Question, 1889-1892', *Canadian Journal of Political Science*, Vol. 34, (3), (2001), pp. 451-486.

[26] Wade, F. C., *The Manitoba School Question*, (Printed at the Manitoba Institution for the Deaf and Dumb), 1895, and Ewart, J. S., *The Manitoba School Question: A Reply to Mr Wade...*, (Manitoba Free Press), 1895.

[27] McLauchlin, Kenneth, "Rising The Protestant Horse': The Manitoba School Question and Canadian Politics, 1890-1896', CCHA, *Historical Studies,* Vol. 53, (1986), pp. 39-52.

[28] Little, J. I., 'New Brunswick Reaction to the Manitoba Schools' Question', *Acadiensis*, Vol, 1, (2), (1972), pp. 45-58.

Canadians for failing to assimilate with the majority and of frustrating the dream of a homogeneous country.

The validity of the 1890 legislation was twice upheld by the Judicial Committee of the Privy Council. *Winnipeg v Barrett* (1892) considered whether the Public Schools Act conflicted with the constitutional protection for denominational schools contained in the Manitoba Act 1870, s22. The Judicial Committee held that s 22(1) guaranteed the right of religious groups to establish and run their own schools but did not guarantee public funding of those denominational schools since, in 1870, all schools in Manitoba were funded by the religious groups that ran them. The use of taxation to fund denominational schools was only established after the founding of the province and was not guaranteed in s22(1) of the 1870 legislation. This meant that the provincial legislature could end taxpayer funding of denominational schools and establish taxpayer-funded non-sectarian schools without breaching s22(1). *Brophy v Manitoba* (1894), the second case, related to the remedial powers of the federal government under s93(3) of the Constitution Act 1867. This legislation made education an exclusively provincial matter although there was a special power for the federal government in relation to separate schools. It allowed an appeal to the Governor-General in Council where any provincial legislation affected the right and privileges of Roman Catholics and Protestants in relation to education. If a province failed to comply with the decision of the Governor-in-Council, then the federal government had the power to introduce remedial legislation. It was unclear whether the changes introduced in the 1890 Act were sufficient to justify the federal government doing this, but the Judicial Committee affirmed the federal government's power to restore the lost school privileges. The outcome of these two judgements was that Manitoba's government had the right to remove public funding from denominational schools and establish a non-sectarian public school system but the federal government had the authority, if it chose to use it, to pass remedial legislation to protect denominational education.

Delays followed as the weak federal Conservative government sought an acceptable solution and in February 1896, it finally introduced remedial legislation. The draft legislation was disliked intensely by some of the Conservative caucus and its introduction resulted in a further political crisis. In April 1896, Prime Minister Mackenzie Bowell was forced to call an election and to resign. Charles Tupper became Prime Minister and led the Conservatives into the election. Wilfrid Laurier, the Liberal leader faced by virulently anti-French and anti-Catholic voices forced the remedial bill's withdrawal. The issue lay at the heart of the federal elections in June 1896 when Laurier defeated the government largely by winning 49 of the 65 seats in Quebec.[29] *L'Électeur*, official newspaper of the Liberal Party, commented, 'the electoral campaign has taken the character of a type of holy war...Never before had our country witnessed such criminal and scandalous exploitation of religion.'[30]

Laurier sought to deflect attacks from the Catholic hierarchy, who were accused by Canadian politicians and the Pope of interfering in politics, by promising a less prickly solution. In late 1896, he and Greenway reached a compromise that was included as an amendment to the Schools Act 1897. This did not restore separate schools, but it allowed Catholic teachers to be employed in certain circumstances and gave some religious-instruction privileges within the public schools. Many of the Canadian Catholic hierarchy were opposed to this compromise and appealed to Pope Leo XIII who, having sent an observer in early 1897, agreed with Laurier that while the compromise was inadequate, it was the fairest solution given the small number of Catholics in the province. In reality, the Manitoba Schools' Question was far from being 'settled' in 1896-1897 and it was not until the late 1970s that more equitable arrangements were made.[31] For many in modern Quebec, the Manitoba Schools' Question is regarded as the most significant loss of French and Catholic rights beyond Quebec.

Although the continuance of separate denominational schools was enshrined in the Constitution Act 1867 when provinces were given exclusive jurisdiction over its own educational structures, their existence remained a source of contention between Catholics and Protestants. In Quebec, a dual confessional public school system was developed composed of Catholic and Protestant schools that controlled their own curriculums, teacher training and inspection through their confessional section of the Council of Public Instruction. Ontario, Saskatchewan and Alberta established a sectarian separate-school system parallel to a common non-sectarian public school system. Nova Scotia, New Brunswick and Prince Edward Island each officially had a non-sectarian public school system but, in practice, Catholic schools did receive state funding and by default a separate-school system came into being. Newfoundland provided support exclusively for denominational schools while British Columbia funded no religious-based schooling until 1977.

The decade after the rebellions in the late 1830s saw widespread change in the Canadas. Political changes, modifications in established

---

[29] Crunican, Paul, *Priests and Politicians: Manitoba schools and the election of 1896*, (University of Toronto Press), 1974.
[30] *L'Électeur*, 21 June 1896.
[31] Cook, G. R., 'Church, Schools and Politics in Manitoba, 1903-12', *CHR*, Vol. 39, (1), (1958), pp. 1-23.

political ideologies and crises in social policy especially in education were issues in which the Catholic Church with its growing self-confidence had little choice but to be involved. In the aftermath of the rebellions, it was the Roman Catholic Church that provided many in Lower Canada with a focus for their faith but also for their political and cultural aspirations. Though conservative clerical nationalism was not fully formed by 1850, its roots were clearly identified in the growing ultramontanism of the Church and in its increasing appeal to many French-Canadians as the protector not simply of their faith but also of their cultural heritage.

In Europe and especially in France and Italy during the 1820s and 1830s a Catholic revival linked to ultramontanism was increasingly important and reached in Quebec during the 1840s. Bourget, who had close links with the Papacy, restructured the Church to increase its presence in the social and political spheres as part of the campaign to strengthen French-Canadian faith and willingness to adhere to Catholic doctrine. To achieve this, he initially needed to resolve the problem of the shortage of priests in the province and recruited priests from religious communities in Europe. This led to an increase in the number of priests per head of population from 1:1800 in 1830 to about 1:1000 by 1850. This gave the Church a greater presence in the lives of parishioners with priests becoming more involved in charitable work, education and the organisation of religious processions, retreats and temperance societies.

La lutte que se sont livrés mutuellement l'Église et l'État au XIXe siècle, aussi bien en Europe qu'au Canada-français, n'a été en fait qu'une transposition, au niveau des institutions, d'une opposition fondamentale entre deux groupes sociaux aux intérêts divergents, soit le clergé, d'une part, et la bourgeoisie, d'autre part.[32]

Initially Bourget was wary of the reformist politics of Louis-Hippolyte LaFontaine but by the mid-1840s, he recognised the value of an alliance with the dominant political grouping especially with the introduction of responsible government in 1848. The advent of a professional bureaucracy gave governing political parties access to extensive patronage. This led to closer ties between the Catholic Church and LaFontaine's Reform Party and this was reflected in important changes at local level. Social legislation and the bureaucracy necessary to manage it provided opportunities for professional men in

---

[32] Eid, Nadia F., *Le clergé et le pouvoir politique au Québec, une analyse de l'idéologie ultramontaine au milieu du XIXe siècle*, (HMH, Cahiers du Québec, Collection Histoire), 1978, p. 26.

French-Canadian rural society. The new political and bureaucratic structures also strengthened the political power of French-Canadians since their representatives were now ministers in the Executive Council. Participation in local government and school affairs gave individuals status within their communities as well as potential access to lucrative patronage positions.

Bourget's spiritual revival, closely linked to his political agenda for the Church, would have greater influence over the lives of the people if those lives were being structured and monitored by Catholic clergy. The French-Canadian *petite bourgeoisie* also saw the advantage of allying with the clergy to strengthen their position in relation to British middle-class commercial power. Following Bourget's lead, local clergy involved themselves in Church initiated social activities as a further way of influencing the lives of their parishioners. For both the professions and the Church, the social initiatives introduced by the state provided important opportunities. It was this new alliance and the declining prestige of the traditional *seigneurs* that led to their alliance with *habitants* over state-imposed taxation. This represented a reversal of the situation in the 1830s when it was the alliance of *habitants* and professionals that confronted the Church and *seigneurs*. Education itself was not the issue; it was a matter of who should control it. In seeking these alliances, Bourget was:

> ...l'un des premiers leaders ecclésiastiques à saisir l'importance de cette entreprise comme facteur d'intégration et de cohésion à la fois idéologique et administrative au sein de la communauté religieuse canadienne.[33]

Bourget was largely responsible for the assertion of the rights of the Church over their parishes and schools and over birth, marriage and death, the critical events in people's lives that were independent of the state.[34] Education was seen first as a means of training good Christians and only secondly intelligent and educated individuals.[35] Bourget's position was reinforced by the elevation in 1846 of Pius IX who was more open to innovation than his predecessor. He went to Rome to ask for the establishment of an ecclesiastical province and to recruit clergy who were prepared to go to Canada and, as a result a new diocese was set up in Toronto.

---

[33] Ibid, Eid, Nadia F., *Le clergé et le pouvoir politique au Québec, une analyse de l'idéologie ultramontaine au milieu du XIXe siècle*, p. 32.

[34] Ibid, Eid, Nadia F., *Le clergé et le pouvoir politique au Québec, une analyse de l'idéologie ultramontaine au milieu du XIXe siècle*, p. 37.

[35] Ibid, Eid, Nadia F., *Le clergé et le pouvoir politique au Québec, une analyse de l'idéologie ultramontaine au milieu du XIXe siècle*, p. 201.

European ideas of secularisation and anticlericalism were not without their supporters in Lower Canada in the 1840s and 1850s. The *Parti Rouge* supported the abolition of the dime in 1849 that would have severely weakened the economic position of the clergy and the Church in general. The return of Papineau from exile in 1845 and the emergence of the Rouges as a radical, nationalist party reasserted the role of education and liberalism in the development of French Canadian nationalism.[36] Faced by this, the Church responded that the French-Canadian nation was defined in terms of its language and religion restating its links with French-Canadian people and its loyalty to the British Crown.[37]

The Church was also concerned by the influx of largely Protestant immigrants into Lower Canada at the same time that many French-Canadians migrated to the United States. Like other elite groups, the Church was concerned about cultural survival and consequently promoted the colonisation of new lands in Canada where French-Canadian communities could be established beyond the influence of Protestant anglophones. The settlement of French-Canadians in the Eastern Townships was stimulated by the establishment of the Association pour l'établissement des Canadiens français dans les Townships du Bas-Canada in 1848.[38] Father Bernard O'Reilly, Catholic missionary at Sherbrooke until 1848, exposed the poor condition of the Eastern Townships colonists in newspaper articles especially in *Le Canadien* and speeches and called for some sort of association to organise their settlement as an alternative to emigration. His plea was taken up by the Institut Canadien de Montréal, an avant-garde group of young intellectuals and the Association was launched in April 1848 at a substantial meeting of 8,000 sympathisers.[39] The Association was short-lived and its concrete

---

[36] Bernard, Jean-Paul, *Les rouges: libéralisme, nationalisme et anticléricalisme au milieu du XIXe siècle*, (PUQ), 1971, pp. 6, 39.

[37] Ibid, Eid, Nadia F., *Le clergé et le pouvoir politique au Québec, une analyse de l'idéologie ultramontaine au milieu du XIXe siècle*, p. 231.

[38] LaBrèque, Marie-Paule Rajotte, 'Un 150e anniversaire; L'Association des Établissements Canadiens des Townships (1848)', *Journal of Eastern Townships Studies/Revue d'études des Cantons de l'Est*, n° 7, (1998), pp. 75-81. See also, Little, John I., 'The Catholic Church and the French-Canadian Colonization of the Eastern Townships, 1821-1851', *Revue de l'université d'Ottawa*, Vol. 52, (1982), pp. 142-165, and Little, John I., *Nationalism, Capitalism, and Colonization in Nineteenth-Century Quebec: the Upper St Francis District*, (McGill-Queen's University Press), 1989, pp. 81-92.

[39] Bishop Bourget and Louis-Joseph Papineau were chosen as president and vice-president, respectively. Partisan politics and public disaffection soon

achievements minimal, but it did serve to link O'Reilly's name to the influx of approximately 17,000 French-Canadians between 1844 and 1851.[40] In the 1850s, the Catholic Church purchased lands that it gave to young families of farmers to prevent them from leaving for the United States where it was believed they would ultimately be assimilated. The influence of both the Catholic Church and the Association helped increase levels of immigration and, reinforced by their high birth rate, French-Canadians increased from 25 per cent of the population in 1844 to 48 per cent by 1861 and by the late 1860s they formed the largest social group.

The defence by the Catholic Church of its dominant position was also evident in its attitude to Protestant missionary activity.[41] The Catholic hierarchy was suspicious of Protestant evangelism not simply on theological grounds but also for social and cultural reasons. Protestantism represented a very different way of life and posed a potent threat to French-Canadian heritage. The arrival of Protestantism was considered by some *habitants* as further attack on their traditions and Protestant communities became a legitimate Patriote target. They attacked those who had converted to the religion of the colonial power, for not having taken part in the radical reform movement and of supporting a suspect religion. For instance, the Protestant mission of Henriette Odin-Feller at St. Blaise-sur-Richelieu and the homes of converts were subject to charivaris in 1837.[42] Unable

---

led to the movement's disintegration, but Bourget had time to start a colony at Roxton Falls in Shefford County. Other similar associations undertook various projects and colonisation missionaries remained active for almost a century.

[40] Parent, Gilles, *Deux efforts de colonisation française dans les Cantons de l'Est, 1848 et 1851*, Groupe de Recherche en Histoire des Cantons de l'Est, Département d'histoire, Université de Sherbrooke, 1980.

[41] Campbell, John, *A Concise History of French-Canadian Protestantism*, (Board of French Evangelization of the Presbyterian Church in Canada), 1898, pp. 14-32, considers developments between 1820 and 1890. See the essays in Zuidema, Jason, (ed.), *French-Speaking Protestants in Canada: Historical Essays*, (Brill), 2011,

[42] Cramp, John Mockett, *A Memoir of Madame Feller, with an account of the origin and progress of the Grand Ligne mission*, (Evangelical Society of the Grande Ligne), 1876, pp. 110-122, considers the rebellion. Balmer, Randall, and Randall, Catharine, '"Her Duty to Canada": Henriette Feller and French Protestantism in Quebec', *Church History*, Vol. 70, (2001), pp. 49-72, and 'Henriette Feller, The Spirit and Mission to Canada', in ibid, Zuidema, Jason, (ed.), *French-Speaking Protestants in Canada: Historical Essays*, pp. 29-48, examine her role as a Protestant missionary. See also, ibid, Hardy, R., *Contrôle social et mutation de la culture religieuse au Québec, 1830-1930*, pp. 30-35.

to establish missions in Montreal or St. Jean where the Catholic Church exercised considerable control, Louisa Roussy, a Swiss missionary and Henriette Odin-Feller established a mission on newly settled lands where the clergy had less control and where the absence of services such as schooling or a doctor favoured establishing good relations with their neighbours. They quickly established a small Protestant community of twenty-five people, most descendants of Madame Lore, a Protestant of American origin who had converted to Catholicism on her marriage. After the charivaris in 1837, Odin-Feller and the families who had converted left St. Blaise for Champlain in the United States. The 1837 rebellion marked an important stage in the development of Protestantism in St. Blaise. It appeared to English and Swiss evangelists of Lower Canada to have removed the influence of the clergy, the most significant obstacle to their conversion of French-Canadians. On her return two months later, she distributed food and medicine to local people, stopped further action against those who had burned the converts' houses, and went to Napierville to speak to Richard McGinnis, charged by the government with taking depositions and examining witnesses, on their behalf. She wrote:

> En général, l'esprit du peuple est tellement changé envers nous, qu'il n'est, je crois, aucune maison de la Grande Ligne dans laquelle je ne puis entrer maintenant.

However, her actions did not prevent nine properties being destroyed during Loyalist reprisals in November 1838.

For evangelicals, attitudes in Quebec seemed to prove much of their Catholic conspiracy theory. Liberty of expression was not a characteristic of French Quebec and evangelicals were powerless in the face of the total political and social control of the Catholic hierarchy. This was evident in evangelical journals where any expression of anti-Protestantism by Catholic leaders in Quebec was widely publicised. Stories of persecuted French converts from Catholicism were publicised across the evangelical world and the threat of violence, loss of employment and censorship blamed on the direction of Catholic priests and bishops. The Catholic clergy sought to protect their often ignorant and confused flock from anti-religious and anti-Catholic writings and speech through Catholic pastoral letters and the threat of excommunication where individuals endangered the position of the Church.

Roman Catholicism engaged in a war of words when it was externally threatened by the aggression of the anglicising colonial state or from those within the Roman Catholic community between those who adhered to the conservative religious, social and political teachings of the Church and those who questioned that orthodoxy through a broadly anticlerical and liberal ideology. Both posed a challenge to the doctrinal and cultural hegemony of the Roman Catholic Church, but they also posed difficulties for the state for whom the support of the Church was essential to maintain control over French-Canadian society.

An effective presence since the 1763 Treaty of Paris ceded most of the Franco-American empire to Britain, the Anglican Church had decidedly establishment ambitions. Officially recognised as a legally established church by the Constitutional Act of 1791, the Anglican Church was seen as a vital conservative bulwark against republicanism and revolution in British North America. After 1815, John Strachan, later bishop of Toronto believed that the survival of a hierarchical society and a political order defined by executive rule depended less on the venerable constitution than upon the rational traditions of the Anglican Church. Despite legal, social and economic advantages, for a variety of reasons Anglicanism did not evolved into the naturally acknowledged Church of Canada envisaged by British elites in the wake of American independence. Initially it enjoyed extensive privileges in both the Maritimes and Upper Canada but it was never exclusively English in composition and experienced vibrant competition from extremely popular evangelical societies, most notably the Methodists. In Upper Canada, there were more Irish than English Anglicans and the church drew many of its clergy and laity from Ireland. At the same time, many among the humbler ranks of Irish Protestants were resolute Tories who clung to the church as a familiar badge of identity against the dangers of Roman Catholic immigration, while many English immigrants were political reformers and dissenters. In addition, the Loyalist influx after 1783 imported the religious pluralism of the American colonies, a process exacerbated by the later immigration of American settlers.

The claims of the Church of England, especially over the Clergy Reserves, emerged as a divisive issue in the mid-1820s and led to an intense 'war of words' within Protestantism.[43] After 1791, Anglicans insisted successfully that '*a* Protestant clergy' meant 'the' Protestant clergy of the Church of England as the established church and that the Church of England alone had a right to the benefits of the Clergy Reserves. Any attack on the Reserves met with their spirited defence especially by John Strachan, who in 1819 had been instrumental in establishing the Upper Canada Clergy Corporation to manage the

---

[43] A brief discussion of religion and education in the 1820s and 1830s can be found in Craig, G. M., *Upper Canada: the formative years, 1784-1841*, (McClelland & Stewart), 1963, pp. 165-187.

lands.[44] The position of the Church of England was, however, far from dominant in Upper Canada. In 1819, there were only 10 Anglican clergymen and 2 Anglican chaplains in the province while there were 6 Presbyterian ministers and 6 Catholic priests plus an unspecified number of itinerant Methodists.

The same year, following the request of a Presbyterian church in the Niagara District for financial assistance, Lieutenant-Governor Sir Peregrine Maitland asked the Colonial Office to determine whether the Church of England, as Strachan claimed, had the exclusive right to the Reserves under the Constitutional Act.[45] The British Attorney-General and Solicitor-General concluded that Presbyterian clergy could be included in the definition of 'Protestant Clergy' under the act.[46] Maitland, however, did not agree and first attempted to prevent publication of the law officers' opinion in Upper Canada and then to evade its implication by suggesting that the Church of Scotland be limited to 'occasional' assistance. He, like Strachan, believed that only through exclusive support of the Anglican Church and a system of education controlled by its clergy could Upper Canada overcome dangerous republican ideas which, they thought, were infiltrating the province through American Methodist clergymen and teachers.[47] There was increasing division of opinion between those who thought that the Reserves should be fairly distributed to support all Protestant clergy and those who wanted the lands secularised with the money used for public services such as schools and roads.

Because Methodists and Presbyterians formed a large and vocal segment of the population, the exclusive claims made by the Church of England could not escape becoming entangled in the political struggle between Maitland's administration and the anti-government

---

[44] *The Christian Recorder*, Vol. 1 (1), (1819), pp. 13-16. See also, Strachan, John, *Canada church establishment: copy of a letter addressed to R. J. Wilmot Horton, Esq. by the Rev. Dr. Strachan, archdeacon of York, Upper Canada, dated 16th May, 1827, respecting the state of the church in that province*, (London: s.n.), 1827.

[45] The argument is contained in, *The Canadian Miscellany, or, The Religious, Literary and Statistical Intelligencer*, Vol 1, (1), (1828), 'A Pastoral Letter from The Clergy of the Church of Scotland in the Canadas to Their Presbyterian Brethren', pp. 2-24.

[46] Moir, John S., 'John Strachan and Presbyterianism', *Journal of the Canadian Church Historical Society*, Vol. 41, (1999), pp. 81-97.

[47] Bethune, A. N., *Memoir of the Right Reverend John Strachan, D.D., LL.D., first bishop of Toronto*, (Henry Rowsell), 1870, pp. 87-129, considers Strachan in the 1820s.

opposition.[48] In 1827, Maitland informed William Huskisson that he was not prepared to see 'the national church' degraded to a sect and all denominations 'placed on a level.' He admitted that Methodists 'exceeded greatly' Anglicans and Presbyterians, but like Strachan, he believed that many who were nominally attached to other denominations could be won over to the Church of England if it received the proper support.[49] Maitland's support for the Church of England and for Strachan proved damaging especially as the religious issue became a focus of public attention. Partly to divert criticism and hoping to increase the revenue of the Church of England, Strachan, with Maitland's approval, went to London in 1826 to continue negotiations with the Canada Company for the sale of the Clergy Reserves.[50]

At the same time he sought, with Maitland's active support, a charter for a provincial university under the control of the Church of England.[51] While in London, Strachan prepared an 'Ecclesiastical Chart' that exaggerated the Anglican Church's position in Upper Canada but this and his continuing attacks on Methodists were strenuously challenged on his return to Canada in the summer of 1827. [52] The charter for a university was attacked and even some of his fellow-churchmen were disturbed by his actions. Maitland did not abandon his principles but was concerned that Strachan's dogmatism had exacerbated the religious situation. Reports circulated of a break

---

[48] See, for instance, the debate on 22 December 1826, *Journal of the House of Assembly of Upper Canada, from the 5th December, 1826 to the 17th February, 1827....: being the third session of the ninth provincial Parliament of this province*, pp. 23-25.

[49] French, Goldwin, *Politics & Parsons: The Role of the Wesleyan Methodists in Upper Canada and the Maritimes from 1780 to 1855*, (Ryerson Press), 1962, and the more general Semple, Neil, *The Lord's Dominion: The History of Canadian Methodism*, (McGill-Queen's University Press), 1996, pp. 71-99, remain central on this issue.

[50] *An Act to Authorize the Sale of a part of the Clergy Reserves in the Provinces of Upper and Lower Canada*, (G. Eyre and A. Strahan), 1827.

[51] Strachan, John, *An Appeal to the Friends of Religion and Literature, in behalf of the University of Upper Canada*, (R. Gilbert), 1827, provoked widespread opposition especially his assertion that the university should be a 'missionary college'.

[52] Strachan's 'Ecclesiastical Chart' in printed in *Appendix to Journal of the House of Assembly of Upper Canada*, (Toronto: s.n.), 1828. See also, Strachan, John, *Canada church establishment: copy of a letter addressed to R. J. Wilmot Horton, Esq. by the Rev. Dr. Strachan, archdeacon of York, Upper Canada, dated 16th May, 1827, respecting the state of the church in that province*, pp. 4-5.

between the two and Maitland made clear that he had not anticipated the bitterness the issue had aroused. The *Upper Canada Herald* saw it as an attempt to impose an illiberal and exclusive 'clerico-political aristocracy' alien to the Upper Canadian situation.[53] In December 1827, a petition of 8,000 signatures challenged Strachan's position on both the Clergy Reserves and the university and in March 1828, the Assembly sent a petition to the Colonial Office requesting revocation of the university charter.[54] At the end of Maitland's administration, Strachan had clearly become a liability. The Lieutenant-Governor ignored Strachan's 'Ecclesiastical Chart' and attempted instead to blame much of the agitation on those who misrepresented the Church of England. But in the election of 1828 the province registered its disapproval of Maitland and his advisers. 'There can be no question,' Samuel Peters Jarvis wrote to W. D. Powell in December 1828:

> ...that much of the odium, which has fallen to the share of many of those who were conspicuous in the late administration, was caused by his [Strachan's] uncompromising disposition.

The new Lieutenant-Governor, Sir John Colborne remained distant from Strachan whom he thought had injured 'to a very large degree the interests of the Episcopal Church and, I am afraid, of religion also' and was critical of his active political role but was not prepared 'to be evasive about his own religious convictions.'[55] In 1828, he had been unwilling to accept Strachan's proposal for a university or respect Strachan's tactics in strengthening the bond between his church and the interests of society.

Anglican privileges drew increasing criticisms from other growing church bodies and especially from Methodists. Upper Canadian Methodism was far from united in the 1820s. The first Methodist missionaries in the province were Americans accredited by a New York state Methodist Episcopal conference but after 1815 British Wesleyan Methodists also sent missionaries to Canada. To avoid competition, the two Methodist bodies agreed a geographical division in 1820 with Lower Canada reserved for the Wesleyans and Upper

---

[53] *Upper Canada Herald*, 9 October 1827.
[54] The Report of the Select Committee on the petition is printed in ibid, *Appendix to Journal of the House of Assembly of Upper Canada*. Strachan vigorously defended his position in the Legislative Council in early March 1828: *Speech in the Legislative Council, 6th March 1828: On the subject of the Clergy Reserves*, (Robert Stanton), 1828.
[55] Colborne to the bishop of Quebec, 1829, cit, Hayes, A. L., *Anglicans in Canada: Controversies and Identity in Historical Perspective*, (University of Illinois Press), 2004, p. 64.

Canada for the Americans. This proved difficult to maintain and by 1828 a Canadian Methodist Episcopal Conference was established to which many of the British Wesleyans in the province objected. In York, for instance, the Methodist congregation split with the Wesleyans organising a separate chapel. The problem was not simply one of organisation. The Wesleyan Methodists was hierarchical in structure and loyalist in attitude while American Methodism was less liturgical and more emotional in its forms of worship, less structured and more free-spirited and incorporated notions of the separation of church and state.

Rooted among both Loyalists and post-Loyalist Americans and strong in the countryside, American Methodism was strengthened by immigrant Wesleyan Methodists and this challenged the dominance of the Anglican Church. In 1826 a sermon, delivered the previous summer at the funeral of Bishop Jacob Mountain by John Strachan, was published.[56] It traced the rise of the Anglican Church in the colony as the established church and attacked Methodists as ignorant American enthusiasts, unsound in religion and disloyal in politics. None of these arguments were new, but on this occasion the Methodists in York chose not to remain silent and Egerton Ryerson, a young minister of Loyalist family was one of those invited to frame a reply.[57] In a long letter printed in the *Colonial Advocate* in May 1826, he challenged all of Strachan's assertions mounting a vigorous defence of the loyalty of all Methodists.

No less than Strachan, Ryerson wanted a society that was both Christian and British. He rejected charges of ignorance by citing the intellectual training required of all Methodist preachers and also challenged the contention that most were Americans. This letter and the subsequent debate in the provincial press drew attention to Ryerson's outstanding abilities as a publicist for the Methodist cause. The following year, Strachan again put forward his claims in a series of letters written in England to garner support for both the Church of

---

[56] Strachan, John, *A Sermon preached at York, Upper Canada, third of July, 1825, on the death of the late Lord Bishop of Quebec*, (James Macfarlane), 1826. See also, Moir, John S., 'John Strachan's sermon on the death of Bishop Mountain: a question of motives', *Journal of the Canadian Church Historical Society*, Vol. 40 (1998), pp. 179-186.

[57] Ryerson, Egerton, *The Story of My Life*, (W. Briggs), 1883, is a useful, if slanted autobiography. Sissons, C. B., *Egerton Ryerson: His Life and Letters*, 2 Vols. (Clarke Irwin), 1937, remains the standard biography. Gidney, R. D., 'Egerton Ryerson', *DCB*, Vol. 11, pp. 783-795, takes account of more recent work.

England and the colony's newly chartered university [58] In the public uproar that followed, Ryerson was one critic among many, but in eight letters, published first in the *Upper Canada Herald* in June 1828 and later as a pamphlet, he again defended the character of Methodism, argued the case for religious equality and broadened his attack to include the educational policies of what he claimed to be an Anglican-dominated executive.[59] This coincided with the end of the monopoly of the Church of England in Britain with repeal of disabilities against Nonconformists and Catholic Emancipation in Britain by the Tory Government in 1828 and 1829 and the introduction of what some have called a 'free trade in religion', strengthening his argument. In 1829, Ryerson became the combative first editor of the Methodist *Christian Guardian* in which he campaigned against religious privilege in church, law or public education and he and some Methodists became powerful allies of the Reform movement until the mid-1830s.

Between 1826 and 1832, Ryerson was gradually associated in the public mind with those who saw themselves as political Reformers. Many of the constitutional issues that roused Reformers were also of concern to Methodist leaders: the disposition of the Clergy Reserves, the right to solemnise marriages, the control over many of the educational institutions by the Church of England and the question of denominational equality. Ryerson's spirited attacks on Anglican ascendancy, his leading role in organising and drafting the petition of the Friends of Religious Liberty in December 1830 and his censure in 1831 of Sir John Colborne, who harboured doubts about the loyalty of Canadian Episcopal Methodists, and who accused Methodists in general of political meddling, all identified him not just as a leading Methodist but also as a leading Reformer.[60] This is misleading. Ryerson and his co-religionists occupied the middle ground in provincial politics between the Tories and the more radical reformers. Conservative and Loyalist as regards political change, they were only

---

[58] Sissons, C. B., 'Four early letters of Egerton Ryerson', *Canadian Historical Review*, Vol. 23, (1942), pp. 58-64, and 'Canadian Methodism in 1828: a note on an early Ryerson letter', *Douglas Library Notes*, Vol. 12, (3), (1963), pp. 2-6, are useful on Ryerson's early foray into politics.

[59] Ryerson, Egerton, *Letters from the Reverend Egerton Ryerson to the Hon. and Reverend Doctor Strachan...*, (Printed at the Herald Office), 1828, originally published in the *Upper Canada Herald*.

[60] Smith, William, *Political Leaders of Upper Canada*, (Ayer Publishing), 1977, pp. 198-201, considers the Colborne episode. See also, *Report of the Select Committee to which was referred the petition of Donald Bethune and others of Kingston, complaining of the increasing influence of a foreign priesthood, & etc*, (Toronto: s.n.), 1831, consisting largely of Ryerson's combative defence of Methodism.

firmly reformist in matters of Anglican dominance, land policy and education.

The 1820 agreement between Episcopal and Wesleyan Methodists broke down in 1832 when, with Colborne's support, twelve new British Wesleyan missionaries arrived in York. The Canadian Episcopal Conference accepted that a revival of the rivalry between the two groups would weaken the Methodist movement as a whole and that the burden of missionary work was stretching its limited resources. However, a more formal association with the Wesleyans was unattractive as it threatened its autonomy and political activities. Despite this, there were strong arguments for considering a union with the Wesleyans: it would allow the Conference to access British Wesleyan resources of money and manpower, elevate its social status and help remove the stigma of disloyalty. In addition, Colborne suggested that state aid for missionaries might be available. He had already covertly encouraged the British Wesleyan leaders to resume their Indian missions. This also fulfilled his goals of strengthening the anti-American and anti-republican spirit of Upper Canada and of challenging 'natural' conservatives like Ryerson to moderate their opposition to church establishment. After some months of negotiation and fierce criticism from some prominent preachers, a union plan was proposed and Ryerson was appointed to carry out final negotiation. Early in 1833, he left for England seeking change not to the state but to the church. He also sought support for the new Methodist College in Cobourg, part of his plan for his church to have a well-educated clergy. His mission was successful. The union permanently joining Upper Canadian Methodism with British Wesleyan Methodism, providing the recognition, respectability and funding he sought for Canadian Methodists and, though not without resistance and dissent, this was ratified by the Canadian Methodist Conference in October 1833

The moderate conservatism of Ryerson's political views became increasingly apparent when he returned from England in the autumn of 1833 and his most important statements on the constitution were drawn directly from the observations he made in London. Throughout the negotiations, the Wesleyans had stressed that the *Christian Guardian* must become an exclusively religious journal, free from direct criticism of the Government, not opposed to state aid for the extension of religion and Ryerson began immediately to move the newspaper in that direction. He became convinced that the more radical colonial reformers wanted to destroy the 1791 Constitution and end the connection with Britain. In the first of a series of *Impressions of England*, published in the *Christian Guardian* on 30 October, he attacked English radical leaders such as Joseph Hume and John

Arthur Roebuck, who were close allies of Canadian Reformers, as infidel, republican and anti-Methodist and for encouraging sedition in Canada.

> Radicalism in England appeared to us to be but another word for Republicanism, with the name of King instead of President. This school, however, includes all the Infidels, Unitarians, and Socinians in the Kingdom; together with a majority of the population of the manufacturing districts.[61]

The following year, he published his letters in a pamphlet.[62] The *Impressions* led to a sharp break between Methodists and other radicals and Ryerson appeared to reverse direction and commit himself to Toryism. The Reform press condemned him as a traitor and many of his Methodist brethren agreed. William Lyon Mackenzie, journalist and leader of the radical reformers in Upper Canada, was damning in his criticism:

> The *Christian Guardian*, under the management of our rev. neighbour Egerton Ryerson, has gone over to the enemy, press, types, & all, & hoisted the colours of a cruel and vindictive priesthood....The Americans had their Arnold and the Canadians have their Ryerson. [63]

Mackenzie, who regarded Ryerson as a trusted friend and ally, was particularly stung by his attack on Hume and responded with visceral anger:

> I was the dupe of a Jesuit in the garb of a Methodist preacher...as subtle and ungrateful an adversary in the guise of as old and familiar friend as ever crossed the Atlantic.[64]

For Mackenzie, Ryerson had sold out to the colonial government and the new Methodist Union had been rewarded with £900 in state aid with a further £1,000 promised.[65]

---

[61] *Christian Guardian*, 30 October 1833.

[62] 'A Canadian', *The Affairs of the Canadas in a Series of Letters*, (J. King), 1837.

[63] *Colonial Advocate*, 4 November 1833.

[64] *Colonial Advocate*, 4 November 1833.

[65] Raible, Christopher, "'I was the dupe of a Jesuit in the garb of a Methodist preacher': The collapse of the alliance between William Lyon Mackenzie and Egerton Ryerson', unpublished paper, pp. 13-16, details Mackenzie's vehement attack. I am extremely grateful to Chris for sending me a copy of this valuable paper.

To Ryerson, however, the change was one of emphasis, not principle and he responded to Mackenzie's rebuke in the next issue of the *Christian Guardian*. He had not written his *Impressions* casually, his attack on Hume was deliberate and by praising Hume, Mackenzie had shown his own 'want of discernment or of honesty'.[66] Despite his denials that he had altered his opinions, the public perception was that Ryerson had shifted from left to right. The Tory press was jubilant. In the *Courier*, for instance:

What shall we say, however, of the Egerton Ryerson of the *Christian Guardian*! The great high priest of the republican faction in Canada! who, in one short movement, has come to 'the left about face', and turned outright Tory. We can hardly believe the evidence of our senses.[67]

David Mills suggests:

The focus of Ryerson's loyalty was the colonial Governor, who symbolised both the balanced constitution and the imperial connection: [The] colonial Governor, who administers the laws of a state according to its constitution is the minister of God...if he makes no attempt to change the constitution, nor break the compact between him and the people; there is, therefore, no legal round of opposition to his civil authority.[68]

His passionate presentation of the grievances of Upper Canada masked a profoundly Loyalist view of the balanced constitution.[69] Ryerson was now convinced that the main enemy was the Reform movement not the administration. He did not dispute there were still justifiable complaints but argued that appeals to the Crown and the imperial parliament were bringing redress.[70] To Ryerson, the cause of Reform had been largely won and Reformers were no longer seeking to remedy real grievances but to introduce fundamental constitutional

---

[66] *Christian Guardian*, 6 November 1833.

[67] *Courier*, 2 November 1833.

[68] Mills, David, *The Idea of Loyalty in Upper Canada 1784-1850*, (McGill-Queens University Press), 1988, p. 58.

[69] Ducharme, Michel, *Le Concept de Liberté au Canada a l'Époque des Revolutions Atlantiques, 1776-1838*, (McGill-Queen's University Press), 2010, pp. 168-169, 188-189.

[70] On Ryerson's ideas, see Riddell, R. G., (ed.), 'Egerton Ryerson's views on the government of Upper Canada in 1836', *CHR*, Vol. 19, (1938), pp. 402-410, and Pearce, Colin D., 'Egerton Ryerson's Canadian Liberalism', in Ajzenstat, Janet, and Smith, Peter J., (eds.), *Canada's Origins: Liberal, Tory or Republican?*, (Carleton University Press), 1995, pp. 181-208.

change. The division between Mackenzie and Ryerson left a legacy of distrust and division and Christopher Raible suggests:

> Undoubtedly Ryerson was more calm and level-headed in his attitudes than was Mackenzie, but they shared many values in common. Ryerson, by abandoning further involvement with the cause of political reform, meant that it more readily moved in a more radical direction.[71]

The tensions between Ryerson's Methodism, Mackenzie's Presbyterianism and the Anglicanism of Strachan reflected the political divisions between moderation, radicalism and Toryism in Upper Canada.

The Anglican Church may have sought to replicate the British pattern of a single dominant church that enjoyed a privileged relationship with the state but it failed. British North American society enjoyed a significant degree of religious pluralism where political loyalty did not require doctrinal unity. The censuses of early 1840s divided the population of Upper Canada was into four equally vibrant religious denominations: Anglicans (22 per cent), Methodists (17 per cent), Presbyterians (19 per cent) and Roman Catholics (13 per cent) with 17 per cent claiming 'no religion', or rather not members of the institutional churches recognised by census takers. Roman Catholics made up 82 per cent of the population of Lower Canada but Protestants made up the bulk of the English-speaking population. This pattern of religious pluralism and competition in which religious allegiance was divided into a small number of larger institutional churches was replicated in the Maritime Provinces. This set Canada apart from the United States where religious identities were more fragmented. Canadian religious identities remained fluid and flexible and the authority of the institutional churches and the state were weaker.

Upper Canada was more pluralist in character than Lower Canada and different Protestant churches vied with each other for position and influence. Roman Catholics formed a substantial minority and Catholic leaders estimated that they made up almost one quarter of the population in the province for much of the nineteenth century.[72] Many of the Catholics were from Ireland, but there was a considerable Catholic Scottish settlement in Glengarry, a

---

[71] Ibid, Raible, Christopher, "'I was the dupe of a Jesuit in the garb of a Methodist preacher", p. 21.
[72] Bull, William P., *From Macdonell to McGuigan: The History of the growth of the Roman Catholic Church in Upper Canada*, (Perkin Bull Foundation), 1939, remains useful.

number of French-Canadian pioneers in the Detroit River region and along the Ottawa valley, as well as a small Catholic German community in Waterloo County. Unlike in Lower Canada, Catholics were confronted by a largely Protestant population. Many contemporaries, some less than sympathetic to Catholicism, commented favorably on the piety of Catholic clergy and the loyalty of the Catholic population to the Crown. *The Mirror*, the province's leading Irish Catholic newspaper made this clear during the 1837 rebellion:

> The Clergy of our religion have always, to our certain knowledge, recommended submission to the higher powers, and a respectful obedience to the laws of the land, for which they have been sometimes censured-but it is plain now, that their object was in accordance with the rules laid down by the Apostles, and as dictated by a meek and merciful Saviour, whereas there is not one of them even suspected, and very few of their hearers who paid attention to their instructions, concurred in the work of devastation, confusion, or blood.[73]

However, growing Catholic, especially Irish immigration, saw an extension of Catholic schools and convents in Protestant areas and calls for separate schooling leading to anti-Catholic reactions from the Orange Order.

Anti-Catholicism was part of the development of definitions of citizenship and civic institutions on the local and provincial levels. At an ideological level, 'Popery' was a foil for a free Protestantism and many Upper Canadians felt that a 'Papist' was by definition foreign and threatening. The print culture of the period illustrated the inherent anti-Catholicism of their Protestant loyalist nationalism. Tracts, pamphlets, novels, exposes and histories for both children and adults contained anti-Catholic themes. Anti-Catholicism, far from being a fringe ideology, was a central building block of the way many people in Upper Canada viewed themselves as well as in their position within the narrative of world history. Suspicion of Catholic theology, Catholic clergy, Catholic laity and the Pope in Rome permeated that narrative, infused their systems of education and permeated their public words.

The social unity that the established church intended to develop in this new British society was consequently seriously undermined. A powerful Roman Catholic presence in Lower Canada and a rapidly expanding Methodist movement in the newly settled lands of Upper Canada made such monopolistic pretensions unsustainable. Although Anglicanism retained a certain social status and elite influence, it

---

[73] *The Mirror,* 16 December 1837.

acknowledged the denominational character of Canadian religious life long before its legal disestablishment by the Clergy Reserves Act of 1854. Questions such as the right of non-Anglican clergy to perform marriages and of dissenting churches to incorporate, build churches and own burial grounds had been largely settled by the early 1830s through legislation that affirmed the rights of all Christian religions at the expense of a supposed Anglican establishment.

The rhetoric of Catholic and Protestant discourse during the nineteenth century, whether aimed at fellow-religionists or those of different faith played a significant role in Canada's 'wars of religion'. It established the parameters of the debate within and between Catholicism and Protestantism over the authority of religions in Canada and their place in defining individuals' places in an increasingly pluralistic and secularising religious environment. It buttressed the authority of faith among their different social and ethnic constituencies and provided a combative framework within which those constituencies defined their places in Canadian society. It also provided a means of protecting the doctrinal and historical heritages of religious groups when faced with the opposition and evangelical aggression of other religious faiths.

4 Performative action as 'wars of religion'

There were a series of incidents in Belleville, Kingston, Aurora and Toronto during Edward, the Prince of Wales' visit to Canada in 1860. Both the Orange Order and the Roman Catholic Church had a firm grasp on the social landscape of Canada West. The Duke of Newcastle, Secretary of State for War and the Colonies who accompanied the Prince on his visit to Canada and the United States, refused to allow the Prince to receive addresses from representatives wearing Orange insignia or to parade under arches decorated with Orange emblems.[1] The Montreal *Pilot* maintained that the Duke was wisely taking a firm and consistent line against all secret societies and had also refused to allow the Prince to share a platform with Masons in their regalia. But that was not the view of many Upper Canadians and effigies of Newcastle were burned by Toronto Orangeman. The politics of the street reached a climax in Toronto 'the Belfast of Canada' and especially in Kingston, known at the time as 'the Derry of Canada', the centre of activities in eastern Upper Canada for both Catholics and Orangemen. The Prince could not disembark from his steamer because of thousands of Orangemen dressed in their brilliant regalia and waiving their banners. At the heart of the dispute was different understandings of the right of an organisation to demonstrate that brought the Orange Order into conflict with Roman Catholics. They objected to what they saw as royal recognition of the Orange Order that had caused so much conflict in Ireland and threatened Catholic rights in Canada. What should have been public ceremonies to boost imperial relations and rituals to demonstrate loyalty and community ended up exposing persistent social tensions and acted as triggers for confrontation between rival religious groups.

Sectarian violence was an important populist and emotional feature of Canada's 'wars of religion', a publicly aggressive expression of the claims of one religious grouping against another. It took the 'war of words', which despite its often fiery rhetoric was largely conducted by clergy and the educated middle-classes, on to the streets and reflected a stylised version of belief by dividing those involved into 'them' and 'us'.[2] To call someone a 'Papist' was not just a religious

---

[1] Radforth, Ian W., *Royal Spectacle: The 1860 Visit of the Prince of Wales to Canada and the United States*, (University of Toronto Press), 2004, pp. 139-140, 164-205.

[2] Goheen, P. G., "The Ritual of the Streets in Mid-19th-Century Toronto', *Environment and Planning D: Society and Space*, Vol. 11, (2), (1993), pp. 127-146, and 'Negotiating Access to Public Space in Mid-Nineteenth

label but included implications about that person's political views, their family life, their level of education and most importantly, their definition of authority. Catholic and Protestant violence, though often orchestrated and manipulated by educated elites with their own political agendas, almost invariably emerged from set-piece, ritual-laden confrontations often in the street involving the comparatively uneducated and easily motivated working-classes. Most of the major sectarian violence in nineteenth century Canada was linked to the central issue of who held power and control. Protestants wanted to maintain or protect their position over Roman Catholics especially the threat from what they saw as 'French domination' while Catholics wanted to preserve their church's position in society and reverse the historic attempts at anglicisation and assimilation that were at different times and to different degrees central to colonial policy. Sectarian contention was grounded in conflicting visions of how Canadian society should be structured and how it should develop and when either group perceived that changes might occur in local, regional or national power relations, they responded by taking to the streets asserting their strength in ritualised public demonstrations that could easily degenerate into ritualised violence.

British North American nativism was complex and varied but the dramatic increase in Catholic Irish immigrants breached an acceptable 'threshold' altering North America's political, economic and social landscapes. Unlike the United States, the overwhelming majority of the Irish who had settled in British North America by 1850, had arrived before the Famine, a substantial majority were Protestant and most worked on the land. However, they were the main English-speaking ethnic group in the Canadian colonies. In Newfoundland, Irish immigrants were largely Catholic and made up over half of the population.[3] On Prince Edward Island, one in four inhabitants was from an Irish background by 1850. Nova Scotia by 1828 had an Irish-Catholic population of 40,000. The predominance of Irish immigrants in New Brunswick, one-third of the total population before the Famine more or less evenly divided between Protestants and Catholics, led to it sometimes being called 'New Ireland'. In Canada West, the Irish accounted for over two-thirds of the residents in its five largest towns especially in Toronto. Though the Irish population of Canada East was smaller, they were more concentrated than in Canada West with

Century Toronto, *Journal of Historical Geography*, Vol. 20, (4), (1994), pp. 430-449, provide valuable local studies of the politics of the street.

[3] Lambert, Caroline, "Tho' Changed Be Your Climate, Unchanged Are Your Hearts: Support for Irish Causes in St. John's, Newfoundland, 1840-86', *Canadian Journal of Irish Studies*, Vol. 34, (2), (2008), pp. 47-55.

over half living in Quebec or Montreal. Yet, the image of Irish Catholics in Canada has been inspired largely by the 'famine motif' of Irish Catholic poverty, intemperance, and violence.[4] For instance, in the early 1870s Toronto's Irish Catholics were described as an urban-dwelling peasantry, uneducated and unskilled, to whom 'drunkenness and alcoholism were endemic, almost genetic.'[5]

It was conflict between Orange and Green, who brought their sectarian divisions with them from Ireland that produced substantial demonstrations of sectarian violence in Canada. Processions enabled a large number of collective identities to develop and the street provided a symbolic space in which these identities were negotiated and re-configured especially where there was no concentration of Irish-Catholics but also in segregated communities that were defended against Orange assault. They were supremely visual events, as newspapers makes clear; public display was their major function. Personal demeanour, forms of dress, banners and flags and, on occasions, the dressing of the streets themselves were central features of these events. They tended to coalesce around Catholic celebrations on St. Patrick's Day on 16 March and the Orange Order's commemoration of William III's historic victories over Catholic James II at the Boyne on 12 August. Yet, Catholics and Protestants had many other holidays and the nineteenth century calendar was filled with partisan festival days providing ample opportunities for communal exhibition and provocation that reflected their contrasting views of their histories and their different world-views.

Sectarian attitudes in Canada, stoked by the Protestant press, were strongly influenced by events in Britain.[6] The implications of Catholic Emancipation in 1829, the agitation over the state endowment of Maynooth seminary in Ireland in 1845, the 'masked popery' of the Oxford movement and the 'papal aggression' of 1850 were of as much concern to Protestants in the colonies as they were to Protestants in Britain. This was evident in their transplanting of Orangeism from Ireland after 1830 though the Canadian Orange

---

[4] On this issue see, Fegan, Melissa, *Literature and the Irish Famine, 1845-1919*, (Oxford University Press), 2002, especially, pp. 10-34, 164-206.
[5] Nicholson, Murray, 'The Other Toronto: Irish Catholics in a Victorian City 1850-1900', in Stelter, Gilbert A., and Artibise, Alan J., (eds.), *The Canadian City: Essays in Social and Urban History*, (McGill-Queen's University Press), 1984, pp. 328-359, cit, p. 335.
[6] Walker, F. A., 'Protestant Reaction in Upper Canada to the Popish Threat', Canadian Catholic Historical Association, *Report*, Vol. 51, (1951), pp. 91-107, and Miller, J. R., 'Anti-Catholic Thought in Victorian Canada', *CHR*, Vol. 66, (1985), pp. 474-494.

Order was significantly transformed from a narrowly anti-Catholic sectarian organisation into a broadly Loyalist and Pan-British fraternal organisation that was, according to its historians, more benign than its equivalent in Ireland.[7] It was the Orange Order rather than the Fenian Brotherhood or the Hibernians that became the archetypal Irish institution in Canada. The response in Canada combined violence with anti-Catholic rhetoric expressed in graphic and provocative terms. The Catholic Church was the Antichrist and Catholics as a body were universally condemned. For instance, in 1842 an article by James Douglas printed in Toronto:

> ...instead of the true church, which is a spiritual body with Christ at its head, Popery is but a putrifying and noisome carcass...a collection of unregenerate men, the doers of every evil work with those who love and those who make a lie, with the Pope, not the Saviour, for their head.[8]

Anti-Catholicism was not confined to conservative Protestants but the fear of Catholic dominance in Upper Canada, a spectre reinforced by the existence of the Catholic dominated Quebec had a significant influence even on moderates. Ryerson, for instance, attacked Reformers in Upper Canada for seeking an alliance with Papineau's Parti Patriote and deplored the possible introduction of American democracy into the colonies:

> ...it appears evident beyond a doubt, that the introduction of the institutions of the United States into Lower Canada is advocated because it will place the supreme power in the hands of the *Catholic* majority. In case of independence or elective institutions, the Catholics would constitute the numerical majority in both Provinces—and then comes the reign of Popery![9]

Anti-Catholicism intensified from the 1840s largely because the Famine migrants fundamentally shifted Canada's demographic profile that, with the exception of its indigenous peoples, blacks and pockets of European immigrants, had previously been largely homogeneous and where Anglo-Saxon and Gallic influences dominated.[10] However,

---

[7] Wilson, David A., (ed.), *The Orange Order in Canada*, (Four Courts Press), 2007, pp. 25-41.
[8] *The Wesleyan*, Vol. 2, (16), 20 April 1842, p. 121.
[9] *Christian Guardian*, Vol. 6, (25), 29 April 1835, p. 98.
[10] See, Scott, 'An Unprecedented Influx: Nativism and Irish Famine Immigration to Canada', *American Review of Canadian Studies*, Vol. 30, (4), (2000), pp. 429-453, reprinted in Mulrooney, Margaret M., (ed.), *Fleeing the famine: North America and Irish refugees, 1845-1851*, (Greenwood Publishing), 2003, pp. 59-78.

the sectarian violence that accompanied it had very different impulses. Economic considerations, especially where labour was threatened by new and cheaper sources played an important role in nativist responses to immigration. Irish Catholics in the Maritime Provinces as well as in the province of Canada, reinforced existing concerns and economic questions took on an increasingly sectarian character.[11] In New Brunswick, for instance, half of those who arrived at St. John, its leading port, settled in the province. In Fredericton, its provincial capital 45 per cent of households claimed Irish birth in 1851. Growing competition for employment caused by Irish immigrants exacerbated labour relations in the port of Quebec though the common religious roots of French-Canadians and Irish may have reduced the intensity of the nativist reaction.[12] Ontario's economic and political landscape was transformed as a result of immigration and its nativist response mirrored that of the Maritime Provinces. In both areas, the 'dumping' of immigrants by the British Government was highly criticised and a powerful coalition of Protestants sought to isolate Irish Catholics and contain the spread of their religion and culture.[13]

This led to escalating sectarian violence. In St. John, where skirmishes between Catholics and Orangemen predated the Famine, concerted and organised violence erupted in 1847[14] and 1849 when troops were deployed to keep the two sides apart.[15] After the 1849

---

[11] Punch, Terence M., 'Anti-Irish prejudice in Nineteenth-Century Nova Scotia: The Literary and Statistical Evidence', in Power, Thomas P., *The Irish in Atlantic Canada, 1780-1900*, (New Ireland Press), 1991, pp. 13-22.

[12] Spray, William A., 'Reception of the Irish in New Brunswick', in Toner, P. M., (ed.), *Historical Essays on the Irish in New Brunswick: New Ireland Remembered*, (New Ireland Press), 1988, pp. 11-26.

[13] See regards Canada's riots as 'manifestations of larger North American and transatlantic issues': See, S. W., 'Nineteenth-Century Collective Violence: Toward a North American Context', *Labour/Le Travail*, Vol. 39, (1997), pp. 13-38, p. 22. See also his *Riots in New Brunswick: Orange Nativism and Social Violence in the 1840s*, (University of Toronto Press), 1993, and 'The Orange Order and Social Violence in Mid-Nineteenth Century Saint John', in ibid, Toner, P. M., (ed.), *Historical Essays on the Irish in New Brunswick: New Ireland Remembered*, pp. 71-89.

[14] *The Loyalist*, 24 September 1847, indicates the scale of the riots in its report of those tried on 15 September for riot and assault. Seventy-eight men were present in court while eight men were described as 'absent'.

[15] Wynn, Graeme, 'Ideology, identity, landscape and society in the lower colonies of British North America 1840-1860', in Baker, Alan R. H., and Biger, Gideon, (eds.), *Ideology and landscape in historical perspective: essays on the meanings of some places in the past*, (Cambridge University Press),

riot, civic authorities banned Orange parades from the streets and urban violence diminished in intensity. An economic revival, the end of the Irish Famine migrations and an official local accommodation with the Irish-Catholics assured peace in the 1850s. Tensions continued but there were no more large-scale clashes. Control of the provincial press and the widespread activities of the Orange Order in Ontario and New Brunswick and the Protestant Alliance in Nova Scotia proved effective in excluding the Irish from the power structure during the 1850s and later.[16] For example, in Ottawa by the mid-1850s, municipal councillors were all Protestant and as late as 1897, few municipal, judicial or police positions were held by Irish Catholics. This Orange-Tory faction controlled patronage, civic offices and exercised municipal powers including tax assessment and collection, labour for municipal work, relief, police and licensing of taverns, carters and cabmen. Until the police were professionalised in the 1850s, the Orange-dominated council could count on a monopoly of violence through its control of the police, magistracy and city's fire companies.[17] Attempts by Reformers to restrict the powers of the Orange-Tory coalition through legislation to ban secret societies, control processions and elections and outlaw the carrying of weapons in parades resulted in the development of a new bourgeois consensus with the Orange-Tory coalition over public order but this made little inroad into its dominance over Toronto's politics until the 1880s.

Sectarian violence was also a persistent feature of Canadian politics especially during elections to the Assembly where political disagreement had an important religious dimension. Election results were of material importance because of the economic and social benefits of patronage to the victors and drew public attention to contentious issues. In addition, political divisions coincided with other areas of religious, social and economic conflict. Electoral conflict

---

1992, p. 199, Gordon Winder, 'Trouble in the North End: The Geography of Social Violence in Saint John, 1840-1860', *Acadiensis*, Vol. 29, (2), (2000), pp. 27-57

[16] Houston, C. J., and Smyth, W. J., *The Sash Canada Wore: An historical geography of the Orange Order in Canada*, (University of Toronto Press), 1980, is the fullest treatment of the Canadian Orange tradition. See also, ibid, Wilson, David A., (ed.), *The Orange Order in Canada*, and Senior, Hereward, *Orangeism in Ireland and Britain, 1795-1836*, (Routledge & Paul), 1966.

[17] Ibid, See, Scott, 'An Unprecedented Influx: Nativism and Irish Famine Immigration to Canada', p. 70, Kealey, G. S., 'Orangemen and the Corporation: The politics of Class during the Union of the Canadas', in Russell, V. l., (ed.), *Forging a Consensus: Historical Essays on Toronto*, (University of Toronto Press), 1984, pp. 41-86.

served as an outlet for intergroup hostility as political campaigning mobilised and polarised opinion. In the Ottawa Valley and in the New Brunswick woods, rival patronage networks in the timber trade divided along ethno-religious lines, and groups of male workers clashed over elections.[18] In Lower Canada, in the 1830s most of the supporters of the reformist Patriote party were Catholics and were faced by a largely Protestant British party. In Upper Canada, Anglican Tories were opposed by often Dissenting reformers.

There was, for instance, widespread sectarian violence between the Irish Catholic supporters of Daniel Tracey, an immigrant Irish doctor and journalist and his opponent Stanley Bagg, a Protestant Tory and businessman during the by-election for the second seat in Montreal West in 1832.[19] Traditionally the seat went to a British Montrealer, but Louis-Joseph Papineau, who held the other seat, had backed Tracey to secure Irish-Catholic support for the Patriote movement. The election began on 25 April and the poll ended on 22 May after twenty-three days marred by numerous acts of violence between partisans of the two candidates. The most serious violence took place on Monday 21 May when magistrates asked the garrison for assistance in suppressing disturbances at the poll and the Riot Act was read. *La Minerve* and *The Vindicator* both stated that reinforcements to the troops having arrived from le Champ de Mars, the Tracey faction was followed along the street by Bagg's supporters and the soldiers. In the exchange of missiles from one faction to the other, some of the soldiers were struck, and on command of their officers, they fired into Tracey's followers killing three French-Canadians and wounding about twenty others. *The Vindicator* shortly after the election riot said:

> We have frequently expressed in our columns the horrors taking place in Ireland and the wholesale slaughter of the people. We can assure the public that there is little difference between those who precipitated the recent

---

[18] Cross, M. S., 'The Shiners' War: Social Violence in the Ottawa Valley in the 1830s', *CHR*, Vol. 54, (1), (1973), pp. 1-26, S. W., 'Polling Crowds and Patronage: New Brunswick's 'Fighting Elections' of 1842-3', *CHR*, Vol. 72, (2), (1991), pp. 127-156.

[19] Senior, Elinor Kyte, *British Regulars in Montreal: An Imperial Garrison, 1832-1854*, (McGill-Queens, University Press), 1981, pp. 11-23, provides the best account of the riots and their aftermath. See different analyses in Galarneau, France, 'L'élection partielle du quartier-ouest de Montréal en 1832: Analyse politico-sociale', *Revue d'Histoire de l'Amérique Française*, Vol. 32, (4), (1979), pp. 565-584, and Jackson, James, *The Riot That Never Was: The military shooting of three Montrealers in 1832 and the official cover-up*, (Baraka Books), 2010.

happenings in this city and those whose crimes are of a public nature; and unless opposition be legally had to this terrible state of affairs, it will be little time before we too are exposed to a similar fate.[20]

For Catholics, this was the Protestant colonial state supporting the interests of a Protestant candidate with armed force. Tracey nonetheless won by a narrow margin of four votes on the strength of his obtaining 84 per cent of the French and 71 per cent of the Irish vote. Tracey's supporters, almost all Irish or French, included Louis-Hippolyte LaFontaine and most of the craftsmen, farmers, carters, and day-labourers in the riding. Bagg had mustered the businessmen and office holders, only a few of whom, for instance Pierre-Édouard Leclère, were Irish or Canadian. This proved a short-lived triumph as Tracey died of cholera on 18 July 1832 caught while attending patients before he could take his seat.

However, two years later in Quebec, the Tories called on the Irish Catholics of Quebec City's Upper Town to vote along language lines and link the shamrock to the rose in a battle against disloyal Patriotes.[21] This appeal worked: most Irish Catholics, who made up 6 to 8.5 per cent of eligible voters, gave their support to the Conservatives. The extremist behaviour of some French-Canadians and the conservative stance of the clergy, in addition to their own realisation that they no longer needed the French-Canadians as a crutch in society, drew the Irish majority into the Tory camp and into associations where they could pursue legitimate constitutional reform. This further distanced many of the Irish from the cause of the French-Canadians leading to acerbic comment in the Patriote press:

How is then that enlightened men in this country dare to consider as protectors of this religion, the government that oppresses it in Ireland. This is a blindness that is hard to conceive of. No! These are not the sons of Erin.[22]

In Canada East, the first election after Union in 1841 was marked by considerable sectarian violence especially in marginal seats. In Vaudreuil, armed supporters of the British candidate attacked and held the poll for unionist voters killing two men. At Chambly, 'the Irish boys' captured the poll and managed to get enough voters to gain a majority of ten for the British candidate. In Terrebonne, LaFontaine

---

[20] *The Vindicator,* 25 May 1832.
[21] De Brou, David, 'The Rose, the Shamrock and the Cabbage: the Battle for Irish Voters in Upper-Town Quebec, 1827-1836', *Histoire sociale,* Vol. 24, (1991), pp. 305-334.
[22] *Écho du Pays,* 7 May 1835.

withdrew his candidacy to prevent a pitched battle. Despite French-Canadians outnumbering British voters by ten to one, the British candidate was elected. The toll: one dead in Montreal, two in Vaudreuil and three in Beauharnois. In Canada West, Compact Toryism still had significant support especially among the 20,000 members of Orange lodges who were roused to fight for the 'British connection'.[23] There was rioting in some constituencies and several deaths in Toronto and in the counties of Durham and Halton West.

Electoral violence continued after Confederation. Violence made polling impossible in Kamouraska in Quebec, Alexander Mackenzie was chased from a meeting by a 'howling mob' and during Cartier's election campaign in 1872 in Montreal the militia was called out to restore order. Although the introduction of the secret ballot in the 1870s ended the use of intimidation to directly affect votes, the practice of intimidating candidates by seeking to keep known supporters away from the polls and disrupting and breaking up meetings continued.

During late 1840s there was a proliferation of crises across the Atlantic world. In Britain, Ireland, Canada and the United States, as well as across Europe, the old certainties were challenged and either swept aside or repressively maintained. Virtually every facet of life was transformed in British North America during the 1840s by movements that touched beliefs, modified habits and founded institutions, changing the face of the United Province as well as its role in a Canadian polity. Religious enthusiasm and evangelism were revitalised among Roman Catholics and Protestants and the groundwork laid for Catholic ultramontanism and aggressive Protestant anti-Catholicism whose fundamental tenet was superiority of religious over secular power. The 1840s also saw the establishment of sectarian management of asylums, hospitals and correctional institutions and sectarian division in the schools of Quebec. Economic pressures were linked with outbreaks of violence, notably electoral violence in March 1841, March 1842, April and December 1844 (a stabbing and two deaths), April 1845 and April 1846 (two deaths). Violence accompanied repression of strikes on the Beauharnois canal works in 1843 (eleven deaths)[24] and labour unrest on the Lachine canal in January and March

---

[23] Beer, Donald R., 'Toryism in Transition: Upper Canadian Conservative Leaders, 1836-1854', *Ontario History*, Vol. 80, (1988), pp. 207-225, is valuable on changing Conservatism.

[24] LaFontaine to Baldwin, 16 June 1843, Aubin, Georges, (ed.), *Louis-Hippolyte La Fontaine, Correspondance générale, Tome I: Les Ficelles du Pouvoir, Correspondance entre Louis-Hippolyte La Fontaine et Robert*

1843, April and August 1844, followed by canallers' 'outrages' in October. Oratory and journalism were exceptionally virulent between February and August 1849 with provocations by the Anglo-Protestant merchant élite reaching a peak with the burning of the hall of Legislative Assembly on 25 April 1849. In each incident where lives were lost and formal inquests held, contemporaries identified ethnic rivalries as a factor: French versus British, French versus Irish, and Catholic versus Protestant.

Concerns over Irish Catholic loyalty were particularly evident in 1848 when the newly responsible government faced attempts by some dissident politicians to fashion an alliance between French-Canadians and Irish Catholics, something that was egged on by some republican Irish-Americans. The authorities were seriously alarmed by reports of Irish Catholics taking secret oaths and preparing for rebellion as a prelude to American invasion.[25] In 1848, one of the leaders of the Irish Republican Union declared:

> Canada contains hundreds of thousands of patriotic Irishmen and of Canadians, who sigh for annexation to this great and glorious republic....It is therefore our manifest duty to Ireland, to Canada and to Freedom, to send such agencies as we deem most efficient to prepare the people of that oppressed colony for annexation to these United States, and thus complete the work that Washington began.[26]

In fact, the response from Irish Catholics in Canada was lukewarm. The Irish Republican Union established in the province floundered and its newspaper, the Montreal *United Irishman*, lacked the energy and invective of Ireland's nationalist papers. Moderate Catholic Irish opinion was outraged by attempts to import Irish politics into Canada. Concerns persisted into 1849 in the context of the Rebellion Losses legislation and the publication of a Tory manifesto

---

Baldwin, 1840-1854, (Varia), 2002. p. 57, wrote of the confrontation on the Beauharnois canal. See, Way, Peter, *Common Labour: Workers and the Digging of North American Canals*, (Cambridge University Press), 1993, and Bleasdale, Ruth, 'Class Conflict on the Canals of Upper Canada in the 1840s', *Labour/Le Travail*, Vol. 7, (1981), pp. 9-39.
[25] Doughty, Arthur, (ed.), *The Elgin-Grey Papers, 1846-1852*, 4 Vols. (King's Printer), 1937, Vol. 1, pp. 209-210.
[26] Belchem, John, 'Nationalism, Republicanism and Exile: Irish Emigrants and the Revolutions of 1848', *Past and Present*, Vol. 146, (1995), pp. 103-135, at p. 118.

supporting annexation to the United States but what support there may have been for republican Irish nationalism evaporated.[27]

The Irish Catholic population was sufficiently large in Montreal and Quebec to be organised politically, a situation made possible by the Church's nurturing of nationalism.[28] Cultural nationalism demonstrated a renewed vitality with the founding of a branch of the Ossianic Society in London, Canada West. The formation of the Young Men's Saint Patrick Association in Toronto in 1855 largely free from church control heightened fears that nationalism was taking a more radical turn.[29] The growing concentration of Irish Catholics led to a defensive reaction from the Protestant culture resulting in the rise of the power of the Orange Order. A third of all Canadian Orange Lodges established in the nineteenth century were created between 1854 and 1860 and most of them were in Canada West. Orangemen began to attack St. Patrick's Day processions, partly as a reaction to attacks on their 12 July parades. The immigration boom in the 1850s was largely responsible for this: new Protestant immigrants created new Orange Lodges and new Catholic immigrants encouraged previously neutral Protestants to join them.

This increased sectarian tension, especially in Toronto known as 'the Belfast of North America' because it was the only major North American city to receive more Irish Protestant immigrants than Irish Catholic. On St. Patrick's Day in 1858, Matthew Sheedy, a Catholic was killed in Toronto and the ground floor the *O'Donoghue National Hotel* was wrecked during brawls between Orangemen and Catholics.[30] The Orange police force failed to identify any Protestant rioters, and the wall of Protestant silence was such that the Police Magistrate, George Gurnett (himself an Orangeman), complained in

---

[27] Pollard, Derek, and Martin, Gerald Warren, (eds.), *Canada 1849: a selection of papers given at the University of Edinburgh Centre for Canadian Studies Annual Conference, May 1999*, (University of Edinburgh), 2001, and Warner, Donald F., *The Idea of Continental Union: Agitation for the Annexation of Canada to the United States 1849-1893*, (University of Kentucky Press), 1960, pp. 9-32.

[28] 'Resolutions of the St. Patrick's Society', *The True Witness & Catholic Chronicle*, 30 October 1857, passed by Irish Catholics in Montreal embodied 'the entire policy of Irish Catholics of Canada...'

[29] *New York Times*, 19 April 1856, suggests that tensions between Catholics and the Orange Order in Toronto were exacerbated by the decision in 1856 to carry 'the Host through the public streets for the first time in Toronto' and that 'Religious animosities, most unhappily, are every day becoming more embittered in this Province.'

[30] *New Era*, 25 March 1858, p. 2, prints McGee's speech responding to the violence.

his report that 'other obligations' had prevented witnesses from telling everything they knew.[31]   Thomas D'Arcy McGee was sufficiently influential in persuading Toronto Catholics to stop St. Patrick's Day parades for three years though he refused to insist that legislation should be passed banning the Orange processions on 12 July. What he wanted was a voluntary repudiation by both sides.

It was in this context that Michael Murphy and other prominent Irish Catholics in Toronto established the Hibernian Benevolent Society, a combination of social, sports and benefit club that organised Irish Catholics against Orangeism on the streets of Toronto and later developed into a Fenian front organisation.[32] The Society grew rapidly and branches were soon established in both Canada East and Canada West. This represented a shift in Irish-Canadian radical nationalism away from largely middle-class organisations such as the Young Men's Association towards lower-class organisations, for the authorities a worrying departure in the Canadian political sphere especially as they also enjoyed some support from the clergy.

Irrespective of the extent to which the Hibernians became a Fenian organisation in the 1860s, tensions with the Orange Order remained high during the 1860s especially in the aftermath of the Fenian invasion in 1866 and D'Arcy McGee's assassination in 1868. Street violence continued, especially in Toronto, between Catholic and Protestant groups into the 1870s but it became less intense, more limited in scope and rarely caused loss of life or property. The number of street fights declined in the face of popular pressure for greater public order and because the Orange Order acted in a more restrained manner in its efforts to present a more respectable public image. By 1900, Orange lodges in Toronto had become places were notions of duty, masculinity and respectability were inculcated among young Protestant men. This did not prevent the Order continuing its fight against what it saw as a global papist threat in its struggles against Home Rule in Ireland and French Catholic rights in Canada but it was now a war fought more often through words than street violence.[33]

Sectarian violence was essentially a communal and populist response to the participants' relationship to the structures of power in

---

[31] Trigger, Rosalyn, 'Irish Politics of Parade: The Clergy, National Societies and St. Patrick's Day Processions in Nineteenth-century Montreal and Toronto', *Histoire sociale/Social History*, Vol. 37, (2004), pp. 159-199, provides a valuable context for these issues.

[32] Neidhardt, W. S., 'Michael Murphy', *DCB*, Vol. 9, pp. 587-589.

[33] McLaughlin, Robert, *Irish Canadian Conflict and the Struggle for Irish Independence, 1912-1925*, (University of Toronto Press), 2013, pp. 51-76, considers Orange Canadian Unionists and the Home Rule crisis, 1912-1914.

Canadian society and their need to maintain or to prevent losing their position in that society by defending religious rights that were under attack. Although it existed throughout the nineteenth century, it was at its most intense between 1840 and 1880. Its decline reflected changes in public attitudes to the acceptability of public violence, the development of a professional police force capable of containing its worst excesses and the adaptation of a more respectable character by organisations that had previously sponsored street violence. To dismiss this violence as simply representing a diffuse sense of rage neglects the extent to which those involved had well-defined objectives.

5 Rebellion as 'wars of religion'

Between 1837 and 1885, Canada experienced several periods of intense inter-communal violence when minority groups rose in rebellion to protect their heritage and culture. In 1837 and 1838, French-Canadians twice rebelled in attempts to achieve constitutional change or independence from the colonial state and people had to make a choice between their religious and political convictions. Although the division between rebel Roman Catholics and loyalist Protestants is simplistic since there were rebels and loyalists of both religions, the religious dimension has been neglected. The same may be said of the rebellions in Upper Canada where rebels and loyalists were both largely Protestant although some rebels were from the smaller Protestant sects while loyalists were part of the Protestant mainstream.

There is evidence of Protestant and Catholic conflict between loyalists and rebels in 1837 and 1838. Properties of known Patriotes were destroyed in both the Richelieu valley and the Deux-Montagnes but, with the exception of the church at St. Eustache attacked because it was a Patriote stronghold, there is no evidence for destruction of church property.[1] In many respects, the critical religious dimension lay within Catholicism. The Patriotes had an incisive liberal and emancipating ideology that questioned the position of the Church. The *fabriques* crisis of 1831 had threatened to carry democratic values into the government of the Church and during the anti-coercive meetings of 1837, some of the speeches of Papineau, Wolfred Nelson and other Patriote leaders were uncompromisably anti-clerical in tone. This was also evident in Robert Nelson's Declaration of Independence in February 1838 repeated in November 1838:

> That all ties between Church and State are declared abolished, and every person has the right to freely exercise the religion and the beliefs dictated to him by his conscience.

---

[1] The Appendix to the First Report of the Commissioners appointed to inquire into the losses occasioned by the troubles in Canada, during the years 1837 and 1838, and into the damages arising therefrom;—containing a list of the names of the said claimants, referred to in a marginal note of the papers relative to the Rebellion Losses in Canada, ordered by The House of Commons to be printed 2 May 1849, *Sessional Paper*, No. 253, lists the 2,167 who made claims including the Church of St. Eustache at £6,812.

The Roman Catholic Church's definition of the French-Canadian nation explicitly refuted that of the Patriotes as emphasised by a clerical ideologist in the 1840s:

> ...it is not borders, nor even laws or political administrations which make a nationality; it is a religion, a language, a national character.[2]

The Roman Catholic hierarchy threw its weight behind a policy of compromise and the colonial authorities successfully exploited antagonism between radical Patriotes and the Church.[3] The Church was strongly identified with conservative, anti-revolutionary and anti-democratic forces. Lartigue's first injunction was dated 24 October 1837, two days after a demonstration by 1,200 Patriotes in front of the Cathedral of St. Jacques protesting against Lartigue's sermon on 25 July at the ceremony when Ignace Bourget[4] was consecrated as his coadjutor with the right of succession.[5] Lartigue had reminded the congregation of the Catholic Church's attitude to rebellion against lawful authorities.[6] On 27 July, *La Minerve* responded telling the clergy to 'de se renfermer dans les bornes de leurs attributions et de ne pas se mêler de politique' whilst the previous day, *Ami du peuple* headed its article on Lartigue 'La Religion contre M. Papineau'. The first pastoral letter restated the traditional doctrine of the Church to 'the obedience due to authority' casting serious doubt on the wisdom of the radicals' policy that he considered imprudent as well as

---

[2] Cit, Dumont, F., *Genèse de la société québécoise*, (Boréal), 1993, p. 227, and Lamonde, Y., *Histoire sociale des idées au Québec, 1760-1896*, (Fides), 2001, p. 286.

[3] Correspondance de Mgr Jean-Jacques Lartigue (1836-1840), in *Rapport de l'archiviste de la province de Québec*, Vol. 25, (1944-1945), pp. 173-266, Vol. 26, (1945-1946), pp. 47-134. Pouliot, Léon, 'Lord Gosford et Mgr. Lartigue', *CHR*, Vol. 46, (1965), pp. 238-246.

[4] Sylvain, Philippe, 'Ignace Bourget', *DCB*, Vol. 11, pp. 94-105.

[5] Chaussé, Gilles, *Jean-Jacques Lartigue: Premier eveque De Montreal*, (Fides), 1980, p. 199. See also, Chause, Gilles, and Lemieux, Lucien, 'Jean-Jacques Lartigue', *DCB*, Vol. 7, pp. 485-491, Proulx, Louis, *Defense du Mandement de Mgr. L., Evêque de Montréal, en date du 24 Octobre 1837*, n. p., n. d. [1837], for a defence of Lartigue's denounciation of the Patriote leaders.

[6] Ouellet, Fernand, 'Le mandements de Mgr Lartigue de 1837 et la réaction libérale', *Bulletin des recherches historiques*, Vol. 58, (2), (1952), pp. 97-104. See also, Langlois, Jean-Pierre, 'L'Église face aux Patriotes en 1837-1838', *Société canadienne d'histoire de l'Église catholique*, Sessions d'étude, Vol. 51, (1984), pp. 19-37.

harmful.[7] However, Lartigue did not threaten ecclesiastical sanctions against those in his diocese who did not respect his instructions. This letter was not well received by Patriotes. *La Minerve* on 30 October was particularly critical:

> Comme gardien de la morale chrétienne sans invitation aucune de la part du pouvoir exécutif, sans l'espoir de récompense qu'il repousse, monseigneur se dit forcé de dire quelles sont les maximes de la morale chrétienne. Il cite nombre des textes bien connus et souvent répétés pour dire: qu'il faut être soumis aux puissances: au prince; et qu'il n'est pas permis de se révolter.[8]

It acknowledged the principle put forward by the Church:

> Vous avez raison et nous sommes d'accord, mais malheureusement vous oubliez qui a commencé la rébellion! Vous ne vous rappelez pas que c'est cette puissance exécutive à laquelle vous prêchez obéissance et soumission? Vous êtes assez au fait des événements du jour pour savoir que c'est la puissance exécutive qui s'est rebellée contre la loi...

La Minerve accepted that the mandement protected a certain view of Christian morality but deplored the submission of the Church to the will of a colonial executive that, it believed, was responsible for the popular Patriote agitation. For *La Minerve*, Lartigue's mandement defended the aggressor at the expense of the abused and advocated 'Soumission et obéissance passive à la puissance, au prince, au gouvernement.'

The *Ami du peuple*, by contrast, took a constitutionalist stance in its editorial on 30 October 1837:

---

[7] To support of his position, Lartigue cited the classical texts of St Paul and St Peter, the witnesses of the Fathers of the Church and also used passages from two more recent texts by Pope Gregory XVI: encyclical *Mirari vos* of 15 August 1832 that condemned the propositions, deemed revolutionary, that La Mennais, who had shifted from ultramontanism to liberalism, had developed in his Paris paper *L'Avenir* and the Bull to the bishops of Poland of July 1832. He rejected the argument, which he judged as fallacious, in favour of popular sovereignty evoking the 'horreurs d'une guerre civile, les ruisseaux de sang inondant vos rues et vos campagnes' and adding that 'presque sans exception, toute Révolution populaire est une oeuvre sanguinaire comme le prouve l'expérience. Finally he turned to Jean-Jacques Rousseau, 'l'auteur du *Contrat social*, le grand fauteur de la souveraineté du peuple qui dit quelque part qu'une Révolution serait achetée trop cher, si elle coûtait une seule goutte de sang.'

[8] *La Minerve*, 30 October 1837.

Depuis longtemps nous attendions quelques démarches de la part des autorités ecclésiastiques, nous étions surpris que dans ces temps de trouble et de désordre l'église ne vint point interposer sa puissance bienfaisante et faire des efforts pour arrêter les malheurs qui menacent le peuple; nous avons eu satisfaction de voir que si noire attente a été un peu longue elle n'a pas été vaine et que le chef de l'église de Montréal vient de se prononcer d'une manière qui n'est nullement équivoque...

It was more favourably disposed to Lartigue's intervention arguing that he had taken a moral not a political stance:

Si la politique se bornait ici à des discussions parlementaires ou à des discussions de gazettes, si chacun selon son opinion s'efforçait de faire triompher son parti, sans porter atteinte à l'ordre public et à la morale, nous sommes assurés que notre clergé ne songerait nullement à intervenir...

Recent actions by the Patriotes especially the boycott of colonial goods to reduce duties paid to the colonial administration extended the agitation that began in the Assembly and the *Ami du peuple*, maintained that Lartigue was justified in registering his opposition to the challenge to the established order.

Ce n'est pas en effet sous le rapport politique que le clergé et l'évêque de Montréal envisagent la question des affaires du jour, c'est sous le rapport moral et religieux, et certes ils en ont le droit.

With very few exceptions, the clergy disavowed the reflexive anticlericalism of Patriote nationalism. The letter reminded clergy and laity of their religious responsibilities.[9] Étienne Chartier, priest of St. Benoît challenged the argument on which the pastoral letter was based.[10] According to Gilles Chaussé:

...although the clergy disassociated itself from the views expressed by the curé of St. Benoît, nonetheless a significant section of the clergy entertained

---

[9] Ibid, Chaussé, Gilles, *Jean-Jacques Lartigue: Premier eveque De Montreal*, p. 200.

[10] Chabot, Richard, 'Etienne Chartier', *DCB*, Vol. 8, pp. 140-146, and ibid, Messier, Alain, *Dictionnaire encyclopédique et historique des patriotes 1837-1838*, pp. 104-105, more generally Chabot, Richard, 'Le rôle du bas clergé face au mouvement insurrectionnel de 1837', *Cahiers de Sainte-Marie*, Vol. 5, (1967), pp. 89-98. See also, Boileau, Gilles, *Etienne Chartier: La colére et le chagrin d'un curé patriote*, (Septentrion), 2010, and Audet, F. J., 'L'abbé Étienne Chartier', *Les Cahiers des Dix*, Vol. 6, (1941), pp. 211-223

serious doubts about the action of their bishop and on his view of the doctrine of unconditional obedience to the Crown and its representatives.[11]

It is difficult to estimate the influence of the Roman Catholic Church on the failure of the rebellions but Lartigue's response appears to have some effect. As a result of lack of funds, silver from the church at St. Denis was seized, an action that caused serious divisions among Patriotes.[12] Support for the movement was largely nationalist, something militant Patriotes in 1837 and 1838 did not recognise and reactions to this overt attack on the clergy showed their limited success in getting across their social message. Not only were many *habitants* deeply disturbed by the seizure, but local priests were no longer in any doubt as to Lartigue's warning of 24 October. In the aftermath of the Patriote victory at St. Denis on 23 November 1837, the curé of St. Denis was instructed by Lartigue to refuse the sacraments to rebel supporters. Although the message was intercepted and treated with some disdain, when it was read aloud to the rebels it had the desired effect and local support quickly dwindled. When the Patriote leaders woke on Monday 27 November, they found that most of their men were gone.

Lartigue had made the position of the Church very clear in his first pastoral letter and this was reinforced in his subsequent actions. If first letter was both 'doctrinal and paternal', the tone of the second pastoral letter was far more assertive.[13] Dated 8 January 1838, a little less than a month after the Patriote defeat, the document demanded expiatory actions:

...pour faire à Dieu réparation publique de tous les sacrilèges, meurtres, pillages, trahisons et autres crimes commis dans ce district, pendant la crise insurrectionnelle que nous avons éprouvée.

He called for the celebration of a solemn mass followed by sermons exhorting congregations to fast, give alms and pray 'appraiser la colère de Dieu' and called on priests 'exciter leurs peuples à la pénitence'. He attacked the Patriotes as brigands and rebels and

---

[11] Ibid, Chaussé, Gilles, *Jean-Jacques Lartigue: Premier eveque De Montreal*, p. 211.

[12] Allaire, J.-B.-A., *Histoire de la paroisse de St. Denis-sur-Richelieu*, (Courrier de St. Hyacinthe), 1905, pp. 376-377, explains that the silver was recovered and kept by Nelson. *Résumé impartial de la discussion Papineau-Nelson sur les évènements de Saint-Denis en 1837*, (Montreal), 1848, p. 6, stated that Captain Jalbert was instructed by Papineau to seize the silver.

[13] Ibid, Chaussé, Gilles, *Jean-Jacques Lartigue: Premier eveque De Montreal*, p. 200.

accused them of having 'égaré une partie de la population de son diocèse à force de sophismes et de mensonges', but also of having spread disorder, arson and civil and religious disobedience. He admonished them for having made themselves rich from plunder and for demoralising the young and above all he accused them of killing in cold-blood people who 'n'avaient d'autres torts à leurs yeux, que celui de ne pas partager leurs opinions politiques'. Lartigue evidently did not consider this the right occasion to remind his congregations of his previous pastoral letter and finished with a revealing phrase:

> Mais vous n'oublierez plus à l'avenir que, lorsqu'il s'agit d'éclairer votre conscience sur des questions difficiles, délicates, et qui regardent le salut de vos âmes, c'est à vos Pasteurs qu'il faut vous adresser...

Lartigue also sent three circular letters to the clergy of the diocese of Montreal about the rebellions. The first, on 26 December 1837 concerned an address signed by all the Protestant clergy indicating their loyalty and that of their congregations to the British Crown. The other two dealt with the celebrations of masses for actions of grace (6 February 1838) and for public order (20 November 1838) because of the 'derniers troubles civils qui malheureusement ont éclaté dans notre Diocèse'.

Events vindicated Lartigue.[14] After suffering defeats at St. Charles and then at St. Eustache, *habitants* lost faith in their now absent or dead political leaders. Despite the initially unfavourable reactions to his intervention, Lartigue soon appeared as a true leader, independent, lucid and capable of proposing a more realistic programme than the Patriote leaders. Two developments convinced the French-Canadians of the selflessness of Lartigue and their other religious leaders, who had rallied around him. On 9 November 1837, at the request of the parish priests from the Richelieu valley, he endorsed a petition for the rights of French-Canadians that all the priests in Lower Canada signed. He and Bourget also provided support to the families of those who were imprisoned, particularly after the abortive uprising in early November 1838 and they sought amnesty for the rebels winning widespread public admiration.

In late January 1838, Lartigue had interceded with Lord Gosford to persuade the metropolitan government not to impose union of the two Canadas. When Lord Durham's *Report* endorsed legislative

---

[14] Pouliot, Léon, 'Mgr. Lartigue et les troubles de 1837, I. Mgr. Lartigue avant 1837', *Canada français*, Vol. 23, (1937), pp. 413-421, 'Mgr. Lartigue et les troubles de 1837, II. Pendant l'orage', pp. 517-529, and Mgr. Lartigue et les troubles de 1837, III. Après le mandement du 24 octobre', pp. 613-615.

union and a system of non-denominational schools in 1839, Lartigue encouraged his clergy to sign a new petition to the Queen and Parliament opposing the plan. It failed to prevent union in 1841 but showed that when French-Canadians felt abandoned and misled by their political elite, their religious leaders had stepped in and put themselves at the service of the nation. In the aftermath of the rebellions, it was the Roman Catholic Church that provided many in Lower Canada with a focus for their faith but also for their political and cultural aspirations. Though conservative clerical nationalism was not fully formed until the 1850s, its roots were evident in the growing ultramontanism of the Church and in its increasing appeal to many French-Canadians as the protector not simply of their faith but also of their cultural heritage.

The Fenian movement, though non-sectarian in its ideology, gained much of its support from Roman Catholics in the United States and Canada. This made it an issue on which the Roman Catholic hierarchy, even if it sympathised with the objective of an independent Ireland, took an ambiguous opposition. It was not the political objectives of the Fenians that the Church opposed but its methods, conspiracy and violence directed at legitimate authority. Catholic bishops, encouraged by their colleagues in Ireland especially Paul Cullen, the archbishop of Dublin, declared that the Fenian organisation was condemned by the church as a secret society. Although the bishops had been anxious in 1865 to have the backing of Rome for their anti-Fenian stance, their position was more cautious and the hierarchy in the United States opposed the papal condemnation of Fenianism in 1870 issued at the request of the Irish bishops. The church in America and Canada laboured under various disadvantages that hampered its ability to deal resolutely with the Irish nationalist discontent in its midst. Fenianism was regarded as a threat to the Church as much as a threat to the Canadian state.[15]

One of the major problems that bedevilled attitudes to Irish-Canadian nationalism was the divergent attitudes of the Catholic hierarchy. Thomas Connolly, bishop of New Brunswick in 1852 and archbishop of Nova Scotia seven years later, was the most influential Catholic cleric in the Maritime Provinces.[16] He believed that his first duty was to care for 'our people' in the colonies and that Irish Catholics who were not content with life in British North America should go elsewhere. He recognised that the life of Irish Catholics in British

---

[15] Raffety, Oliver, 'Fenianism in North America in the 1860s: The Problems for Church and State', *History*, Vol. 84, (1999), pp. 257-277.

[16] Flemming, David B., 'Thomas Louis Connolly', *DCB*, Vol. 10, pp. 191-193.

North America left much to be desired because of sectarian attitudes, but felt that their position was still superior to that facing Irish Catholics in the United States. For Connolly, the Irish enjoyed a liberal society in which their rights were respected and consequently owed loyalty to Canada and its government.[17] A supporter of Confederation, his position was made clear in late 1865 in an open letter to Sir Arthur Gordon Lieutenant-Governor of New Brunswick in which he reassured non-Catholics that Irish Catholics in British North America had nothing to gain from the Fenians, 'that pitiable knot of knaves and fools.'[18] It is not surprising that revolutionary nationalism made little progress in the Atlantic colonies. Connolly's position led the editor of the *Irish Canadian* to argue that the Church should not involve itself it political matters publishing several letters from Catholic priests in Ireland against Church involvement in political societies.[19]

By contrast, John Joseph Lynch, bishop in 1860 and archbishop of Toronto a decade later, took a more aggressively nationalist stance and periodically denounced British policy in Ireland.[20] Of Toronto's population of 45,000 in 1851, Catholics, largely of Irish birth, numbered 12,000, their strength exceeded only slightly by members of the Church of England and Catholic numbers were increasing faster than the population as a whole. This aggressive growth of Catholicism and its institutions in the 1850s resulted in a sectarian Protestant response that led to violence. Lynch thought that Irish-Canadians owed their primary allegiance to Ireland, a country the victim of iniquitous laws and tyrannical oppression. He painted a bleak picture of the lives of most Irish immigrants to and in his pastoral letter, *The Evils of Wholesale and Improvident Emigration from Ireland*, documented the social miseries of immigrants who filled the prisons, poor houses, hospitals and streets with 'miserable creatures' stripped

---

[17] This view was echoed in the Irish-Canadian press, for instance, in 'Fenianism', *Canadian Freeman*, 10 August 1865, p. 2.

[18] Connolly, T. L., 'The archbishop of Halifax on the Irish in British and in republican America', in McGee, T. D., *The Irish position in British and in republican North America: a letter to the editors of the Irish press irrespective of party*, 2nd edition, (M. Longmoore & Co.), 1866, appendix B.

[19] 'The Fenians and the Priests', letter from a parish priest to the *Cork Examiner*, *Irish Canadian*, 15 February 1865, p. 3, 'The Fenians', letter to the *Universal News*, from a Thomond Priest, *Irish Canadian*, 15 March 1865, p. 3.

[20] Humphries, Charles W., 'John Joseph Lynch', *DCB*, Vol. 9, pp. 535-538.

of their religion.[21] For Lynch, a free Ireland would gain greater respect for immigrants from Canadians.[22] His nationalist views, which may have (as he used as a defence) reflected the views of a large proportion of his flock, led him to support the activities of organisations such as the Hibernian Benevolent Association and to ignore the existence of conspiratorial or secret organisations. His example was followed by parish clergy who began to cooperate with Hibernians in organising social activities. Lynch certainly appeared to be giving moral support to radical nationalism especially because of his links with Michael Murphy, the Hibernians' leader.[23] Though the extent to which the Hibernians was a Fenian organisation is hotly debated, Lynch's action in providing encouragement to Toronto's revolutionary nationalists contributed to the growth of Irish nationalism, put at risk the Church's relationship with the government and revived suspicions over the loyalty of Irish Catholics in Canada West.[24] It was not until August 1865 that Lynch censured the Hibernians and Murphy and advised all good Catholics to quit the Society that had now fallen away from Catholic principles and was governed by imprudent men.[25]

The sheer scale of the largely Catholic Famine immigration into Canada and especially the United States irrevocably altered the nature of Irish nationalism in North America providing a cohesiveness and coherence that Irish communities had previously lacked. Nationalism wedded demands for Irish sovereignty with republican rhetoric

---

[21] See, Stortz, Gerald J., (ed.), 'Archbishop Lynch's *The Evils of Wholesale and Improvident Emigration from Ireland*, (1864)', *Eire/Ireland*, Vol. 18, (1983), pp. 6-16, and Stortz, Gerald, "Improvident Emigrants': John Joseph Lynch and Irish Immigration to British North America, 1860-88', in Murphy, Terence, and Stortz, Gerald, (eds.), *Creed and Culture: The Place of English-Speaking Catholics in Canadian Society, 1750-1930*, (McGill-Queen's University Press), 1993, pp. 171-184.

[22] See, McKeon, H. C., *The Life and Labours of John Joseph Lynch, First Archbishop of Toronto*, (Sadler), 1886, pp. 248-260, for discussion of Lynch and emigration.

[23] Neidhardt, W. S., 'Michael Murphy', *DCB*, Vol. 9, pp. 587-589, and Stacey, C. P., 'A Fenian interlude: the story of Michael Murphy', *Canadian Historical Review*, Vol. 15, (1934), pp. 133-154.

[24] Clarke, Brian P., *Piety and nationalism: lay voluntary associations and the creation of an Irish-Catholic community in Toronto, 1850-1895*, (McGill-Queen's University Press), 1993, pp. 168-198, examines the Hibernians and Fenians in Toronto while Sheppard, George, "God Save the Queen', Fenianism and Fellowship in Canada West', *Histoire Social/Social History*, Vol. 10, (1987), pp. 129-144, takes a broader canvas.

[25] 'Hibernian Benevolent Society of Canada', *Irish Canadian*, 16 August 1865, p. 4.

offering a powerful opportunity for identity formation outside traditional assimilation routes. The Fenians' espousal of such rhetoric made important claims about Irish-American ethnicity and identity.[26] The events of 1848, with the exile of many Young Ireland leaders to the United States, meant that Irish nationalism and independence had now become a transatlantic issue and that the United States, rather than France, had become the natural ally of the nationalists. In Canada, by contrast, this rhetoric posed a fundamental dilemma since linking Irish-American nationalism with the republican credentials of the United States raised the spectre of invasion and annexation as a potential means of achieving America's long-standing aim of bringing Canada into the union. Calls for the liberation of Ireland, whether through constitutionalist or revolutionary means, posed a potent threat to the continued existence of a Protestant Canada.

Increasingly, 'Hibernian' and 'Fenian' were used interchangeably and both groups were seen as enemies of Protestantism In 1860, Fenians only made up about 10-15 per cent of the 600 members of the Hibernian Society in Toronto.[27] Two years later, the Fenians established a small circle in Montreal and in either 1864 or 1865 a Fenian circle was established in Quebec. There is some evidence suggesting that Fenian circles were formed in Ottawa, Halifax, St. John and Charlottetown during the mid-1860s. Although not as obvious or numerous as urban members, Fenians in rural locations and small towns such as Sarnia, Stratford, Guelph Adjala, Puslinch and Aberfoyle were given an important role in the Fenians' invasion plan in 1866. [28] In Adjala, for instance, support for the Fenians reflected and reinforced sectarian tensions between Irish Protestants and Catholics in the area. This was especially evident in Toronto in late 1864. As Orange celebrations wound down on Guy Fawkes Day, an festival held every year on 5 November, 'about four hundred armed, masked Hibernians gathered near Queen's Park, keeping a nucleus there and sending columns to the east and west of the city' with the

---

[26] Lynch, Timothy G., "A Kindred and Congenial Element': Irish American Nationalism's Embrace of Republican Rhetoric,' *New Hibernia Review*, Vol. 13, (2), (2009), pp. 77-91.

[27] A highly unfavourable account of the development of the Hibernian Benevolent Society in Toronto is found in *The Canadian Freeman*, 17 August 1862.

[28] Nash-Chambers, Debra L., 'In the Palm of God's Hand? The Irish Catholic Experience in Mid-Nineteenth Century Guelph', CCHA, *Historical Studies*, Vol 54, (1984), pp. 67-87.

columns firing rifles as they marched.[29] A week later, armed Hibernians interrupted another Orange march and burned effigies of Protestant leaders and a short time later vandalised an Orange meeting hall, desecrating the epitome of Anglo-Protestant symbols: the Bible, the Union Jack and a painting of the Queen.[30] The public response was furious. Catholics were maligned especially after bishop Lynch refused to condemn their actions though he did label them 'foolish and unwarranted'.[31] sweeping detention powers were given to magistrates to maintain public peace and Toronto police officers suspected of being Hibernians were dismissed.[32] Irish Catholic tavern keepers were arrested for storing pikes at their bars.[33] The extent of the division over the demonstration on 5 November is clear with the *Globe* condemning the demonstrators as seeking 'the subversion of an existing government' while the *Irish Canadian* and *Canadian Freeman* saw them as valiant defenders of the Catholic faith.[34] The *Globe's* editor, George Brown came in for particular criticism: it was part of his relentless war against Catholics in Upper Canada and his willingness to keep alive 'the smouldering embers of religious strife'. [35]

It is easy to suggest that Fenians were of marginal importance and that the Fenian scares were exaggerated to the point of paranoia.[36] The Fenians were very much a minority in Irish Catholic Canada. Even in their main centres in Toronto and Montreal, the combined number of sworn Fenians was thought to be less than a thousand in 1865-1866,

---

[29] Senior, Hereward, *The Fenians and Canada*, (Macmillan of Canada), 1978, p. 69. For contemporary comment see, 'Fifth of November—Almost a Serious Disturbance', *Globe*, 7 November 1865, 'The Fenians and the Fifth', *Globe*, 8 November 1865, p. 2, 'The Fenians', *Leader*, 8 November 1864, p. 2, and 'Fifth of November', *Irish Canadian*, 9 November 1864, p. 4.

[30] *Globe*, 12 November 1864.

[31] See, 'Bishop Lynch's Letter', *Globe*, 12 November 1864, p. 2.

[32] Ibid, Senior, Hereward, *The Fenians and Canada*, pp. 70-71, 87.

[33] Cameron, Edward Robert, *Memoirs of Ralph Vansittart*, (Musson Book Company), 1924, p. 210.

[34] 'The Lynch-Law Advocates', *Globe*, 12 November 1864, p. 2.

[35] 'Mr Brown's Remedy', *Irish Canadian*, 16 November 1864, p. 4.

[36] This was, for example, evident when rumour of the invasion in early 1866 quickly spread throughout all of Canada. Panic set in as banks in villages along the border sent their cash to the interior and scores of families moved further into the Canadian interior. The expected date for the expected invasion was St. Patrick's Day and as it approached, the Canadian provincial government and Britain mustered troops to the Fenians' well-publicised points of entry into the country. One enterprising Canadian sold 'Fenian Telescopes' with a guarantee to be able to spot Fenians five miles away.

just under 5 per cent of the Irish Catholic population in both cities. In Canada as a whole, there were probably no more than 3,000 Fenians out of an Irish Catholic population of over 250,000. This was despite the boasts of Michael Murphy, by then Head C entre of the Fenians in Canada, that over 100,000 men were ready to rise against the Canadian government in the winter of 1865-1866. This can be contrasted with the Orange Order that had 50,000 members in Canada West alone. Irrespective of this, there was widespread concern in Protestant communities about the Fenians. For instance, the citizens of Orangeville heard and probably believed rumours of Fenians burning Presbyterian churches and 'putting all Protestants to the sword, regardless of age or sex.'[37]

Fears of a Fenian uprising against Protestants encouraged the Orangemen in Canada West to increase their efforts in defence of Protestantism and in surveillance of Catholic activities. John Hillyard Cameron, Grand Master of the Orange Lodges of British North America, labelled the Hibernians as 'Fenians'[38] and Ogle R. Gowan, a Past Grand Master, advised all the brethren to join an established militia unit or arm themselves privately in preparation for the impending Fenian raid.[39] This call by a leading Orangeman for the use of arms created considerable disquiet among the Catholics in Toronto. The calling of the Orange Order to arms naturally constituted a challenge to the Irish Catholics to do the same.

Suspicion that Fenianism was widespread among the Irish Catholics in Toronto and the *Irish Canadian's* admission of Fenian sympathy among members of the Hibernian Benevolent Society increased Protestant concerns over how widespread Fenianism was in Canada West's Irish Catholic community. The continued threats by Irish-American Fenians of a raid on Canada exacerbated this situation. Many Protestants feared that if a raid took place the attacking Fenians would receive assistance from sympathetic Irish-Canadian Fenians in Toronto. Canadian citizens and newspapers became alarmed by these growing threats of attack and that some defence measures should be adopted. The Canadian government seemed to confirm this view when it despatched the militia and then 10,000 volunteers to the border as a precautionary measure for a possible raid on St. Patrick's Day 1866. The Protestant press adopted a more conciliatory tone

---

[37] Stacey, C. P., 'A Fenian Interlude: The Story of Michael Murphy', *CHR*, Vol. 15, (1934), p. 139.
[38] 'The Orange Grand Master', *Irish Canadian*, 14 December 1864, p. 4.
[39] 'To the Members of the Loyal Orange Association: letter to the Orange Brethren from Ogle R. Gowan, Nebo Lodge, Toronto, 1 November 1865', *Irish Canadian*, 8 November 1856, p. 5.

than usual with the *Globe* assuring the Protestant community that if a Fenian plot existed, it would not succeed because of the 'respectable, order-loving portion of our Roman Catholic fellow-citizens'.[40]

The Hibernian procession on 16 March passed without incident but within a month Michael Murphy and five others were arrested reported on route to join the Fenians in the Campobello incursion.[41] This reignited Protestant suspicions over Irish Catholic loyalty and Catholic concerns about the legality of Murphy's arrest and possible trial before Protestant magistrates. The problem for the government was that it had little evidence against Murphy and it is probable that a trial would have exposed this weakness. This became irrelevant when Murphy and the other prisoners were, according to Stacey, allowed to escape. Tensions between Irish Catholics and Protestants reduced from late April but revived with the Fenian invasions in June 1866, something that came as a shock to the government, despite intelligence to the contrary, and to the Irish Catholic community that had been assured by the Catholic press that no invasion was planned.

Although exaggerated, the idea of Irish-Canadian support for the Fenians was widely reported in the press. This was reinforced by the discovery of arms caches, for instance, in Griffintown and wild rumours that the Fenians would be given a 'warm reception' on their arrival. Many Irish Catholics suffered from charges of disloyalty as well as insults and even threats of violence. The *Canadian Freeman* regretted that such tactics were encouraged by Orangemen who urged that many Irish Catholics, whom they considered rebels and Fenians, be driven from the country.[42] The raids were subject to extensive press coverage during June but this declined in the weeks after. The divisions between Protestants and Catholics occasioned by the raids, however, lasted much longer. The Protestant fear was that there would be significant Irish Catholic support for the Fenians. The support given was largely in terms of intelligence and was later acknowledged by Irish-American Fenians leaders and by some contemporary military analysts as of tactical importance, but no large-scale Irish Catholic support materialised. The *Canadian Freeman*, which had discounted the danger from the Fenians the previous autumn,[43] expressed a clearer and more forceful opposition to the Fenian 'marauders'.[44] The feeling of disgust and indignation that spread throughout the province

---

[40] 'St. Patrick's Day', *Globe*, 9 March 1866, p. 2.
[41] 'Arrest of a Fenian', *Globe*, 11 April 1866, p. 2.
[42] 'The Social Persecution of Orangeism', *Canadian Freeman*, 28 June 1866, p. 2.
[43] 'Panic Writing', *Canadian Freeman*, 23 November 1865.
[44] *Canadian Freeman*, 7 June 1866.

was equally shared by the many Irish Catholics who were as ready as Protestants to affirm their duty of loyalty and allegiance to Canada.

Public perception of a Fenian-Catholic alliance was misplaced. The Fenians accepted support from all denominations. Irish Protestants held prominent positions in the Fenian Brotherhood, the main Fenian generals were all Protestant and the *Barrie Examiner* noted a quarter of imprisoned Fenians at Brantford were Protestants.[45] McGee drew a sharp line between Fenians and Irish Catholic Canadians but this proved difficult to maintain in an atmosphere of paranoia and when Canadian Fenians still seen as a major threat to security.[46] However, some Canadians disagreed with this pessimistic analysis:

> A Montreal special says the rumors of a Fenian invasion create no excitement here; the people laugh at the reports, and look upon them as a very transparent attempt to hoax the Canadians and oh eat us out of the custom duties.[47]

The case for the Fenian invasions being a 'war of religion' is less clear than in the rebellions in 1837 and 1838 and in the North-West in the 1880s. As in 1837 and 1838, there was a clear division between the attitudes of the Church hierarchy and those Irish-Canadians willing to take up the Fenian cause and between 1860 and 1866 there was an intense and vitriolic debate within the Irish Catholic press over the precise character of the Hibernians. The Protestant press, popularised and often articulated through the *Globe*, created a climate of mistrust and fear among many Protestants and the government believed that there was a widespread Fenian conspiracy within Canada as well as in the United States though publicly it emphasised the external nature of the threat. The response of Protestants and particularly the Orange Order was conditioned by this belief. The extent of the Fenian threat within Canada is unclear but was sufficient to rouse Protestant concerns that the Fenians, despite the fact that they never articulated one, had a Catholic agenda for Canada.

Until 1869, the 'wars of religion' were confined largely to Quebec but the decision by the new federal government to acquire the Hudson's Bay Company's land in the north and west of Canada brought conflict with the French Catholic Métis living in those

---

[45] *Barrie Examiner Extra*, 7 June 1866.
[46] See, *Canadian Freeman*, 20 September 1866.
[47] The *Deseret News*, 4 June 1867.

regions.[48] The terms of political authority were unresolved in the 1868 legislation and a political and legal vacuum existed in the territory. If, in retrospect, Métis resistance was understandable, it should have been foreseen and there were warnings. French Catholic Métis were lukewarm about Confederation. Fearing floods of agricultural settlers whose presence would make their hunting life that was already under threat unsustainable, they would have preferred the continuance of Hudson's Bay Company rule. With uncertain government and land rights, political tension rose.[49] The Canadian government and Protestant expansionists paid little attention to the Métis as it was assumed that their attitudes were the same as other segments of Red River society and consequently, they were ignored. Macbeth commented:

> ...the Canadian authorities seem to have blundered by overlooking the fact that the new territory had a population of some ten thousand people, who ought at least to have been informed in some official way of the bargain that was being made and of the steps being taken to secure and guard their rights and privileges.[50]

What became a crisis for the Métis began in the 1850s with a fundamental shift in how the western interior of Canada was perceived.[51] For some, it was no longer a wilderness but as a potential location for settler expansion. Rising land prices in Ontario and the explosion in railway construction that eventually led to the building of Canadian Pacific Railway created visions of commercial wealth that

---

[48] Discussion of the confrontations between the Métis and the federal government between 1869 and 1885 is in my *Rebellion in Canada, 1837-1885, Volume 2: The Irish, the Fenians and the Métis*, (CreateSpace), 2012, pp. 294-433.

[49] Sprague, Douglas N., *Canada and the Métis, 1869-1885*, (Wilfrid Laurier University Press), 1988, pp. 19-66. See also, Teillet, Jean, *The North-West is Our Mother: The Story of Louis Riel's People, The Métis Nation*, (Patrick Crean Editions), 2019.

[50] MacBeth, Roderick George, *The Making of the Canadian West, being the Reminiscences of an Eyewitness*, (W. Briggs), 1898, pp. 29-30. MacBeth, (1859-1934) was former lawyer turned Presbyterian minister and provides eye-witness accounts of Riel's Resistance and the later rebellion.

[51] Owram, Doug, *Promise of Eden: The Canadian Expansionist Movement and the Idea of the West, 1856-1900*, (Toronto University Press), 1980, pp. 38-78, explores the expansionist campaign 'new worlds to conquer' between 1856 and 1869.

could only be achieved by western expansion.[52] For Canadian propagandists, the western interior was the keystone in the arch of the Canadian empire:

> The NOW of this country finds a territory of immense extent occupied by about 14,000 civilized people; the THEN of ten years shall see a population of 500,000...Now the eye wanders, without a resting place over our unoccupied plains, then it shall be arrested by the happy homes of thousands which dot the horizon.[53]

From the early-1860s, Anglophone Protestants settlers arrived from Ontario, generally insensitive to Métis culture, hostile to Roman Catholicism and many were advocates of Canadian expansionism. Morton concluded that it was not immigration that was the Métis' chief fear but the immigrants' language and Protestant religion.[54] For the Roman Catholic bishop Alexandre Taché, the sudden immigration of settlers from Ontario threatened to expose the Métis to the more secular, commercial and Protestant Anglo-Saxon civilisation.[55] Although the clergy made no attempt to delay the transfer, Taché was able to use the Resistance to obtain safeguards to protect his people from the shock of opening the North-West to settlement. The *Globe* took a more critical position on the role of the Church:

> This movement has the sanction of the clergy...the Catholic clergy have taken a great part, but it is a political, not a religious movement.[56]

At the same time, many Americans migrated to the North-West, some of whom favoured annexation of the territory by the United

---

[52] Warner, Donald F., *The Idea of Continental Union: Agitation for the Annexation of Canada to the United States 1849-1893*, (University of Kentucky Press), 1960, pp. 99-127, considers the annexationist issues in relation to the Red River Settlement.

[53] *Nor'-Wester*, 21 September 1869. It was Red River's first newspaper, pro-annexationist in attitude. See also Peel, Bruce, *Early Printing in the Red River Settlement 1859-1870; and its Effects on the Riel Rebellion*, (Peguis), 1974.

[54] Morton, W. L, (ed.), *Alexander Begg's Red River journal; and other papers relative to the Red River resistance of 1869-1870*, (Champlain Society), 1956, p. 2.

[55] Morice, A. G., *Histoire de l'église catholique dans l'ouest canadien du lac Supérieur au Pacifique*, 3 Vols. (Granger Frères), 1911. Dorge, Lionel, 'Bishop Taché and the Confederation of Manitoba, 1869-1870', Manitoba Historical Society, *Transactions*, 3rd series, Vol. 26, (1969-1970), pp. 93-109.

[56] *The Globe*, 6 January 1870.

States. These perceptions of race, class and religion reinforced social divisions in Red River even within the Métis. The English-speaking Métis saw themselves as part of a 'European or agricultural party' and closer to civilisation than the French-speaking Métis who continued to hunt or take part in trading expeditions and who seemed to be veering towards 'the native or aboriginal party'.[57] The problem was that the Canadian image of the Métis was distorted and incomplete.

There was little active opposition to union with Canada in the North-West but equally, there was little active support. Although there had been Canadian immigration to Red River from the late 1850s, it was members of the professions and free-traders who settled at Winnipeg who were the most strident supporters of Canadian annexation and critics of the Hudson's Bay Company's commercial and political monopoly. This small but noisy 'Canadian party' succeeded in making annexation unpopular. But strengthened by a influx of new immigrants from the beginning of 1869, it was to be the principal beneficiary of Confederation rule. This prospect explains why the Métis resisted the transfer of power in 1869.

During the Confederation debates between 1864 and 1867, there had been little enthusiasm for annexing the North-West in either Ontario or Quebec.[58] French-Canadians, who saw Quebec as their homeland, regarded the region with indifference, saw its development as unnecessary when Canada already had significant debts and large areas of undeveloped and accessible land. The North-West was generally viewed by French-Canadians and government supporters as a 'savage land', foreign, desolate, distant and inaccessible for much of the year and an inauspicious location for settlers. Not alone among the French-Canadian press, in 1868 *Le Nouveau Monde*, an ultramontane weekly newspaper in Montreal, published a series of articles portraying agricultural settlement in a less than favourable light as an antidote to the calls for immediate settlement contained in English papers such as the *Globe* in Toronto. Rather than spending money of costly expansion, the federal government should be improving the well-being of its people and developing its own lands that were better suited to settlement.[59]

---

[57] Friesen, Gerald, *The Canadian Prairies: A History*, (University of Toronto Press), 1987, pp. 92-97.

[58] Political parties in Quebec that agreed on little were at one over developing the North-West. *Le Pays*, 6 July 1865, reported that the Rouges thought the whole project 'ridiculous' while *Le Journal de Québec*, 14 August 1865, stated that the Bleus were 'indifferent'.

[59] See Silver, A. I., *The French-Canadian Idea of Confederation*, (University of Toronto Press), 1982, pp. 67-87.

There is a view among some Canadian historians that George-Etienne Cartier, who had negotiated the transfer of land from the Hudson's Bay Company and later authored the Manitoba Act, expected French-Canadians to play an important role in colonising the prairies.[60] However, they did not look upon the North-West as part of their country nor the French Métis as being part of a single nationality. The Métis may have been descended largely from French-Canadians but they had lived apart from Quebec since the eighteenth century and the two ethnic groups now had little in common other than their Catholicism. This was reflected in the muted response of Quebec and Ontarian press to the Resistance in 1869 and 1870. The Métis were seen as 'rebels' whose defeat was essential for the sake of 'the honour of the fledgling Canadian diplomacy'.[61] For French-Canadians at least initially, this was not a French Catholic struggle against English Protestantism rather, if anything, a struggle for local self-determination in which there was an important threat from American annexationists.[62]

Social, economic and religious tensions in the North-West combined with the mishandling of the transfer by the federal government led to Métis resistance directed by Louis Riel.[63] What Riel, the Métis and the clergy feared was the immediate occupation of the Red River Valley by a flood of Protestant immigrants.[64] The Church's official position was to remain politically neutral, but with

---

[60] See, for instance, Sweeny, Alistair, *Goerge-Etienne Cartier*, (McClelland and Stewart), 1976.

[61] *L'Ordre*, 25 November 1869.

[62] Stanley, George F. G., and *The Birth of Western Canada: A history of the Riel Rebellions*, (Longman, Green and Co.), 1936, remains useful but Bumsted, J. M., *The Red River Rebellion*, (Watson & Dwyer), 1996, is the most detailed modern study.

[63] For Riel see, Stanley, George F. G., *Louis Riel: Patriot or Rebel*, (Canadian Historical Association), 1954, Stanley, George F., *Louis Riel*, (McGraw-Hill Ryerson), 1972, Siggins, Maggie, *Riel: A Life of Revolution*, (HarperCollins), 1994, Boyden, Joseph, *Louis Riel & Gabriel Dumont*, (Penguin), 2010, Doyle, David, *Louis Riel: Let Justice be Done*, (Ronsdale Press), 2017, and Thomas, Lewis H., 'Louis Riel', *DCB*, Vol. 11, pp. 736-752.

[64] Ibid, Morice, A. G., *Histoire de l'église catholique dans l'ouest canadien du lac Supérieur au Pacifique*, Vol. 2, pp. 121-205, views the resistance from the viewpoint of the Catholic Church. Lalonde, Andre N., 'The Attitude of the Roman Catholic Clergy towards the Rebellions in 1870 and 1885', *Native Studies Review*, Vol. 1, (1984), pp. 79-81, contrasts the tacit endorsement of Riel in 1869-1870 with its outright condemnation in 1884-1885.

Taché in Rome and Father Superior Lestanc acting in his place, the clergy was allowed considerable latitude in their actions as spiritual advisers and some positively supported the Métis.[65] Lestanc maintained in mid-October that any attempt by the Church to act against the Métis would suggest that 'the Church also was in sympathy with the Government, and so might lead to weakening their influence over their people in a religious point of view'.[66] Once Riel established a provisional government in December 1869, the only way the Métis could be forced to disband was civil war, something all but the Canadian Loyalists were unwilling to countenance or by spending a federal military force, something that could not occur until mid-1870. Riel pre-empted a loyalist uprising by arresting its leaders in December, most of whom were released within a month. However, in February 1870, there was a concerted, but unsuccessful attempt by Canadian sympathisers to oust Riel that was, in part, thwarted by the opposition of Protestant clergy. Having re-established his position, Riel then made what many regard as his greatest mistake, when in March 1870, he allowed the execution of Thomas Scott in many respects, an inconsequential, if volatile, figure. Why Riel agreed to the execution, a disproportionate punishment given Scott's offences, is difficult to determine but it was a political blunder that was to dog him for the remainder of his life.[67]

To Protestant Ontarians, this appeared to be a vindictive act by a 'half-breed papal rabble'. The Ontarian press soon established Scott's Orange Order credentials, but it appears that his execution was not caused by his membership of the Order. There is no evidence that anyone in Red River knew before or immediately after his death that he was a member and Bumsted suggests that had his affiliations

---

[65] Benoit, D. P., *Vie de Monseigneur Taché, Archevêque de Saint-Boniface*, 2 Vols. (Librarie Beauchemin), 1904, remains the most detailed study. For Taché and the Red River resistance see, Huelo, Raymond Joseph, and Huelo, Raymond, *Archbishop A.-A. Alexandre Taché of St. Boniface: The 'good fight' and the illusive vision*, (University of Alberta Press), 2003, pp. 103-142, and Hamelin, Jean, 'Alexandre-Antonin Taché', *DCB*, Vol. 12, pp. 1002-1012.

[66] Dennis, G., 'Memorandum of Facts and Circumstances concerning with the active Opposition by the French Half-Breeds in this settlement to the prosecution of the Government Surveys', *Correspondence relative to the Recent Disturbances in the Red River Settlement*, p. 6.

[67] Rea, J. E., 'Thomas Scott', *DCB*, Vol. 9, pp. 707-709. Bumsted, J. M., 'Thomas Scott's Body', and 'Why Shoot Thomas Scott?: A Study in Historical Evidence', in his *Thomas Scott's Body and Other Essays on Early Manitoba History*, (University of Manitoba Press), 2000, pp. 3-10, 197-210, seek to provide an explanation from the mass of contradictory evidence

been known, it might well have saved his life. The consequence of Scott's execution was a storm of visceral protest in Ontario and *Globe* reported the resolution of Toronto Orangemen:

> Whereas Brother Thomas Scott, a member of our Order was cruelly murdered by the enemies of our Queen, country and religion, therefore be it resolved that . . . we, the members of L.O.L. No. 404 call upon the Government to avenge his death, pledging ourselves to assist in rescuing Red River Territory from those who have turned it over to Popery, and bring to justice the murderers of our countrymen.[68]

Initially the Quebec press far from justifying Riel's actions regarded as an 'abhorrent murder'.[69] Despite this in Ontarian eyes, Quebec was seen as aligned with Scott's murderers while in Quebec the real cause of anger was seen not to be Scott's death but an Ontarian desire to punish not simply Scott's killers but French Catholics in general. The shift towards Ontarian extremism led French-Canadians to conclude that calls for the repression of the Métis were not simply because they were rebels but because they were French Catholics. In this situation, it is unsurprising that Quebec as the French-Canadian province would move towards supporting the Métis. *Le Journal des Trois-Rivières*, for instance, asserted:

> ...the inhabitants of Ontario want to see a policy adopted that will undermine French influence in the North-West...on that point the Province of Québec will have only one answer: to protect and assist our brothers out there.[70]

For Quebec, the fevered response of the Ontarian press had turned what was a local difficulty into a dispute over religion and the place of the French race in Canada.[71] The English wanted to crush the Resistance and the French wanted a province west of Ontario constitutionally supportive of French-Canadian language and culture: 'to please Quebec they negotiated with the Red River delegates; to placate Ontario they dispatched the military force.'[72]

While negotiations were taking place in Ottawa between Riel's delegates and the federal government successfully ending the Resistance, attention turned to the question of amnesty and Scott's

---

[68] *Globe*, 13 April 1870.
[69] *Le Journal des Trois-Rivières*, 18 April 1870.
[70] *Le Journal des Trois-Rivières*, 18 April 1870.
[71] *Le Pays*, 11 March 1870.
[72] Ibid, Stanley, George F., *The Birth of Western Canada*, p. 145.

execution.[73] Faced with angry Protestant opposition in the Maritimes and in Ontario, the Canadian Government could not consider an amnesty that included the death of Scott. The result was evasion with the Canadian Government arguing that the acts requiring amnesty has been committed before Canadian jurisdiction had been established in the North-West and that it was up to the Imperial authorities to exercise the prerogative of mercy. Cartier persuaded Ritchot and the other delegates to sign a petition for amnesty that was forwarded to London on 9 June with a covering despatch from Cartier pleading the necessity of clemency. Although Riel's delegates pushed for written assurances, no one was willing to put a pledge for a general amnesty in writing, much less one that included Scott's death.

Although militarily unnecessary, but important as a means of asserting Canadian authority in the settlement and as a sop to Ontarian nationalists fuming over Scott's death, a Canadian military expedition under British command was dispatched to the Red River on what the Canadian government described as an 'errand of peace', 'representing no party either of Religion or Politics'. The inclusion of imperial troops, a rifle battalion from the 60th Regiment that had been on garrison duty in Canada, was planned before Scott's death to ensure that the force did not become a punitive expedition from Ontario but this not prevent it being seen, with some justification, as hostile to the Métis and punitive in intent. Two battalions of Canadian militia were raised specifically for the task and it was originally envisaged that one would be raised in Ontario, the other in Quebec: the 1st Ontario and the 2nd Quebec Battalion of Rifles. Problems recruiting in Quebec meant that only a quarter of the Quebec Battalion were French-Canadians, the remainder British Protestants. This raised religious and racial issues that had been muted during the Resistance to the fore. Of the thousand volunteers, about half were from Ontario, a third from Quebec and the remainder from other provinces or from outside Canada. The typical militiaman was a young, single, English-speaking Protestant, urban worker.

French-Canadian opposition was regarded in Ontario as a sign of disloyalty and the focus of the conspiratorial analysis of the Resistance

---

[73] Taché, Alexandre A., *L'Amnistie*, (Impr. par le journal 'Le nouveau monde'), 1874, and *The Amnesty Again, or, Charges Refuted*, (Printed at 'The Standard' Office), 1875, examine the corrosive impact of this issue. See also, Jonasson, Jonas A., 'The Red River Amnesty Question', *Pacific Historical Review*, Vol. 6, (1937), pp. 58-66, and ibid, Huel, Raymond J. A., *Archbishop A.-A. Taché of St. Boniface: The 'Good Fight' and the Illusive Vision*, pp. 103-142.

shifted to the role played by priests.[74] Riel and the Métis were increasingly identified with the cause of French rights and among Loyalists there was a widespread belief that Riel was in league with the Fenians. The federal force that arrived at Fort Garry on 24 August consisted almost entirely of the British regulars and the area was already completely secured before the first groups of militia arrived on 27 August.[75] By 4 September, the regular troops had left leaving the Canadian militia to garrison the Fort. This was a recipe for anti-Catholic and anti-French violence by the increasingly confident pro-Canada supporters that now included some of the demobilised militia who chose to stay in Red River. Until the end of 1870, there was periodic violence directed largely against the Métis community. On 13 September, Elzéar Goulet was chased into the Red River by a mob where he either drowned or died from thrown stones or shots fired at him from the riverbank. In October, a second Riel sympathiser was killed when thrown from his horse after it had deliberately been frightened. Canadian troops were involved in these incidents though none were held accountable. There was, according to an American newspaper, 'a reign of terror' directed largely at Métis whether or not they had supported Riel. McKillip concluded:

...part of the decision to fight in 1885 may have resulted from the experience of the Métis with the military forces of Canada after the 1870 rebellion: that the Métis were emboldened to fight, at least in part, by the bad behaviour of the garrison forces of northwest Canada.[76]

The passage of the Manitoba Act in 1870 saw a shift in thinking among some French-Canadians. Although the legislation guaranteed the French language and Catholic schools, French-Canadian newspapers emphasised that it gave the Métis, their co-religionists, their own separate province. The North-West was not an extension to their homeland, but it could become a second French-Canadian province that would become an ally of Quebec in the new Confederation to counter the influence of the more populous

---

[74] *Globe*, 14 April 1870, addressed criticism of Ontarian militancy in the Quebec press: 'If anyone is fanatical in this matter, it is certainly not the people of Upper Canada [Ontario] who desire merely to seek law and order restored in the Territory...the fanatics are the French Canadians who are striving to obtain for themselves peculiar and exclusive privileges.'
[75] This issue of explored in McKillip, Jim, 'Emboldened by Bad Behaviour: The Conduct of the Canadian Army in the Northwest, 1870-1873', in Mantle, Craig Leslie, (ed.), *The Apathetic and the Defiant: Case Studies of Canadian Mutiny and Disobedience, 1812-1919*, (Dundurn Press), 2007, pp. 147-170.
[76] Ibid, p. 150.

Protestant Ontario. The problem was that this did not make Manitoba any more attractive for French-Canadian settlement and by 1872, the French-Canadian press had reverted to a view of the North-West as inhospitable and wild and that the Métis, even though French and Catholic, were half-savage. Many in Ontario held to the same view but this did not prevent them moving west and beginning to settle the prairies.

Scott's execution continued to cast its shadow. In Ontario, Riel was denounced as his 'murderer' and a reward of $5,000 was offered by Edward Blake, the Premier of Ontario for his arrest. Although Riel was twice elected to the federal Parliament such was the opprobrium in which he was held in Ontario that he could not take his seat. Anxious to avoid political confrontation between Ontario and Quebec, Prime Minister Sir John A. Macdonald tried to persuade Riel to remain in voluntary exile in the United States, even providing him with funds. However, Ambroise Lépine, a member of Riel's Provisional Government who presided over Thomas Scott's trial, was arrested, tried and in October 1874 sentenced to death for his 'murder' in the Manitoba Court of Queen's Bench.[77] This sparked outrage in the sympathetic Quebec press and calls for amnesty for both Lépine and Riel were renewed. This presented a severe political difficulty for Alexander Mackenzie, Macdonald's successor as Prime Minister since 1873 who was hopelessly caught between the contradictory demands of Quebec and Ontario. Acting on his own initiative the Governor-General Lord Dufferin commuted Lépine's sentence on 20 January 1875 to two years' imprisonment and loss of political rights.[78] This allowed Mackenzie to secure parliamentary

---

[77] Elliott, George B., and Brokovski, Frederick Thomas, (eds.), *Preliminary Investigation and Trial of Ambroise D. Lépine for the Murder of Thomas Scott,* (Burland-Desbarats), 1874, provides valuable detail on the issue. See also, Bumsted, J. M., 'The trial of Ambroise Lépine', *Beaver,* Vol. 77, (2), (1997-1998), pp. 9-19, and especially Knafla, Louis A., 'Treasonous Murder: The Trial of Ambroise Lépine, 1874', in Wright, Barry, and Binnie, Susan, (eds.), *Canadian State Trials, Volume III: Political Trials and Security Measures, 1840-1914,* (University of Toronto Press), 2009, pp. 297-352.

[78] Buckingham, William, and Ross, Sir George William, *The Hon. Alexander Mackenzie: His Life and Times,* (Rose Publishing Co.), 1892, pp. 386-402, considers the 1875 parliamentary session. See also, Thomson, Dale C., *Alexander Mackenzie: Clear Grit,* (Macmillan), 1960, pp. 221-222, 227, 297, Stewart, George, *Canada under the Administration of the Earl of Dufferin,* (Rose-Belford Publishing Company), 1979, pp. 381-416, and De Kiewiet, Cornelius William, (ed.), *Dufferin-Carnarvon Correspondence,*

approval in February 1875 for an amnesty for Riel and Lépine, conditional on five years' banishment from 'Her Majesty's dominions'.[79] The tragedy for the Métis was that Riel was physically absent in the crucial period of land distribution and, in the absence of a leader with his political vision between 1870 and 1885, the Métis nation began to disintegrate.

After 1874, Riel's religious cosmology and his place within it does change, but only by a small degree.[80] Until his death, he retained the sense of himself as 'Prophet of the New World', devoted to healing the Protestant-Catholic rift in the Christian Church and to his belief in the Métis as a chosen people. Always introspective and strongly religious, Riel became obsessed with the idea that his was a religious mission to establish a new American Catholicism with Bishop Bourget of Montreal as Pope of the New World. While he suffered from sporadic irrational outbursts, he continued his religious writing, mixing Christian and Judaic ideas that included a return to Mosaic Law, endorsement of polygamy and a belief in the Hebraic descent of North American aboriginal groups. He consequently began calling himself Louis 'David' Riel, prophet of the New World, and would pray standing for hours, having servants help him to hold his arms in the shape of a cross. For Mossmann,

---

1874-1878, (Greenwood Press), 1969, pp. 98-129, on the amnesty issue. Dufferin to Carnarvon, 22 January 1875, pp. 128-129, informed London of Lépine's commutation.

[79] Lépine, refused the offer, served out his sentence and was released in late October 1876. He remained active in Métis politics until 1879 when the interests of Riel and the Church began to diverge and he disagreed with Riel who sought to unite the Métis and Indians in the North-West into a confederacy. He had, he said, risked his life once for the Métis cause and was not willing to do so again.

[80] The precise nature of Riel's mental state remains a matter of considerable disagreement. Institutionalised between 1876 and 1878, it is difficult to identify with any clarity what Riel experienced; for some it was delusional, for others madness. For instance, Desjardins, Édouard, and Charles Dumas, 'Le complexe médical de Louis Riel', *L'Union Médicale du Canada*, Vol. 99, (1970), pp. 1870-1878, diagnosed 'a delirious and hallucinatory syndrome of a mystico-religious type', while Littman, S. K., 'A Pathology of Louis Riel', *Canadian Psychiatric Association Journal*, Vol. 23, (1978), pp. 449-462, regarded him as a 'paranoid schizophrenic'. Betts, Gregory, 'Non Compos Mentis: A Meta-Historical Survey of the Historiographic Narratives of Louis Riel's 'Insanity', *International Journal of Canadian Studies*, Vol. 38, (2008), pp. 15-40, provides a recent overview of Riel's mental issues.

Louis Riel in 1885 was primarily a millenarian leader, not a political one.... These movements see the rise of a prophetic leader, who through his charisma strikes a supernatural chord in his mainly peasant or semi-nomadic followers and through his exceptional personality is able to inspire his followers with a desperately needed hope for [his] god-like powers.[81]

For Flanagan, Riel can only be understood if he is seen as a 'spiritual figure, a would-be founder and millenarian prophet'.[82] His religion provided the promise of ultimate escape from domination and was an exaggeration of French-Canadian Catholic theology combining ultramontanism with its recognition of the authority of the Pope over the state and French-Canadian nationalism. It affirmed a providential theory of history in which French Canada had the responsibility for extending the Kingdom of God in North America. Central to Riel's thinking was his reading of the Book of Daniel with its prediction of the rise and fall of four earthly empires, the last for Riel was the British colonial empire, before the emergence of the Kingdom of God. Riel's was an inclusive millenarian vision in which native people, Métis, French-Canadians and European immigrants would ethnically merge and become a 'new race' and with the disappearance of the border between Canada and the United States, a 'new nation'. He had an unfailing certainly about the truth of this transcendental relationship and in his belief that God would ultimately ensure Métis victory in their anti-colonial battles.

In the ten years after 1875, the North-West became a seething mass of discontent with the Canadian government. Both the Métis and the settlers experienced considerable destitution living in the harsh condition on the prairies. The early creation of civil government in the Canadian North-West minimised the frontier violence associated with the territorial expansion of the United States but it failed to provide Métis or white settlers with effective protection for their land or their

---

[81] Mossmann, Manfred, 'The Charismatic Pattern: Canada's Riel Rebellion of 1885 as a Millenarian Protest Movement', in Bowsfield, Harwell, (ed.), *Louis Riel: Selected Readings*, (Copp Clark), 1988, pp. 227-245, at p. 241. This view was also expressed in Martel, Gilles, *Le Messianisme de Louis Riel*, (Wilfrid Laurier University Press), 1984.
[82] Flanagan, Thomas, *Louis 'David Riel': Prophet of the New World*, (University of Toronto Press), 1979, pp. xi, 45-47, 197-198; see also the contrasting discussion in, Reid, Jennifer I. M., "Faire Place à une Race Métisse': Colonial Crisis and the Vision of Louis Riel', in Reid, Jennifer I. M., (ed.), *Religion and Global Culture: New Terrains in the Study of Religion and the work of Charles H. Long*, (Lexington Books), 2003, pp. 51-66.

timber rights.[83] Under John A. Macdonald, the interests of Canada in
the North-West lay in agricultural settlement as an outlet for excess
eastern population and as a stimulus to transcontinental nation-
building.[84] The problem was this process lacked sufficient finances to
develop the province as quickly as settlers wanted and was remote
from the settlers' experience and consequently its willingness to react
to settler demands was sluggish.

By the early 1880s, the three main groups living in the North-
West Territories—the settlers, the Métis and the First Nations—had
grievances against the government of Canada. European and
Canadian settlers accused it of operating the Territory solely for the
benefit of Eastern Canadian business to the detriment of local
interests. Despite this, the settlers, white, Protestant, and English
speaking were aligned to the values of the Anglo-Saxon majority in
Ottawa and when conflict broke out in Saskatchewan, it was these
differences that precluded future cooperation between the two
communities. The life of the First Nations changed irrevocably during
the 1870s with the extinguishing of the buffalo herds that made them
increasingly dependent upon the treaties signed with the federal
government. The government may have allotted reserves of land for
the Indians but for the Métis clinging to their long, narrow river-front
strips, there were no guarantees.

Although the Saskatchewan Métis had complained about their
grievances on several occasions since 1878, they lacked effective
political leadership to put those grievances to the federal government.
This explains why Riel was asked for help in June 1884 and why he
returned to Canada from the United States a month later. He hoped
to establish a united movement across all parties on the Saskatchewan
River and to send delegates to Ottawa to discuss the North-West
Territories becoming a part of the Confederation. Riel was mistaken
in thinking that the approach he has used in 1869 and 1870 would be

---

[83] Pearce, William, *Detailed report upon all claims to land and right to
participate in the North-West Half-Breed Grant by settlers along the south
Saskatchewan and vicinity west of range 26, w. 2nd meridian: being the
settlements commonly known as St. Louis de Langevin, St. Laurent or
Batoche and Duck Lake*, (Roger Maclean), 1886), pp. 8-9, reported that all
the 258 settlers in the area at the time of the Rebellion were able to obtain
patent for his land, that none lost land as a result of government survey and
that timber dues were not onerous.

[84] See, Brown, Robert Craig, *Canada's National Policy, 1883-1900: A Study
in Canadian-American Relations*, (Princeton University Press), 1964, and a
broader analysis in, Fowke, Vernon C., 'National Policy and Western
Development in North America', *Journal of Economic History*, Vol. 16,
(1956), pp. 461-479.

equally successful in 1885. The federal government was in a far stronger position than in 1870 and that may explain why John A. Macdonald, Prime Minister again, was unwilling to negotiate with Riel.[85] In addition, the Catholic Church, stung by Riel's belief that he had a millenarian mission and was God's prophet, did not support his campaign for Métis rights and actively worked with some of the First Nations to prevent their participation in any rebellion.[86] By mid-March 1885, it was clear to Riel that his strategy of negotiating a settlement was unsuccessful and the Métis rose in armed rebellion.[87]

With limited support among the Métis and the First Nations pursuing their own separate armed struggle and with Riel's unwillingness to allow the Métis to use guerrilla tactics that might have delayed a federal victory, this was never going to be a successful rebellion. The federal government quickly mobilised the militia and transported men and resources to the North-West on the Canadian Pacific Railway. By 22 April, over three thousand men had arrived in the North-West. Nearly two thousand were from Ontario, over a thousand from Quebec and nearly four hundred from Nova Scotia. To ensure that French-Canadians were also involved, Sir Adolphe Caron, Minister of Militia and Defence, called on the 9th Voltigeurs from Quebec and the 65th Carabiniers Mont-Royal from Montreal. This was not without its risks and several officers informed Caron that they knew Riel or had links with the Métis and were quickly replaced. Sir Frederick Middleton, who commanded the campaign against the Métis, was concerned about the reliability of the French-Canadian militia and placed them in the Alberta district where they played no active role in the fighting the Métis. The 9th Voltigeurs were responsible for the defence of southern Alberta but the 65th Carabiniers were part of Major-General Thomas Strange's force that

---

[85] McLean, Don, *1885: Metis Rebellion or Government Conspiracy*, (Pemmican Publications), 1985, suggests on the basis of tenuous evidence that either the Canadian government duped Riel into rebellion or deliberately provoked it. Flanagan, Thomas, *Riel and the Rebellion: 1885 Reconsidered*, (Western Producer Prairie Books), 1983, second edition, (University of Toronto Press), 2000, was also savaged by some reviewers.

[86] See, *Riel contre l'eglise catholique: aux Canadiens-français*, (s.n.), 1885, a pamphlet, probably produced by the Conservative Party, that sought to justify Riel's death to French-Canadians by showing that he was opposed to papal authority and includes a letter in Riel's handwriting stating that the members of the Provisional Government had separated from Rome.

[87] Morton, Desmond, *The Last War Drum: The North West Campaign of 1885*, (Hakkert), 1972, and Beal, Bob, and Macleod, R. C., *Prairie Fire: The 1885 North-West Rebellion*, (Hurtig), 1984, are valuable modern accounts.

was deployed against First Nations north of Calgary.[88] As a result, the militia involved in putting down the Métis rebellion consisted largely of Protestants from Ontario.

Mass hysteria made people believe false and sensational rumours, which were based on racist and irrational fears that the Métis, and particularly the First Nations, would behave 'savagely' if given the opportunity. For instance, newspapers such as *The Winnipeg Daily Times* ran unsubstantiated and false stories that including one stating that the 'rebels' had raided Saskatoon and stripped it of all its provisions. Other false reporting involved a story stating that the Dakota Sioux from the local Whitecap Reserve had also attacked Saskatoon.[89] If the critical event in rousing outrage against Riel and the Métis in the resistance in 1869-1870 was the execution of Thomas Scott, the fate of hostages held at Batoche played a similar role in the events of 1885.[90] Initial reactions to the Métis seizure of hostages were mixed with the *Montreal Gazette* regarding it 'of no more consequence than a petty riot in any well settled part of old Canada', but this soon changed and the soldiers who took part in the attack on Batoche regarded freeing them as an important part of their mission. Concern for the hostages can be seen in the excessive descriptions of their plight, living in a cellar as a wretched prison, hourly expecting death and emerging weakened to the cheers of their liberators. Charles Mulvaney left a typical account:

> The prisoners released from Batoche's house all bear the deep imprint of the hardships they have undergone during their long imprisonment, their pale, pinched faces and emaciated forms furnishing indisputable proof of sufferings, both bodily and mental.[91]

---

[88] Strange, Thomas Bland, *Gunner Jingo's Jubilee*, (Remington & Co. Ltd.), 1893, pp. 404-510, for Strange's view of events. Jamieson, F. C., *The Alberta Field Force of 1885*, (Canadian North-West Historical Society), 1931, examines the part played by the Alberta Field Force in defending Edmonton but also pursuing Big Bear. For a more detailed account see, Dunn, Jack F., *The Alberta Field Force of 1885*, (J. Dunn), 1994.

[89] *The Saskatchewan Herald*, 27 March 1885. This story was repeated and embroidered in *The Regina Leader*, 16 April 1885, and *The Manitoba Daily Free Press*, 21 April 1885, and reprinted in almost every Central and Atlantic-Canadian newspaper.

[90] Vance, Jonathan F. W., *Objects of Concern: Canadian Prisoners of War through the Twentieth Century*, (University of British Columbia Press), 1994, pp. 14-16.

[91] Mulvany, Charles, *The History of the North-West Rebellion of 1885*, (A. Hovey & Co.), 1886, p. 277.

This led to calls for Riel to pay with his life for the suffering both of the prisoners and the soldiers who fought to save them. He could have fled to the United States of which he was a citizen but he chose instead to surrender. He hoped to have a trial for treason before the Supreme Court of Canada in Quebec where he could explain his actions to the world but instead he was sent to the jail in Regina before his trial before a stipendiary magistrate.[92] Riel demanded a political trial and perversely that is what he got. As an opposition Quebec newspaper stated just after the sentence was pronounced:

> Riel did not really have a trial. It was a sort of inquisition set up by the government, not for the purpose of enquiring into the guilt or innocence of the prisoner, but only on order to deliver up his head to the fanatics under the cover of a sham trial.[93]

Cut off from the outside world, Riel did not know that some Quebec Liberals had rallied to his defence and hired four respected French and English lawyers, François-Xavier Lemieux, Charles Fitzpatrick, James Greenshields and T. C. Johnstone. Their options were, however, limited. They wanted the charge changed from high treason to treason-felony largely because in cases of treason-felony, the judge and jury had discretion in sentencing. The punishment for high treason had only one outcome, death by hanging. There were sound arguments for trial for treason-felony since as an American citizen, Riel was no longer a subject of the Crown and this posed the question of whether he could be charged with high treason. Treason-felony was introduced into Canadian law in 1868 and extended to the North-West Territories in 1873 but its application to Riel's leadership of an armed rebellion would have been unusually lenient. The difficulty with this approach was that it relied on convincing a jury probably consisting of English-speaking Orangemen. The question of Riel's nationality was barely raised in a trial in which he was tried as both an alien and as a Canadian citizen. The United States had a history of aggressively defending its citizens charged with crimes abroad, even when they were clearly guilty and especially for political militants in Britain and Canada. This had been evident in the aftermath of the Canadian

---

[92] *The Queen v. Louis Riel*, (University of Toronto Press), 1974, with an introduction by Desmond Morton, reprints the proceedings of Riel's trial from 20 July to 1 August. See also, ibid, Flanagan, Thomas, *Riel and the Rebellion: 1885 Reconsidered*, pp. 131-168, and Bumsted, J. M., 'Another Look at the Riel Trial for Treason', in ibid, Wright, Barry, and Binnie, Susan, (eds.), *Canadian State Trials, Volume III*, pp. 411-450, a dissection of why Riel did not receive justice in 1885.
[93] *L'Electeur*, 4 August 1885.

Rebellion in 1838 but particularly following the Fenian incursion in 1866. Yet in 1885, there was a surprising and deafening silence about Riel's American citizenship from his adopted country, a consequence of decisions of courtroom strategy and the internal politics of the United States.[94] Recognising that neither of these strategies was likely to work, the defence lighted on the most obvious approach: Riel was not guilty by reason of insanity. Although fitness to stand trial had been introduced in the Act relating to Procedure in Criminal Trials in Canada in 1869, it had not been extended to the North-West Territories by 1885 and the defence could not call for a pre-trial fitness hearing. They would have to prove their case before a jury.

The lawyers rushed to Regina arriving on 15 July five days before the trial was set to begin and with little time to prepare. The trial judge Hugh Richardson had acted as counsel for the territorial governor and was a member of the Orange Order.[95] His was hardly an impartial appointment though Flanagan argues that his handling of the trial has 'stood up fairly well to the exacting scrutiny of modern historians'. An additional problem for the defence was that trial before a stipendiary magistrate required only six jurors and those selected from the thirty-six empanelled were English and Protestant. On 20 July, Riel was indicted on six counts: three counts of high treason as an alien and three identical charges as a citizen.[96] The defence team tried to have the trial location moved to Winnipeg and the trial delayed to give the defence further time to marshal their case. Initially it appears that the government did consider a trial in Winnipeg but this may have been rejected since there Riel could have demanded a 'mixed' jury of twelve men that might have made conviction more difficult. Adjourned for a week to allow defence witnesses to arrive, the trial began on 28 July and ended with Riel's conviction and sentencing to death on 1 August.

His execution was postponed three times: twice to allow appeals to the Manitoba Court of Queen's Bench on 9 September[97] and the Judicial Court of the Privy Council that ruled against Riel on 22 October,[98] then for a fuller medical examination of his alleged

---

[94] Mumford, J. R., 'Why was Louis Riel, a United States Citizen, Hanged as a Canadian Traitor in 1885?', *CHR*, Vol. 88, (2007), pp. 237-262, examines why the United States did not chose to raise Riel's American citizenship as an issue in 1885.

[95] Flanagan, Thomas, 'Hugh Richardson', *DCB*, Vol. 14, http://www.biographi.ca/009004-119.01-e.php?&id_nbr=7667

[96] *The Queen v. Louis Riel*, pp. 1-6.

[97] *The Queen v. Louis Riel*, pp. 176-198.

[98] *The Queen v. Louis Riel*, pp. 199-200.

insanity.[99] The medical commission was divided on the question of Riel's sanity leaving the final decision to the government; questioning and then dismissing Riel's state of mind was politically expedient. Macdonald's government could have commuted the death sentence knowing just how unpopular allowing the execution to proceed would be for French-Canadians but the decision by his cabinet on 11 November to 'let the law take its course'. This was a political judgement but may also have reflected the increasingly ethnic-nationalist tone of Macdonald's thinking and certainly his need not to alienate Conservative supporters in Ontario.[100] Riel was hanged at Regina on 16 November 1885, an execution that has since divided opinion in Canada.[101]

Macdonald assumed that Riel's religious delusions would neutralise sympathies in Catholic Quebec but he miscalculated. French-Canadians supported the campaign to suppress the Rebellion, and French ministers thought Riel's execution would soon be forgotten but there was widespread outrage in Quebec over Riel's execution that did not abate over time. Macdonald received over 1,200 telegrams pleading Riel's case and petitions received in Ottawa against his hanging had more than 12,000 signatures. There were also petitions from New York, St. Louis and other American cities, a petition from British Catholics in London and from France. Tensions

---

[99] *The Queen v. Louis Riel*, pp. 201-203, prints the petition for a Medical Commission.

[100] Until the early 1870s when racialist theories grounded in Darwinian evolution took root across the Anglo-World, Macdonald held a largely inclusive form of civic nationalism in which he welcomed anyone committed to the principle of maintaining British rule in Canada. By 1885, however, he argued in relation to Chinese immigration that Canada was for 'the Aryan race and Aryan principles'. His view of who could be a loyal British subject was predominantly though not exclusively racial. See, Lorimer, Douglas, 'From Victorian Values to White Virtues: Assimilation and Exclusion in British Racial Discourse, c1870-1914', in Buckner, Phillip, and Francis, R. Douglas, (eds.), *Rediscovering the British World*, (University of Calgary Press), 2005, pp. 109-134.

[101] For instance, Guillet, Edwin C., *Death for High Treason: A Study of the Evidence in The Queen versus Louis Riel, 1885*, typescript, 1944, and Thompson, John S. D., *Discours sur la question Riel: prononcé le 22 mars, 1886 à la Chambre des communes par l'honorable S. D. Thompson*, 1886, are unsympathetic to Riel and suggest that he was fairly tried, convicted and executed while Thomas, Lew, 'A Judicial Murder: The Trial of Louis Riel', in Palmer, Howard, (ed.), *The Settlement of the West*, (University of Calgary Press), 1977, pp. 37-59, views the legal proceedings as biased and that it was a political trial to assuage the 'paranoic fears and passions of Ontario voters'.

between Ontarians and French-Canadians were heightened by what the Orange *Sentinel* called 'the ravings of the French press' and

...we warn our French Canadian neighbors that they stand upon a volcano which at any moment may explode. Riel has been fairly tried and convicted and the sentence of the court must be carried out.[102]

For many Anglo-Ontarians, Riel's actions in 1869, 1870 and 1885 represented a concerted effort to establish a francophone Catholic province in the North-West. When Macdonald declared that Riel would hang though 'every dog in Quebec bark in his favour', he was not simply expressing the view that justice should be seen to be done but reflected a deeper sense of antagonism to Quebec's sympathy for Riel. Wilfrid Laurier's passionate denunciation of the government's action in 1886 was a major step forward in his career. For many French-Canadians, Riel's execution symbolised the weakness of Quebec's politicians in federal government and, in part, contributed to a revival in French-Canadian nationalism from the late 1880s.[103] They also ultimately saw it as the triumph of Anglo-Canadian racism: Riel was only hanged because he was French and Catholic.[104]

The rebellion of 1885 represents the last 'war of religion' in Canada. Riel saw the conflict in messianic terms but there are problems when relating his ideas to the sense of dislocation and marginalisation that caused disaffection among the Métis at Red River and in Saskatchewan. He believed he was a prophet of God sent to prepare the chosen Métis people for their future religious inheritance and that Christ would return to meet his Church in Manitoba and establish his kingdom. There is, however, little evidence to suggest that those who followed Riel in 1885 understood his messianic ideas. Arguably, his views were a constraint on Métis action since they alienated the Roman Catholic Church and, at least initially, French-

---

[102] *Sentinel*, 10 September 1885.

[103] Ibid, Silver, A. I., *The French-Canadian Idea of Confederation, 1864-1900*, pp. 150-179, examines the transition among French Canadians from support for the expeditionary force to criticism of the partiality of Riel's trial and opposition to his execution.

[104] The government initially arrested more than two hundred Métis, whites and Indians on the lesser charge of treason-felony although the government proceeded with only 84 cases. Beal, Bob, and Wright, Barry, 'Summary and Incompetent Justice: Legal Responses to the 1885 Crisis', in ibid, Wright, Barry, and Binnie, Susan, (eds.), *Canadian State Trials, Volume III*, pp. 353-410, examines the trials of the lesser offenders. See also, *Trials in connection with the North-west rebellion, 1885*, (Maclean, Rogers & Co.), 1886.

Canadian opinion. It was Riel's hope that by repeating the strategies he had used in 1869 and 1870, the federal government would accede to his demands. His view was that it was Ottawa that was 'insane and irresponsible':

> I have acted reasonably and in self-defence, while the Government, my accuser, being irresponsible, and consequently insane, cannot but have acted wrong, and if high treason there is it must be on its side and not on my part.[105]

The hanging of Riel rekindled and fuelled Anglo-French tensions in Quebec and led to an immediate protest of 6,000 people in the streets of Montreal. A few weeks later a more organised rally held on the Champ de Mars in Montreal on 23 November garnered 50,000 protesters. One of the speakers was Wilfrid Laurier, who held a cabinet post in the Mackenzie government but had previously not attracted much attention. His moving speech was one of the first steps in a political movement that saw him becoming Canada's seventh and first francophone prime minister. Even though French-Canadians denounced the hanging of Riel, the issues for which he fought were distinct from those of concern to French-Canadians, Nonetheless, the political debates in Quebec were informed by an appropriation of Métis struggle to feed French-Canadian nationalism and eventually led to the dominance of the Liberal Party in Quebec. Honoré Mercier, the leader of the Parti National was strongly opposed to the execution of Riel and to the Conservative government that had held power in Quebec for decades. For many years after 1885, the Conservative Party was known as 'le parti des Anglais'. The public outcry over Riel's execution allowed Mercier and the Liberal party to gain support and in 1886, they won the Quebec provincial election, the first time the Liberal Party had ever held a majority government in Quebec. While its period in power was cut short by scandal the following year, it began a slow process that gradually led in the decline of Conservative power in Quebec. The Liberal landslide victory in 1896 marked a new era of politics in Quebec.

Following the conflict, race became a determining factor in how those living in Saskatchewan began to be treated. Euro-Canadians, both English and French-speaking were privileged over Aboriginal peoples. In addition, the property and homes of Euro-Canadian settlers were protected by the Canadian government whereas Métis homes and property were destroyed and looted by military and volunteers following the conflict. The North-West Rebellion quelled a growing movement of dissatisfaction that western white settlers had

---

[105] Ibid, *The Queen v. Louis Riel*, p. 324.

begun to voice in opposition to the administration in central Canada and was replaced by a movement of Canadian nationalism based on the perceived common 'threat' of Métis and Indian armed rebellion. It marked a further extension of the systematic marginalisation for the Métis and First Nation peoples.

Each of the rebellions between 1837 and 1885 had an important religious dimension. Not 'wars of religion' on a European scale, nonetheless religion played a central role in the ways that participants acted and reacted to each other. Anglo-Protestantism, especially Ontarian Anglo-Protestantism, was privileged over French and Irish Catholicism within the economic and political systems largely because its values were seen as supportive of the development of a capitalist market economy grounded in a Protestant work ethic and of a strong, centralised executive state. Resistance to both was an important feature in each of the rebellions. For French-Canadians in 1837 and 1838, rebellion was a defence of their agrarian values against expansive and aggressive capitalism and of the supremacy of rule by the elected and representative Legislative Assembly, in which they had a majority, over the coercive power of the executive colonial state.

For the Fenians in 1866, 1870 and 1871, their rebellion in Canada was not a direct assault on the Canadian state, though many would have been pleased had the United States used their invasions as a means for annexing the 'fourteenth colony', but a means to achieve independence for Catholic Ireland. The invasions were a political and religious crusade. Although many Irish-Canadians sympathised with this goal, most recognised the futility of the invasions as a way of achieving it and rallied to the loyalist banner. The invasions may have not led directly to Confederation in 1867 but they heightened concerns about Canadian security providing a further justification for bringing the provinces closer together. They also reinforced the development of the Protestant executive state by highlighting the need for a strong centralised state to counter any external threats.

For the Métis in 1869 and 1870 and in 1885, resistance and rebellion expressed their opposition to Protestant Ontarian and expansionist economic and political values. Much as in 1837 and 1838, French-speakers found their economic and cultural heritage under threat from a state determined to exert its authority and willing to use force to achieve this. The agreement between the Métis and the federal government, negotiated in 1870, was a solution forced on government because of the inaccessibility of the North-West to immediate military intervention. In 1885, negotiation with Riel was never an option once the rebellion broke out in mid-March. Troops could now be easily mobilised and transported to put down the Métis and those First Nations who rose in their own separate resistance.

Denied the support of the Catholic Church, which had proved instrumental in getting both sides to negotiate in 1869 and 1870, the Métis faced an overwhelming Protestant crusading force.

Each of the rebellions failed, despite initial military success, because those involved were minorities in the emerging Anglo-Protestant Canadian state. Poor leadership, limited resources and lack of active support even among their natural supporters combined with the strength of the loyalist response to lead to their defeat. Defence of their cultural, economic and religious heritage proved impossible when faced with the coercive power of a modernising state.

6 Rebellion, remembering and forgetting

The question of what it means to remember the past, why the past is remembered and the effect of that remembrance have been areas of fierce debate over the last four decades.[1] There is a sense in which 'a people who do not preserve their memory are a people who have forfeited their history'.[2] Of particular importance in the studies of memory that have emerged since the 1980s, have been attempts to examine the memory of harrowing events of the twentieth century, to consider their legacy and provide a form of therapy and possible closure for troubled aspects of the past. The result is recognition of the importance of memory in constructing individual and collective identity, with aspects of the past utilised to construct a sense of who we are in the present.[3] This recruitment of memory by groups reveal that particular histories are remembered at particular times in particular ways and, in this respect, memory is a flexible device for different social and political agendas.[4] Schudson highlighted how Watergate periodically resurfaces in public discourse not to draw attention to the events themselves but to give definition to other areas of contemporary debate.[5] A return to the past can be used to mobilise the present. It is this, perhaps, that explains why the Canadian rebellions and Eureka are better remembered than the Newport rising in South Wales. In Canada and Australia, the rebellions provided a *liet-motif* for succeeding generations, cited to justify or resist future actions while Newport was in many respects a historical dead-end. It did not lead to political reform and, in its failure, though not forgotten was side-lined by both the authorities and the Chartists.

---

[1] Cubitt, Geoffrey, *History and memory*, (Manchester University Press), 2007, provides a good summary of these debates while Wood, Harriet Harvey and Byatt, A. S., (eds.), *Memory: An Anthology*, (Chatto & Windus), 2008, especially pp. 368-390, contains pithy extracts on public memory.

[2] Soyinka, W., *The burden of memory, the muse of forgiveness*, (Oxford University Press), 1999, p. 58.

[3] Halbwachs, Maurice, *La mémoire collective*, (Presses Universitaires de France), 1950, translated as *The collective memory*, (Harper & Row Colophon Books), 1980.

[4] Novick, P., *The Holocaust and Collective Memory: the American experience*, (Bloomsbury), 2001.

[5] Schudson, M., *Watergate in American Memory: how we remember, forget and reconstruct the past*, (Basic Books), 1992.

One aspect of our collective memory is coming to terms with the past, something that has been in vogue for the past decade.[6] The late 1990s saw a contrite 'Age of Apology' with Bill Clinton apologising for slavery, Tony Blair for the Irish Famine, the Pope for the Crusades and Australia declared a 'National Sorry Day' for past mistreatment of Aborigines. Past sinners are condemned for not thinking and acting as right-minded people do today. Critical tracts 'name and shame' the perpetrators of history's atrocities and demand remorse and redress for victims' heirs. A descendant of Sir John Hawkins, his T-shirt inscribed: 'So Sorry' and 'Pardon', marked the bicentenary of Britain's abolition of the slave trade by kneeling in chains before 25,000 Gambians, asking forgiveness for his ancestor's crimes. Ex-colonial peoples and minorities demand reparations, atonement for the suffering of those deprived of autonomy, repatriation of treasures purloined or pillaged or purchased and compensation for past injustices.[7] Current campaigns to redress wrongs link with widespread public pessimism and refocus attention from the future to the past. The payment of compensation in the 1840s in the Canadas to those affected by the rebellions and the same in Victoria after Eureka was arguably an attempt to draw a line under the rebellions so that the countries could progress. The current and prevailing trend to repair past wrongs reflects the conviction that in the case of the transforming projects of the twentieth century little was left but brutality.

The twentieth century is on the path of becoming a moral memory palace, a pedagogically serviceable Chamber of Historical Horrors, whose stations are labelled 'Munich' or 'Auschwitz' with '9-11' as a...bloody postscript for those who would forget the lessons of the century or who never learned them properly.[8]

---

[6] Cairns, Alan, 'Coming to Terms with the Past', in Torpey, John, (ed.), *Politics and the Past: On Repairing Past Injustices*, (Rowman & Littlefield), 2003, pp. 53-90, and Nobles, Melissa, *The Politics of Official Apologies*, (Cambridge University Press), 2008, are especially relevant for Canada and Australia.

[7] Torpey, John, *Making Whole What Has Been Smashed: On Reparations Politics*, (Harvard University Press), 2006, and Greiff, Pablo de, (ed.), *The Handbook of Reparations*, (Oxford University Press), 2006.

[8] Judt, Tony, *Reappraisals: Reflections on the Forgotten Twentieth Century*, (Heinemann), 2008, p. 4.

The moral merit accorded such claims would astound our ancestors, just as their views now appal those ignorant of history.[9] Many today find it hard to believe that sexism, racism and gross inequality are the usual human condition. We may well lament past misdeeds, but current morality cannot justify anachronistic defamation of their perpetrators, acting by the moral climate of their own day.[10] For historians rather than moralists, the importance of the debate over reparations is not whether a particular group should be compensated or whether politicians should apologise for past events, it is the way in which the debate has introduced new agents into the study of events that have previously been left in obscurity or, in some cases air-brushed out of the story. In this way, historians, as Edward Thompson memorably wrote, rescue individuals or groups from the 'enormous condescension of posterity' and strain to hear those who were previously assumed to be silent. This increases the possibility of contested narratives of events and, in that respect, takes our understanding of the past forward. In constructing historical narratives describing change, we must confront the gaps and distortions inherent in trying to reconstruct the past. The richness of human life depends on our ability to recapture the past, yet our memories are selective and incomplete.

Three films about the Lower Canadian rebellions in 1837 and 1838 give the impression of a terrible tragedy. Nothing in the films minimises the miserable fate of Patriote characters or the general impression of a crushing defeat. *Quand je serai parti, vous vivrez encore* (The Long Winter) a film from 1999 by Michel Brault highlighted a young, isolated Patriote who hopelessly and helplessly tries to save himself after the rebellion. In 2001, the nationalist director Pierre Falardeau released his film *15 février 1839* about the imprisoned Patriotes awaiting their execution that climaxes with the tearful separation of De Lorimier and his wife. In *Quelques arpents de Neige*, the Patriotes are poor habitants who live 'a dog's life' and have nothing to lose. The hero of the film no longer believes in the political struggle and does not want to fight any more. Nevertheless, he is pursued by the British and after the woman he loves dies, he

---

[9] Black, Jeremy, *The Curse of History*, (Social Affairs Units), 2008, especially pp. 1-56, provides a devastating critique of the political abuse of history. Macmillan, Margaret, *The Uses and Abuses of History*, (Viking Canada), 2008, pp. 33-54, is also relevant.

[10] Maier, Charles S., 'Overcoming the Past? Narrative and Negotiation, Remembering and Reparation: Issues at the Interface of History and Law', in Torpey, John, (ed.), *Politics and the Past: On Repairing Past Injustices*, (Rowman & Littlefield), 2003, pp. 298-303.

commits suicide trapped between British and American soldiers. *La complainte des hivers rouges*, a theatrical drama written by Roland Lepage in 1974 is a long list of complaints from French-Canadians during and after the rebellions. In writing his work, Lepage was inspired by Laurent-Olivier David, *Les Patriotes de 1837-1838*. It recounts the daily life and the struggle of the Patriotes who rose up against the English occupation in Quebec during 1837 and 1838. In each case, the British were one-dimensional figures generally malicious, inhuman and cruel persecutors. These representations of the rebellions provide a 'victim' discourse in which the British are characterised as bastards and French-Canadians as gallant but heroic losers.[11]

Historians often minimise the importance of the rebellions in the history of Quebec. It was a contingent event that fitted no notion of historical necessity and was consequently of little significance. It could have been avoided with a little more goodwill on both sides and what was being demanded by Patriotes could have been achieved by reform. The fact that historians talk of 'rebellions' rather than 'revolution' led some to suggest a desire to limit the significance of the event. 'Every rebellion,' Elinor Kyte Senior argued 'is a story of failure, for if the insurgents are victorious, it is no longer rebellion but revolution'.[12] Yet for Lionel Groulx, even the word 'rebellion' was too strong as he could never admit that the virtuous French-Canadians could give themselves over to revolutionary impiety.[13] The Patriotes may have been defenders of the nation but were mistaken in their anticlericalism and calls for democracy. For Groulx, in 1837 there was no rebellion but resistance to a police operation that began with the failed attempt to arrest the Patriote leaders in Montreal. The exaggeration of the dramatic character of the rebellions as portrayed in film combined with a sense of the historical remoteness of the rebellions demonstrate the difficulty of constructing a balanced representation of these events.[14]

For a long time, the rebellions appeared either as a taboo subject or as a case for special pleading. In a history textbook used for several

---

[11] Brown, Richard, *Three Rebellions: Canada 1837-1838, South Wales 1839 and Victoria, Australia 1854*, (Clio Publishing), 2010, pp. 719-733, provides a more detailed discussion of remembrance.

[12] Ibid, Senior, Elinor Kyte, *Redcoats & Patriotes: The Rebellions in Lower Canada 1837-38*, p. 1.

[13] Boily, Frédéric, *La Pensée nationaliste de Lionel Groulx*, (Septentrion), 2003.

[14] See, Létourneau, Jocelyn, *Passer à l'avenir: histoire, mémoire, identité dans le Québec d'aujourd'hui*, (Boréal), 2000.

decades with young children, Guy Laviolette presented the history of Canada using twenty themes but although discussion of the first half of the nineteenth century included the battle of Chateauguay in 1812 and the restoration of parliamentary and responsible government by LaFontaine in 1848, there was no mention of the rebellions.[15] Criticism was made of this book in the following terms:

> Pour survivre et prendre la place qui nous revient au Canada, il va falloir d'abord que nos jeunes connaissent objectivement l'histoire des deux Canadas et celle du reste du monde. Une meilleure connaissance de leur pénible évolution historique depuis la conquête et une plus grande maturité intellectuelle devraient leur permettre, en cette deuxième moitié du vingtième siècle de faire leur option avec une plus grande lucidité.[16]

Laurent-Olivier David saw the rebellion as a 'glorious war' led by 'most honourable men' but such musings suggested that he encouraged the rejection of authority. In 1892, curé Louis-Eugène Duguay complained that his *Les Patriotes de 1837-1838*, a seditious book, was being given as a prize in the schools in his diocese. Clearly, the rebellions were a subject for adults. Children needed to be protected from the issue largely because of the criticism of the Church by the Patriotes and because, until after 1945, conservative Catholicism dominated the historiography. In many countries there are historical subjects that are difficult or even painful for their populations but rarely are historical subjects reserved for adults. In Quebec, however, the issue of the rebellions is not a case of collective guilt that a society refused to recognise or pleaded ignorance in the interests of a particular conservative governing class.

Today, control by the Church has lessened, conservatism no longer dominates Quebecois society and people no longer defend the doctrine that resistance to established authorities is unacceptable and unchristian. Since 2002, the Journée des Patriotes has been celebrated in May. The Société St. Jean-Baptiste and other organisations in Quebec had long wanted a day in honour of the Patriotes of 1837-1838. On 27 November 2001, Bernard Landry, then Prime Minister of Quebec proposed a motion to the National Assembly to establish the Journée nationale des Patriotes. He regarded the rebellions as important in three respects:

---

[15] Laviolette, Guy, *Histoire du Canada*, (Frères de l'Instruction chrétienne), 1951.
[16] http://www.bibl.ulaval.ca/ress/manscol/1962.html

...in recognising our nation, for her political liberty and for the establishment of democratic government.

He continued stating:

Our collective memory will never forget the tragic and bloody end of this episode...or the profound significance of the fighting on the lives of men and also women...The battle was for responsible government.

Landry then drew brief comparisons with the Upper Canadian rebellion as 'similar to that of the Patriotes' and finally placed the rebellion in the context of:

...the movement for national emancipation that affected Europe and South America at the same time...from 1804 to 1830, Serbia, Greece, after years...of oppression, Belgium, Brazil and Bolivia...[17]

Landry's speech reflected the ways in which the rebellions were seen by the establishment in Quebec. They were about achieving responsible government, something he equated with contemporary movements for national emancipation. In doing so he appears to confuse the rebellions as a means of political change and the rebellions as an expression of revolutionary principles. Responsible government was realised within a decade of the rebellions, but whether it was a direct result of them or something that would have occurred anyway is debatable. National emancipation is something that has yet to be achieved: Quebec may have a form of home rule but it does not have its independence.

Official recognition of the place of Patriotes in the history of Quebec ended the long-term refusal to accept the historical importance of the rebellions. However, it took 164 years before this occurred including sixteen years when the Parti Québécois, the spiritual descendent of the Parti Patriote, both sought the political sovereignty of the Quebecois people, was in power.[18] Even then, it was unwilling to create a new public holiday by recognising the Patriote festival that occurs on 25 November, the anniversary of the battle of St. Denis. The Journée des Patriotes took the place of the fête de Dollard that itself had replaced the fête de la Reine Victoria. For many the establishment of the Journée des Patriotes came too late and it is

---

[17] Assemblée nationale, 'Souligner l'importance de la lutte des Patriotes de 1837-1838', *Débats de l'Assemblée nationale*, 27 Novembre 2001.
[18] Tourigny, J.-D., *Fêtes Patriotoques*, (De La Salle), 1921, is particularly useful on the development and context of holidays.

not surprising that there was significant outrage at the ingratitude of government for the sacrifice of those who had given their lives for their country.

It is not the first time that Patriote commemoration has been approached in this way. Political and social leaders use monuments to guide sentiments of patriotism among their citizens. They help define the nation through the common past its members share or imagine they share. Communities adopted different approaches to monuments and rarely sought to commemorate an objective past. They celebrated a version of the past that reflected the values, attitudes and objectives of their promoters. Monuments that had been largely built in cemeteries up to 1890 took on an increasingly public role: only 7 had been built but between 1890 and 1930 a further 39 were added.[19] In 1895, the first monument a statue to Jean-Olivier Chénier, the heroic leader at St. Eustache in 1837, was unveiled.

The debate over Patriote monuments began forty years earlier. In 1853, prompted by the success of the Rebellion Losses Act four years earlier, there were demands for a monument for the Patriotes in Montreal. E.-R. Fabre,[20] the president of the Institut-Canadien took up the challenge organising a committee that proposed a threefold commemoration: a monument in Montreal to commemorate the 12 Patriotes executed in 1838 and 1839; a second at St. Denis in memory of his brother-in-law, C.-O Perrault and his companions who were killed in the battle, and finally a monument to Chénier and the Patriotes of St. Eustache. The committee called for donations to fund the monuments from members of the Institut and others across the province. Even so the amount collected was insufficient and only the monument to the executed Patriotes was built in Montreal's cemetery and unveiled in 1858. The Societé St. Jean Baptiste initially subscribed $100 to the fund but this decision was overturned by eight conservative members and nine liberals left the Societé in protest. Only a thousand people were present when the monument was installed in contrast to the over 10,000 who attended the ceremonies when an identical obelisk was unveiled in the memory of Duvernay three years earlier. His obelisk, erected by conservative members of the Societé, makes no mention of Duvernay's role as a Patriote and effectively removed him from the rebellions. In many respects, these two monuments caught the tensions between liberals and conservatives and help to explain why the rebellions remained such a contested issue within

---

[19] Ibid, Gordon, Alan, *Making Public Pasts*, pp. 32-33.
[20] Roy, Jean-Louis, 'Édouard-Raymond Fabre', *DCB*, Vol. 8, pp. 282-286, Messier, p. 183, and Roy, Jean-Louis, *Edouard-Raymond Fabre, Libraire et patriote canadien (1799-1854)*, (Hurtubise), 1974.

French-Canadian politics. Some gathered subscriptions for memorials while others opposed the commemoration of figures who reminded them of divisive struggles in the past.

From the 1850s through to the 1880s, ultramontane nationalism dominated French Canada and after Confederation liberal nationalism was increasingly marginalised. Nevertheless, liberal nationalism did not die out and its electoral support hovered around 40 per cent during the 1870s and 1880s. Though there were significant differences between the two approaches to French-Canadian nationalism, the two groups did cooperate during the 1880s over proposals for a national theatre in Montreal that would act as a meeting place for nationalists whatever their political hue. Originally the Monument-National was planned to back on to the Champ de Mars, where a balcony would allow speakers to address crowds at the traditional site for political rallies. Inadequate funding led to be project being abandoned in 1884 but five years later it was revived by L.-O. David and the Societé St. Jean Baptiste and was successfully opened in 1893 on a different site.

The early 1890s also saw increasing demands for a commemoration of Chénier led by Dr David Marcil, a legislative councillor and former mayor of St. Eustache. In 1891, he exhumed Chénier's remains from their location in the St. Eustache cemetery reserved for babies who died unbaptised and sought to have them interred at the Patriote monument in Montreal. This was opposed by Édouard-Charles Fabre, bishop of Montreal who said that since Chénier had ignored the commands of Lartigue he could not be buried in consecrated ground.[21] The Club Chénier, founded by liberal supporters of Marcil, established a fund to carry out the ambitions of the Institut Canadien of 1853 to build him his monument. This proved far from easy. While there was sympathy from Montreal's liberal middle-class, church opposition to the veneration of the Patriotes remained a serious obstacle. La Minerve, normally supportive of the Patriote position, was highly critical of what it saw as a partisan effort for revenge against the clergy. As a result, Marcil's scheme proved less than popular. Contributions came exclusively from Montreal's middle-class, the same group that made up most of its opponents.

The Club Chénier abandoned the highly regarded plans for the monument by Philippe Hébert, a renowned sculptor in favour of a

---

[21] Marcil and later his son kept the bones in an urn. They were passed to Henry Birks, a goldsmith in 1924 who kept them in one of his vaults until 1954 when they were given to the Saint-Jean Baptiste Society. They were finally buried, with the agreement of the Church, in the cemetery at St-Eustache in July 1987.

dull monument designed by Alfinso Pelzer, an obscure American artist. Its unveiling in 1895 showed the extent to which the rebellions remained divisive. Marcil spoke at the Monument-National later that evening and made links between 1837 and the more recent North-West rebellion of 1885 and other speakers noted similarities between Chénier and other 'freedom fighters' around the world. However, the speeches of the Toronto MP J. D. Edgar and the criminal lawyer Henri St. Pierre expressed a more moderate stance noting that Chénier represented the idea of 'Canada first' and that Canadians were one people. This confused discourse was exacerbated by the audience cheering the memory of both the Patriotes and the Queen at the end of the service. For conservatives, the Patriotes were seen as an expression of the liberal nationalism they opposed. For some liberal nationalists especially supporters of Henri Bourassa who regarded Confederation as a compact between two founding people, they represented a multicultural 'Canada first'.

In the first twenty years of the twentieth century, this position was strengthened by the threat to British-French equality that was finally shattered by the conscription crisis during the First World War. As Bourassa's vision of expansive bicultural nationalism evaporated, it was replaced by the ideas of Lionel Groulx, the first professor of Canadian history at the University of Montreal.[22] For Groulx, nationalism was grounded in his belief that God had assigned the French-Canadians a specific national task and he fused Roman Catholicism with the ethnic core of the nation so completely that for several decades, the two were inseparable. This was a nationalism reunited by faith. The Dollard monument unveiled in 1919 was typical of his approach to nationalism but it was also extended to the Patriotes who were re-Catholicised. The Patriotes were no longer guilty of anti-clerical liberalism but seen as heroes of Catholic nationalism. Groulx effectively rewrote the history of the rebellions with a Catholic slant and in the 1926 Patriote monument expiated their sins. He argued that Lartigue had not excommunicated the Patriotes but was sympathetic to their position and that parish priests had also sided with the Patriotes. Groulx's exoneration ignored the fact that the 1926 monument commemorated those executed in 1839 for rebelling twice and trying to establish a republican Lower Canada where there would have been separation

---

[22] Groulx, Lionel, *Mes Mémoires*, 4 Vols. (Fides), 1970-1974, is a valuable autobiography while Giguère, Georges-Émile, *Lionel Groulx, Biographie*, (Bellarmin), 1978, and Boily, Frédéric, 'Catholicisme et nationalisme chez Lionel Groulx', *Canadian Studies*, Vol. 51 (2001), pp. 187-199, provide a more critical stance.

between Church and State. His approach to the rebellions was selective and this enabled him to rehabilitate the Patriotes.

After ninety years, the Patriotes had become martyrs of French-Canadian liberty and were now appropriate subjects for a patriotic monument. The earlier monuments of 1858 and 1895 were ignored largely because they were the product of a divided French-Canadian nationalism: the Chénier monument celebrated one small episode and the Institut Canadien monument was tucked away in a cemetery. The 1926 Patriote monument sanitised the memory of the movement establishing a national and public memorial reflecting Groulx's vision of a united and Catholic nationalism. In 1895, hundreds attended the unveiling of the Chénier monument; in 1926 an estimated 250,000 people were present when the monument to Papineau, De Lorimier and Wolfred Nelson was inaugurated. This merging of competing nationalisms was reflected in public history and public memory.

Commemoration was not confined to Montreal and in the major locations of rebellion in 1837 and 1838, public memories are reinforced through plaques, streets and other locations named after prominent Patriote leaders, the preservation of important contemporary buildings and monuments.[23] At St. Charles, for example, the maison Chicou-Duvert, the location for the assembly of the Six-Comtés on 23 October 1837 is preserved. There is also a plaque opposite the house erected by the Commission des Monument Historiques du Québec celebrating the assembly with an inscription in English and French: 'the assembly...that set forth the principles of responsible government'. In the Parc des Patriotes, a Patriot Monument was built by the Comité de L'Action Patriotique in 1937 listing those killed in the battle on 25 November 1837. In 1982, the Comité des Patriotes erected a plaque to commemorate the Column of Liberty of 23 October and five years later the Commission municipale put a plaque on the wall of the local church listing the 24 Patriotes buried in its cemetery. Commemoration of the rebellion extends to New South Wales where 58 French-Canadians were transported. Place names like Canada Bay and Exile Bay and the Patriot monument at Cabarita Park in Concord, Sydney, unveiled in May 1970, by Pierre Trudeau, attested to their presence in Australia.

Parallel to the growth in commemoration, there has been a trend to minimise those things that arouse public interest in the rebellions. Both among historians and in some teaching programmes, there has been a tendency to minimise the spectacular, enthralling and romantic episodes in the rebellions in favour of those things that are less heroic.

---

[23] The Patriote website has over forty pages devoted to monuments: http://cgi2.cvm.qc.ca/glaporte/index.shtml

So it was better to forget the battles and concentrate on the Ninety-Two Resolutions as if they give people a better understanding of what 1837 means to modern Quebeçois society and its history. Is it surprising that the Quebeçois are less interested in their history though they take their history more seriously than in British Canada?[24] The problem is that assertions about the rebellion and the Patriote project tend to be qualified by the need for historical if not emotional veracity.

Avant comme après l'insurrection de 1837-1838, ce sentiment [national], de plus en plus accusé, a trouvé des expressions intellectuelles et politiques très disparates, voire contradictoires, en deçà desquelles on peut toutefois déceler une sorte de dénominateur commun [prenant la forme d']une volonté d'aménager sur le territoire québécois un espace francophone doté des institutions nécessaires à sa survie et dont [ces élites] seraient les titulaires légitimes.[25]

This is an abstract rationalisation of the situation that lacks concrete reference to character or event reflecting much modern writings on Quebec by her historians. The focus is not on producing a coherent narrative of 'our' history in which the actions, behaviour and motivation of people is central, the traditional approach to history, but on abstractions such as ideologies, economic crises and social classes and class consciousness. Dealing with ideas may well be easier than dealing with people but the result is an editing out of the humanity of the rebellions. This removes the awkwardness and unpredictability of people and the absurdity of events by placing them beneath a veil of scientific rationality. Yet it is the very awkwardness and unpredictability of people and the absurdity of events that are central to an understanding of history: we should never forget that the past was a messy place despite our attempts as historians to impose a sense of logic. Representations of the rebellions remain problematic within Quebeçois historical thinking and the difficulty of building an adequate representation of these events may reflect a collective trauma.

In Upper Canada, while there was considerable effort on the part of its political leaders in the mid-nineteenth century to invent a Loyalist

---

[24] Osborne, Ken, 'Teaching history in schools: a Canadian debate', *Journal of Curriculum Studies*, Vol. 35, (5), (2003), pp. 585-626; Jedwab, Jack, *Influencing Quebec and Canada's Futures and Pride in the Past*, (Association for Canadian Studies), 2007.

[25] Bouchard, Gérard, 'Une nation, deux cultures: Continuités et ruptures dans la pensée québécoise traditionnelle', in Bouchard, Gérard, (dir.), *La construction d'une culture: le Québec et l'Amérique française*, (PUL), 1993, p. 5.

past, the rebellions and its participants played a less significant role in this process.[26] Public monuments in Upper Canada served a promotional role and within the Loyalist, as much as in the Patriote tradition communicated traditions and beliefs across the generations and from one class to another. It is this Loyalist tradition that helps to explain why public monuments commemorating the rebellions did not become part of Ontario's usable past until the twentieth century. The rebellions rejected everything that Loyalists believed: fidelity to Britain, anti-Americanism and anti-republicanism. As a result, most nineteenth century public monuments commemorated events such as the War of 1812 or the contribution of politicians after 1840 in the move towards Confederation. This was evident in the building of a tower to commemorate Sir Isaac Brock regarded by many Loyalists as the saviour of Upper Canada and who died during the British victory at Queenston Heights in 1812. Begun in the 1820s, it was incomplete when in 1840 an explosive charge was set off by Benjamin Lett in the base of the column in one of the last acts of the Upper Canadian Rebellion. A campaign to rebuild the monument began almost immediately but it was not completed until 1856. When the Prince of Wales (later King Edward VII) unveiled the Brock Monument in 1860 he said:

> Every nation may, without offence to its neighbours, commemorate its heroes, their deeds of arms and their noble deaths. This is no taunting boast of victory, no revival of long passed animosities, but a noble tribute to a soldier's fame; the more honourable because we readily acknowledge the bravery and chivalry of that people by whose hands he fell.

The problematic nature of public monuments to the rebellions in Upper Canada can be seen in the Clifton Gate Memorial Arch that commemorated the inception of responsible government following the rebellion of 1837.[27] Those involved in the Upper Canada rebellions, were sent to Van Diemen's Land and there are two monuments in Hobart commemorating the Canadian convict presence. One is at Sandy Bay, unveiled by Douglas Harkness, former Minister of National Defence of Canada on 30 September 1970 and the other is in Prince's Park, Battery Point unveiled on 12 December 1995 by High Commissioner Brian Schumacher. In Hobart,

---

[26] Knowles, Norman, J., *Inventing the Loyalists: The Ontario Loyalist Tradition and the Creation of Usable Pasts*, (Toronto University Press), 1997, pp. 26-47.

[27] Coutu, Joan, 'Vehicles of Nationalism: Defining Canada in the 1930s', *Journal of Canadian Studies*, Vol. 37, (2002), pp. 180-203.

Tasmania, there are two historical plaques erected by the Canadian government to commemorate the 92 prisoners from Canada who were exiled for their part in the rebellion and the invasions of 1837 and 1838. 'Their struggle,' one of the inscriptions says, 'was a significant factor in the evolution of responsible government in Canada and Australia'.

In both Ontario and Quebec, commemoration of the rebellions remains a contested issue. The historiographical confusion over what the rebellions were had spilled over into what is commemorated and the ways in which remembrance is expressed. Nevertheless, in both provinces for different reasons at different times, the rebellions are visually remembered. In Ontario, the British heritage and its opposition to the threat from American republicanism, the basis for commemoration until 1945, has declined in importance. This is reflected in the widening scope, for example, of plaques especially since 1960. In Quebec, the continuing and contested importance of the rebellions and of history generally contributes to and in turn is reinterpreted by the debate over the future direction of the province within or outside the federalist Canadian state.

The Red River Resistance of 1869 and 1870 was, in many respects, a relatively minor event in a remote area of British North America that lasted less than a year. Nonetheless, explaining what happened in Red River and why has generated considerable historical discussion.[28] Broadly, there are two main schools of thought on the Resistance. The first centred in Ontario regarded the events in Red River as illegal and causing unnecessary problems for the government of Canada in transferring the lands of the Hudson Bay Company to the new Confederation. It does not acknowledge the legitimacy of the Resistance or the Provisional Government and insisted that the French Métis never had the full support of other groups within the community. This tradition was hostile to Riel, raised Thomas Scott from nobody to political martyr and made heroes of those such as Schultz, Mair and Boulton who upheld Canadian aspirations in the North-West, a position reinforced by their own memoirs. It did not matter that Sir John Macdonald's government had blundered in its dealings, or rather lack of them, with Red River that precipitated the crisis or that its negotiations with the Red River delegates in April 1870 were duplicitous, what was important was the imperial expansion of

---

[28] Bumsted, J. M., (ed.), *Reporting the Resistance: Alexander Begg and Joseph Hargrave on the Red River Resistance*, (University of Manitoba Press), 2003, pp. 9-16, and Bumsted, J. M., *The Red River Rebellion*, (Watson & Dwyer), 1996, pp. 245-254, provide a detailed discussion of the historiography.

Canadian nationhood not the particular problems of a numerically insignificant community.

The alternative view sees the Resistance as a justifiable local response to federal obfuscation and mismanagement. The national aspirations of the Métis people of Red River were ignored and were subject to racial and religious hostility and Riel was seen as a victim of Canadian colonial aggression. This view originated from the 1890s in the writings of Catholic clerics like Georges Dugas and Father A. G. Morice.[29] Riel is seen as a flawed leader and that the only Métis who mattered in Red River were the francophone Catholics. From the mid-1930s and especially with the publication of A. H. Trémaudan's *Histoire de la Nation Métisse* and George Stanley's *Louis Riel: The Birth of Western Canada* in 1936, Riel came to be seen as a constructive Métis leader and, echoing the 'frontier' thesis of F. J. Turner, he and his people were caught halfway between the 'primitive' and 'civilisation' suggesting that events in Red River were a cultural rather than a political response. In the 1940s, Marcel Giraud concluded that the Métis had effectively fused elements of both primitive and advanced societies and had, as a result, thrived. However, this fusion was superficial and was unable to survive the economic pressures that accompanied the end of the fur trade empire of the West. The problem is that both perspectives see events in Red River not in the context of local conditions but from the viewpoint of the national historiography of Canada. Red River was a further expression of the persistent struggle between Anglo-Protestantism and French-Canadian Catholicism for the political soul of Canada.

The debate over Red River was revitalised with the publication in 1956 of W. L. Morton's edition of Alexander Begg's *Red River Journal* and other previously largely ignored sources. Begg's astute daily account of events in the Settlement from November 1869 until July 1870 and his letters to the Ontarian press, later edited by Bumsted, provided a new perspective by focusing on Riel's efforts to find unity between the francophone Métis and anglophone mixed bloods of Red River while preventing the annexationist aspirations of Canadians and, to a lesser extent, of Americans. Métis resistance was based on their justifiable fear of being culturally and religiously overwhelmed by the mass of immigration of English Protestants in the wake of the transition to Canadian rule. The rebellion in 1885 was the product of the failed resistance in 1869-1870. Although Morton and

---

[29] See, Dugas, Georges, *Histoire véridique des faits qui ont preparé le mouvement des Métis à la Rivière-Rouge en 1869*, (Montreal), 1905, and Morice, A. G., *Histoire de l'église catholique dans l'ouest canadien du lac Supérieur au Pacifique*, 3 Vols. (Granger Frères), 1911.

George Stanley in his biography of Riel published in 1963 acknowledged the existence of the anglophone 'half-breeds', they did not take them seriously seeing events in Red River largely in terms of Riel and the Métis.[30] The result, from the 1960s, was analysis of the ethnic mix in the Settlement considering the role of the mixed-bloods. John Foster, Frits Pannekoek and Jennifer Brown focus on the development of a distinct Anglo-Métis identity, grounded in their Anglican communion that was distinctive from francophone and Catholic Métis identity.[31] Brian Gallagher argues that this work exaggerated the racial and religious differences among the mixed bloods and that Foster and Pannekoek have magnified religious strife in the colony. In 1996, Gerhard Ens maintained that there was a continuum across the linguistic-religious divide especially in terms of responses to economic opportunities.[32] Many Métis were not victims of progress but adapted to changes in the economic structures of the colony, co-operated with the anglophones in different ways and were among the Métis not to support Riel. The result of looking at conditions in Red River is a more nuanced appreciation of the nature of the Resistance that challenged the monolithic and determinist interpretations of contemporaries and those historians who had their own nationalist political agendas.

The Red River rebellion was essentially non-violent resistance directed against government policy.[33] It was non-violent, unlike in

---

[30] For Riel see, Stanley, George F. G., *Louis Riel: Patriot or Rebel,* (Canadian Historical Association), 1954, Stanley, George F., *Louis Riel,* (McGraw-Hill Ryerson), 1972, Siggins, Maggie, *Riel: A Life of Revolution,* (HarperCollins), 1994, Boyden, Joseph, *Louis Riel & Gabriel Dumont,* (Penguin), 2010, and Thomas, Lewis H., 'Louis Riel', *DCB*, Vol. 11, pp. 736-752.

[31] Pannekoek, Frits, *A Snug Little Flock: The Social Origins of the Riel Resistance of 1869-70,* (Watson & Dwyer Pub.), 1991, and Brown, Jennifer S. H., *Strangers in Blood: Fur Trade Company Families in Indian Country,* (University of British Columbia Press), 1980.

[32] Ens, Gerhard J., *Homeland to Hinterland: The Changing Worlds of the Red River Métis in the Nineteenth Century,* (University of Toronto Press), 1996.

[33] Whether the events at Red River were a rebellion is a moot point. Morton, W. L., (ed.), *Alexander Begg's Red River journal; and other papers relative to the Red River resistance of 1869-1870,* (Champlain Society), 1956, p 1: 'Not only was [Resistance] frequently employed at the time; it also possesses the merit of describing precisely the spirit and intention of the actions of the *Métis* in 1869-1870, without resorting to the legally accurate but nevertheless misleading term 'rebellion'. There is no doubt that there was resistance to

1885, largely because the physical remoteness of the Red River settlement made an immediate governmental resort to coercion impossible. In fact, the federal government showed considerable restraint in resisting strong Ontarian pressure to avenge Scott's death and succeeded in not provoking the Métis into prolonging their resistance or resisting the advance of the federal Wolseley military expedition. Riel was also able to impose and largely maintain discipline on the armed Métis and sought to secure co-operation with the diverse elements on Red River. The violence that did occur was the consequence of breakdowns in discipline and unity on both sides: for Riel and the Métis, the challenge posed by the Canadian party and the exemplary execution of Scott; for the federal government, McDougall's unauthorised attempt to seize power and possibly some members of the Ontarian militia taking the law into their own hands. There was no official violence between the two sides. In fact, both Riel and the federal government showed a degree of political acumen recognising an awareness of what was possible and what was necessary.[34]

In 1885, Riel thought that he could re-run the 1869-1870 resistance initially seeking to establish a protest movement that included settlers, Métis and Indians. If so, he had not recognised that the context had changed and especially that the building of the Canadian Pacific Railway meant that the North-West was now accessible by military forces in weeks rather than months. John A. Macdonald was again Prime Minister and was not going to be drawn into negotiations to resolve the problems of the North-West, most of which, unlike those in 1870, he did not recognise. His decision to send military forces to put down the rebellion made clear that there

---

the imposition of change by the Canadian government and that that resistance included the use of arms but for there to be a rebellion, it needs to be directed against a legally constituted authority. The critical issue therefore is what was the legally constituted authority in Red River between November 1869 and May 1870? Was it the HBC or the Canadian government in Ottawa or both? Having postponed the transfer on 1 December, legally the HBC remained the constituted authority but, not knowing this McDougall had issued the proclamation of transfer. Or was Riel caught in a constitutional vacuum between the end of one legal authority and the beginning of another? Legally, no but in practice a case could be made for this. Although Canadian expansionists and the Ontarian press certainly saw events in terms of a rebellion, Riel took a more sanguine view seeing resistance as part of a morally and legally justifiable negotiating strategy to achieve defined Métis rights.

[34] Torrance, Judy M., *Public Violence in Canada, 1867-1982*, (McGill-Queen's University Press), 1986, pp. 17-19.

could be no negotiation with rebels and the eventual defeat of both Métis and Indians, while not inevitable, was swiftly achieved. For many Anglo-Ontarians, Riel's actions in 1869, 1870 and 1885 represented a concerted effort to establish a francophone Catholic province in the North-West. When Macdonald declared that Riel would hang though 'every dog in Quebec bark in his favour', he was not simply expressing the view that justice should be seen to be done but reflected a deeper sense of antagonism to Quebec's sympathy for Riel. Wilfrid Laurier's passionate denunciation of the government's action in 1886 was a major step forward in his career. For many French-Canadians, Riel's execution symbolised the weakness of Quebec's politicians in federal government and, in part, contributed to a revival in French-Canadian nationalism from the late 1880s. They also ultimately saw it as the triumph of Anglo-Canadian racism: Riel was only hanged because he was French and Catholic.

At both Red River and in the North-West, Riel's actions reflected the federal-provincial tensions inherent in Confederation. Despite their provincial affiliations, successive federal administrations have sought to persuade Canadians that they are members first of the larger political body dedicated to treating all Canadians fairly wherever they live in Canada. The Métis were broadly committed to Confederation resisting impulses towards either independence or annexation by the United States in 1869-1870 and 1885. They believed that they could exist as a national body within the larger Canadian polity. In that respect, Riel was an early advocate of minority rights and it was the gradual recognition of these rights since the 1960s that has seen a growing sense of remembrance of his life and his mission.

The debate over whether Riel's execution was justifiable or, as Winnipeg Centre MP Pat Martin maintains, he was only executed because he was a 'nuisance', continues.[35] Riel was not, Martin argues, leading a rebellion against Canada but defending the Métis against an impending attack by Canadian forces.[36] This neglects the fact that no expedition would have been dispatched had the Métis not taken up arms. The critical issue is whether Riel should simply be pardoned or whether his conviction should be overturned and the government acknowledge that he was not guilty. While many support the concept of exoneration, many Métis are uncomfortable with a pardon because they understand that it implies guilt, mercy and forgiveness. To these

---

[35] *Winnipeg Free Press*, 31 March 2011. See also, Bumsted, J. M., 'Another Look at the Riel Trial for Treason', in Wright, Barry, and Binnie, Susan, (eds.), *Canadian State Trials, Volume III*, (University of Toronto Press), 2009, pp. 411-450, a dissection of why Riel did not receive justice in 1885.
[36] *Counterweighs*, 17 November 2010.

people, Riel was not guilty of treason and they do not want him pardoned for something he did not do.[37]

More than any other figure in Canadian history, Riel has been used and abused in remarkably diverse ways. Albert Braz examined the many faces of Louis Riel as part of a comparative review of literature stretching back more than a century.[38] Initially, Riel was both a traitor to Canadian Confederation, a symbol of francophone rights and a Catholic martyr. He was later reimagined as what Braz calls 'a pan-American liberator' and a 'pawn of shadowy white forces' as well as the prototypical Prairie maverick, a First Nations hero, a misunderstood intellectual and eventually the founder of Manitoba.[39] The most intriguing of these incongruities for Braz is Riel's transformation in English Canadian culture from the villain of 1885 to hero of an alienated West, spiritual father of Canadian multiculturalism, and, even more astounding, Father of Confederation. Others have characterised Riel as a libertarian defender of property rights, an anarchic anti-industrialist, an eccentric spiritualist and even a racist who believed in the supremacy of the Métis nation. There are shreds of truth embedded within each of these perspectives but none of them fully represented an understanding of the past. Rather they were all part of a contemporary discussion. Riel has come to serve a largely symbolic and often unrecognisable role in the popular iconography of the country which, as a representative of the Métis nation, he held in deep suspicion.

By 1900, Riel had been all but forgotten by Canadian writers and languished in relative obscurity until resurrected as a cultural mediator in the aftermath of World War II. Primarily an Anglo-Canadian phenomenon, the Riel industry began by transforming Riel into a transitional character or a 'go-between' who successfully bridged the gap between indigenous and Euro-Canadian culture. This positive construction of Riel and his activities remained popular until the 1970s, by which time writers were finding it increasingly difficult to celebrate Canadian history through a person that was 'either the

---

[37] For discussion of the question of exoneration see, Flanagan, Thomas, *Riel and the Rebellion: 1885 Reconsidered*, (Western Producer Prairie Books), 1983, second edition, (University of Toronto Press), 2000, pp. 169-189. See also, Teillet, Jean, 'Exoneration for Louis Riel: Mercy, Justice or Political Expediency?', *Saskatchewan Law Review*, Vol. 67, (2004), pp. 359-392.

[38] Braz, Albert, *The False Traitor: Louis Riel in Canadian Culture*, (University of Toronto Press), 2003; see also, Reid, Jennifer, *Louis Riel and the Creation of Modern Canada: Mythic Discourse and the Postcolonial State*, (University of New Mexico Press), 2008.

[39] Ibid, Braz, Albert, *The False Traitor: Louis Riel in Canadian Culture*, pp. i-ii.

country's sworn enemy or a constant reminder of its racism toward the First Nations.'[40] Jennifer Reid argues a case for Louis Riel as *the* ideal unifying figure for Canadian identity because she believes that Canada desperately needs one. She suggests that Canada is *so* fragmented that describing it as a *confederation* is more accurate than the use of the term *nation-state*. She believes that Riel's multicultural and multiregional background positions him as the ideal figure to bridge Canada's current postcolonial divisions.

The creation of Louis Riel Day has simply added a further dimension to previous attempts to define who Riel was and why he should be remembered. It is an annual general holiday in the Canadian province of Manitoba on the third Monday of February though in Alberta, Saskatchewan and Ontario, Family Day is observed at the same time. Manitoba's government introduced a holiday in February in 2007 because of the long period between New Year's Day and Good Friday when there were no holidays. A competition was held among school children to name the day, the winning name was 'Louis Riel Day' and was first held in 2008. It celebrates Riel as the driving force behind Manitoba becoming Canada's fifth province. The date has no special connection to any event in Riel's life. Louis Riel Day is observed on or around November 16, the anniversary of Riel's execution in 1885, in other areas of Canada, particularly Toronto to commemorate his life and to celebrate the Métis' culture, language, heritage and ancestral homeland. There have been calls recently to make Louis Riel Day a national holiday, but Riel remains a controversial and divisive figure. A recent poll in the *Winnipeg Free Press* showed that thirty-six per cent of respondents view Riel as either 'a traitor to Confederation' or 'a cold blooded murderer'. [41] Ever since he was hanged in 1885, Canadians have been trying to define and redefine Riel, sometimes in an honest effort to understand his place in history, but often just to fashion him into some sort of ideological weapon.

Some events in the past acquire a momentum that is appropriated, manipulated and often distorted by succeeding generations. They are interpreted, remembered and acquire a significance in people's heritage that relates more often to current concerns than past realities. They are recreated for entertainment and even apologised for to allay past wrongs and prejudices. It is commonly said that History is written by the winners. But heritage, history shaped to present purposes, is increasingly fashioned by the losers. Events are

---

[40] Ibid, Braz, Albert, *The False Traitor: Louis Riel in Canadian Culture*, p. 117.
[41] *Winnipeg Free Press*, 16 February 2013.

refracted by past and current concerns; villains become heroes and vice versa, rebels become freedom fighters and ideologues, proto-socialists and, in the process, we simplify, modify and romanticise the past. This is how we remember events today yet the past was never like this. It was messy, a confection of peoples (this applies with often more intensity within communities than across societies), ideas (trying to find answers to often unanswerable questions), things happening (not really events until historians get their hands on them) and behind it all the critical question, why?

7 Trauma in Canada

A 'trauma' can be physical or psychological. A wound or fracture causes a physical shock: the greater the shock, the greater the trauma. Psychological trauma is more complex and the relationship between the intensity of an event and its effect can be imbalanced. A person who falls from the tenth floor of a building will invariably die but people who witness traumatic events such as this can be left either with or without serious psychological after-effects. People can also experience serious trauma without being able to identify its cause. Even if the relationship between the violence of an event and its traumatic effects is variable, its impact is never without some link to the individual's emotional psychology and repressed memory. Mental representation has two faces. It is a mental 'reproduction' of the world, but it also has a psychological version that projects itself within the representations of things allowing a degree of objectification. It combines memory and psychological energies that together provide the stimulus through which mental representations can become real for individuals.

Traumas are generally situated between two extremes depending on whether the violence of a traumatic event or its psychological results is more important. Take the case of a meteorite that plunges through the atmosphere and demolishes my house causing me a violent nervous shock. It could have a profound psychological impact but psychological issues played no part in the genesis of my trauma. Its source was external. Trauma of this type has been compared to a tree that has lost in branches. If the tree is healthy and its roots have not been touched, then there is no reason why the branches should not grow again and the tree survive. At the other extreme, there are traumas resulting from predominantly internal psychological problems that become irrationally obsessive. In 1909, Freud published a case-study of this by an individual with obsessional thoughts and behaviours that he felt compelled to carry out known as 'Rat Man'.[1] The case received its name from a torture he had heard about from a military officer, where rats would eat their way into the anus of the victim. The patient was compelled to imagine that this fate was befalling two people dear to him, his fiancée and his father. The irrational and compulsive nature of this obsession is revealed by the fact that the man had the

---

[1] Gardner, Sebastian, *Irrationality and the Philosophy of Psychoanalysis*, (Cambridge University Press), 1993, pp. 90-113, summarises and analyses Freud's paper.

greatest regard for his fiancée and that his revered father had died several years earlier. Freud argued that these compulsive ideas were produced by conflicts that combined loving and aggressive impulses relating to the people concerned.[2] Such was the depth of the trauma that its obsessive character reaches the tree's roots and has the power to destroy it.[3]

All traumas occur between these extremes and, as a result, it is the simultaneous connection between a real traumatic event and its impact that determines the level of psychological dysfunction. There is a considerable difference between the traumatic effects produced by an 'act of God' over which individuals have no control and deliberate actions of individuals or groups. Intentionality in the human agency gives traumatic events significance and determines how they are represented. In some cases, the intentionality behind a traumatic event helps the development of its representation by channelling its effects into a reaction. For instance, the decision to invade Iraq was a direct result of the traumatic events of 11 September 2001. It was a questionable strategic decision but in terms of collective psychology, it helped (at least momentarily) to purge the state of terror into which the United States had been plunged after the attack on the Twin Towers though its longer-term impact combined with continued involvement in Afghanistan and in Iraq is more difficult to assess.

In other cases, intentionality can be an aggravating factor, a way of converting an event into something else; for instance, by developing contempt and hatred for others. The traumatic effect depends not simply on the material event but on the ways in which that event is perceived by individuals and represented by the authorities and with how it is incorporated into individual and collective memory. Historical trauma is the cumulative, emotional and psychological wounding over people's lives and across generations, as the result of a collective trauma and corresponds to a situation where the representation of an event is greater than our capacity to absorb it

Collective trauma is evident in events marked by extreme violence and by the high number of victims. The Holocaust, the Armenian and Rwandan genocides, events in Darfur and the battle of Verdun fall into this category. The defeat of the Patriotes in 1837 and 1838 was not an event of such terrifying human proportions. The

---

[2] Wertz, Frederick J., 'Freud's case of the Rat Man revisited: an existential-phenomenological and socio-historical analysis', *Journal of Phenomenological Psychology,* Vol. 35, (4), (2003), pp. 47-78.

[3] Hunt, Nigel C., *Memory, War and Trauma,* (Cambridge University Press), 2010, pp. 61-80, 114-126, 172-185, and Yael, D., (ed.), *International Handbook of Multigenerational Legacies of Trauma,* (Plenum Press), 1998.

rebellions were confined to the Montreal district. Two hundred were killed, a dozen villages torched, several hundred arrested, twelve executed and sixty or so transported to Australia. The Upper Canadian rebellions were similarly limited geographically to the area round Toronto and, in 1838, to areas adjacent to the border with the United States. The numbers killed were small in 1837, significantly larger in 1838 with executions limited to twenty (2 after the 1837 rebellion and 18 for events in 1838 not including the five rebels summarily executed at Windsor on 4 December) and ninety-two rebels were transported. Things returned to normal quickly after the rebellions; the exiles eventually returned to Canada and, in some cases, to political life.

The Fenian rebellions in 1866, 1870 and 1871 were similarly geographically confined, deaths among the participants were low and, though some Fenians were imprisoned, none were executed. Resistance on Red River in 1869 and 1870 was marked by its peaceful character with only one execution, the questionable and botched shooting of Thomas Scott. The Riel rebellion of 1885 covered a larger geographical area but again deaths among those fighting were small and executions limited to Riel himself and eight Cree warriors.[4] Neither were the rebellions on the same scale as many contemporary events. For instance, the war for Greek Independence between 1821 and 1829 cost 120,000 lives. During the Paris uprising of 1848, several thousand rebels were killed, 1,500 were shot without trial and some 11,000 thrown into prison or deported. The Napoleonic Wars that took place several decades before the rebellions saw the deaths of between 500,000 and 700,000 people. But collective trauma is not simply a matter of scale and this chapter examines its impact on Canada.

Collective trauma was evident in the Lower Canadian rebellions and in the Riel rebellion and they remain areas of contested remembrance. These rebellions were, at least in part, caused by Protestant immigration that challenged the demographic control of Roman Catholic French-Canadians and Métis. By contrast, the Fenian rebellions have until recently barely figured in Canadian remembrance though they are now regarded as part of the Atlantic 'revolution' that sought Irish independence from British colonial rule. They were seen as external rebellions and contributed in an ill-defined sense to the process of Confederation in 1867 and to the question of national security into the 1880s.

---

[4] The rebellion's toll was 53 whites killed, 118 wounded and about 35 First Nations and Métis killed: Magocsi, Paul, (ed.), *Encyclopedia of Canada's Peoples*, (University of Toronto Press), 1999, p. 76.

Traumas of 1837 and 1838

The extent to which the rebellions in 1837 and 1838 constitute successive traumas means looking at the symbolic nature of events. For this reason, the case of the Rat Man is not without relevance since the unbearable death of the father is at the centre of what psychiatrists call failure. What is remarkable in the representation of the rebellions is a crushing sense of failure. This was highlighted Hubert Aquin[5] who argued that the really traumatic event in 1837 was not the defeats at St. Charles and St. Eustache but the victory at St. Denis.[6] It was an unexpected victory involving Patriotes in an unanticipated way in combat where they had to overcome or die and that they were and remained completely paralysed by it. Aquin suggests that as many Patriotes believed that they would never win any conflict with the colonial authorities, it only remained for them to sell their lives as dearly as possible to save their honour. He identified this sense of defeatism among those involved in the rebellions. Yet defeatism was not evident at St. Denis but is a characteristic of ways in which the historical representation of the event was subsequently constructed. This sense of fatalism appears to be a defence mechanism that seeks to reduce the effects of the rebellions by removing references to the unforeseen event at St. Denis.

The Patriotes had to lose because the rebellions could not end differently. Yet the actions of those involved in 1837 showed a quite different state of mind than the quiet demoralisation of Aquin. Take the episode when Georges-Étienne Cartier and his companions braved the frozen waters of the Richelieu under fire to bring ammunition that the rebels in St. Denis needed. Much more than the ultimate defeat of the rebellion, the victory at St. Denis has been pushed into the background. The current festival on 25 November shows that some people believe that the memory of the battle of St. Denis should be celebrated and that rather than allowing people to forget their history we should not just acknowledge those who died for their country but recognise their victory.

---

[5] Aquin, Hubert, 'L'art de la défaite, considérations stylistiques', *Liberté*, Vol. 7, nos 1 et 2, (1965), reprinted in *Blocs erratiques*, (Typo), 1998.

[6] Séguin, Robert-Lionel, *La victoire de Saint-Denis*, (Parti pris), 1964, Boissonault, C.-M., 'Les patriotes a Saint-Denis', *Revue de l'Université Laval*, Vol. 5, (1951), pp. 777-790, and Richard, J. B., *Les événements de 1837 à Saint-Denis-sur-Richelieu*, (Societe d'histoire regionale), 1938, are useful, studies of the battle. See also, ibid, Allaire, J.-B.-A., *Histoire de la paroisse de St. Denis-sur-Richelieu*, pp. 373-403.

Just like the notion of victory, any real sense of courage is absent from representations of events in 1837 while examples of cowardice, escape and panic are ever-present themes. Curé Paquin, author of the *Journal historique de la rébellion à St. Eustache*, used a comic tone when he described the rout of the combatants and the flight of the Patriote leaders.[7] After their expedition to Sainte-Rose was rebuffed by local *habitants*, the Patriotes fled as fast as they could:

> Ils se pressèrent tellement que plusieurs se heurtèrent et se blessèrent même en sautant à la hâte et tous ensemble dans leurs voitures; ils ne ralentirent leur course que quand ils furent au milieu des leurs à St-Eustache, et même là ils croyaient encore avoir l'ennemi à leurs trousses.[8]

The flight of Amury Girod is the model for the anti-hero. His motivation was ambiguous. When faced by British troops, Girod persuaded his men to occupy and defend the church while he fled claiming that he was seeking reinforcements. Instead of aiding the Patriotes of St. Eustache, who faced overwhelming odds, the men of St. Benoit thought only of Girod's flight and wanted to hand him over to the British. His reception from Girouard and the other leaders in St. Benoit was not surprising; they accused him of deserting his men and of being a coward. It was too much for Girod who grabbed a carriage and made off on the northern road towards Sainte-Thérèse, something he could have done earlier had his intention been simply to flee. Girod later committed suicide when cornered by loyalists. The description of the flight of Étienne Chartier, the Patriote curé of St. Benoit is equally comical:

> M. Chartier, qui se trouvait alors au village, fut tellement pressé de se sauver dès qu'il eut entendu quelques coups de canon, qu'il n'eut pas le temps de prendre sa voiture qui était chez le Dr. Chénier, et qu'il se sauva à pied. À quelque distance du village il se jeta dans une traîne qui passait avec deux femmes et cinq ou six enfants en bas âge; mais bientôt, trouvant que cette traîne n'allait pas assez vite, il se remit à courir de plus belle et courut ainsi pendant une demi-heure au moins avec une foule de fuyards, ne le cédant à personne en agilité.[9]

---

[7] *Journal historique des événements arrivés à Saint-Eustache, pendant la rébellion du comté du lac des Deux-Montagnes depuis les soulèvements...,* (Montréal, John Jones), 1838, cit, Globensky, Maximilien, *La Rébellion de 1837 à Saint-Eustache*, 1883, extended edition, 1889, reprinted (Éditions Du Jour), 1974, pp. 41-116.

[8] Ibid., *Journal historique des événements arrivés à Saint-Eustache*, p. 55.

[9] Ibid., *Journal historique des événements arrivés à Saint-Eustache*, p. 61.

Here the comic effect comes from the fact that the leaders were in the vanguard of the panic that affected men, women and children as combatants or non-combatants in a grand chaotic exodus. Rather than standing their ground, the Patriote leaders led the way in attempting to escape.

These scenes of panic are numerous in the historiography of the rebellions. According to Paquin, Féréol Peltier, Hubert and the brothers de Lorimier left St. Eustache before the battle.[10] At St. Charles, it was Thomas Storrow Brown who fled. In the rebellion in November 1838, people remarked on the flight of Côté after the skirmish at Lacolle and Robert Nelson from the battle at Odelltown. It was, however, the escape of Papineau that has taken on such symbolic significance if only because of its visibility. It has become a familiar event, something that the ordinary Quebecois know from the history of the rebellions or from his biography. A matter of controversy at the time and since, it has even become the subject of several songs.

In 1862, Félix Poutré, traitor and police informer published a fraudulent historical account entitled *Échappé de la potence: souvenirs d'un prisonnier d'État canadien en 1838* in which he pretended that he had been one of the main organisers of the rebellion in 1838.[11] For many years, Poutré's account was the best-selling book on Canadian history and his exploits were turned into drama by Louis Fréchette in *Félix Poutré* written in 1892 that was for a long time the most performed play in the Canadian theatre. Analysis of the text revealed the circumstances of the fraud but for the Canadian public it was his role as a forger rather than as a traitor that was recognised. By contrast, Jean-Olivier Chénier, one of the heroes of the rebellion in 1837 was ignored by the public while Poutré's popularity was massive.[12] Even when the significance of Chénier and his history was recognised, there was little emphasis on his courage and heroism. It is striking to compare the paucity of discussion of Chénier with the creative richness of the discourse on Poutré. This reflected the focus of collective representation of the rebellions on a sense of shame to the detriment of a sense of courage and pride.

Behind the denial of Patriote victory, complicity in pessimism and the cult of the traitor lay fear of the Patriote revolutionary agenda. Several works, including those by Gérard Mendel, argue that power

---

[10] Ibid, *Journal historique des événements arrivés à Saint-Eustache*, p. 62.

[11] Collin, Marc, *Mensonges et vérités dans les Souvenirs de Félix Poutré*, (Septentrion), 2003.

[12] Collin, Marc, *Autour de Chénier, les Rébellions et la conscience historique canadienne et québécoise*, thèse de doctorat, Université Laval, 2005.

and authority were grounded in relationships with parental figures.[13] Revolution saw the symbolic death of these figures. Take the representation of the escape of Papineau in Louis Fréchette's drama *Papineau: drame historique canadien en quatre actes et neuf tableaux* first performed in 1880.[14] In the play, Wolfred Nelson ordered Papineau to take cover from the fighting thinking that he was of more value alive than dead. Papineau refused wishing to face death like the others. Then Nelson reproves him for his egotism

Vous ne pensez qu'à votre réputation, alors que vous devriez penser à votre devoir envers le pays!

Papineau, Nelson argued, has a reputation that he should be willing to sacrifice for the good of his country. At that moment, a woman and child make an oath to fight to the death highlighting the self-sacrifice that Nelson demanded of Papineau. This is followed by a passionate speech by Papineau in which he compared what was expected of him with what was required of Christ.

[13] See especially, Mendel, Gérard, *La révolte contre le père*, (Payot), 1968, and *Une histoire de l'autorité: Permanences et variations*, (La Découverte), 2002, in which he developed his ideas on socio-psychoanalysis structured round power and authority. One of the principal merits of Mendel's socio-psychoanalysis is its striving to understand how organisational reality influences individual psychic reality, including in its unconscious dimension. A collective practice, it aims to study how actors, in the framework of their daily professional activity, and organised into specific groups (homogeneous in terms of profession), reflect by themselves on the forces that impact their personality. The working hypothesis of socio-psychoanalysis is that the hold of organisations on individuals is such that the latter have very little power over their acts of work whence the negative psychological effects with their harmful socio-economic consequences. See, Arnaud, Gilles, 'Poweract and Organizational Work: Gérard Mendel's Socio-psychoanalysis', *Organization Studies*, Vol. 28, (3), (2007), pp. 409-428.
[14] Fréchette was the principal literary figure of French-speaking Canada, its unofficial poet laureate, the only nineteenth century French-Canadian writer to be well known outside Canada. His *La Voix d'un exilé*, written in 1866 when he exiled himself to Chicago to protest at Confederation that he saw as marking the end of French Canada, was used as propaganda by the Rouge party in Canada. One twentieth-century critic has called its 'violence of...language' unsurpassed in Canadian literature. According to what may be an apocryphal account, when Fréchette became the province's establishment poet in 1880, he bought up all the copies of *La Voix* he could find and burned them. See, Blais, Jacques, 'Louis Fréchette', *DCB*, Vol. 13, pp. 55-56.

Les femmes... les enfants... Je comprends ce que le Christ a pu souffrir au jardin des Oliviers!

Fréchette ironically contrasted the Garden of Olives where Christ began the process that led to his crucifixion with Papineau's protest that he was being asked to survive. What then was his suffering compared to that of Christ? Certainly, there was no physical suffering but there was moral suffering and what Papineau must suffer will be the loss of his reputation. Unlike the women and children who will fight to the death, he was condemned to live a long life, the butt of sarcasm and ridicule, something reinforced by his escape dressed as a woman. He will never again be a politician of the first rank, and this was a torment for an individual who had known such glory. Fréchette showed us a man who was forced to give up his spiritual roots and who suffered because of this. In doing this Fréchette suggests it is not its children that the revolution devours but its father. The moral misery that exists in Fréchette's Papineau is a survival strategy that poisons the individual's existence. It shows that we cannot escape our social membership and that all individuals alienated from their communities experience the same internal exile, narcissistic suffering and guilt.

The historiography of the rebellions beginning with Papineau's *Histoire de l'insurrection du Canada* published in 1839 is riven by a refusal to accept blame for the revolutionary agenda. The replacement of the battle of St. Denis with a focus on the peaceful Patriote assemblies between May and October 1837 shows that the denial of the revolutionary heritage of 1837 still remains. What defines a revolutionary moment is its aim to reverse established structures through extra-legal means. The independence of Lower Canada could have been achieved through legal, non-revolutionary means but this would have been difficult to realise because it was unable to escape from the contradictions of the colonial system. For a movement that aimed at self-determination for the people, it is necessary to act outside the remit of existing legal systems and this is not only a question of circumstances, it is a matter of structures.

The sovereignty of the people is founded on legal rights but a national revolution that seeks to establish self-determination cannot be constrained by those rights. Illegality is inherent in revolution and in the seizure of sovereignty. Self-determination cannot simply be achieved through reforms while sovereignty is not demanded, it is taken. It is because political change symbolically rests on the 'death' of the figure of parental authority that revolution is violent. Revolutionary violence is not necessary because it is the only way of changing things, it is necessary because it is the only way of representing and resolving the contradictions in the competing symbolic systems of alienation and freedom.

The Patriotes in 1837 and 1838 were arguably involved in a revolutionary movement and the military conflict represented the tension between different sorts of legitimacy. In the eyes of colonial government, taking up arms was an act of high treason while for citizens who no longer recognised the legitimacy of government, direct action was a duty. The transformation of the crimes of lèse-majesté and high treason into heroic acts was the essence of the conflict over legitimacy that was at the heart of the revolution and calls for national independence. The problem in recognising Patriotes such as Chénier as heroes and an unwillingness to accept the significance of the victory at St. Denis is that to do so means accepting the existence of a revolutionary movement for change at work in 1837 and 1838.

This screening of the past reflects the current official ideology that promotes the sovereignty of Quebec through democratic steps and without political violence or recourse to illegality. This explains why the term 'independence' has been replaced by 'sovereignty'. Although there may be little semantic difference between the two terms and their ends might be the same, there are important symbolic differences; independence implies a more militant approach while sovereignty suggests a negotiated constitutional settlement. The refusal to accept that conflict might be necessary has been seen as a weakness by opponents of the sovereignty project and they reinforced the point by emphasising the notion of 'separation'. Those calling for sovereignty made little attempt to counter the separatist argument and this seem to confirm its ability to inspire people to demand change and fear among those opposing it. The refusal of the sovereignty movement to recognise the importance of symbolic violence is a major reason for its failure. The critical question is whether it is possible to establish Quebec as a sovereign power without destroying Canada. In many respects, the referendums in 1980 and 1995 were a repeat of the failure of the rebellions in 1837 and 1838.

The irrational fear of political violence among people who have a limited grasp of its history is a paradox that appears to defy logic. The traumatic character of the rebellions can be explained by the limited extent to which the revolutionary agenda has attached itself to popular representation of the past. The rebellions of 1837 and 1838 remain the only revolutionary event in the history of Quebec and of Canada though a strong case could be made for Louis Riel's rebellion in the 1880s. There is an discrepancy between established symbolic systems and actual experience of revolution and it is this that explains the extent to which the revolutionary agenda has been largely ignored by history.

Fenianism and collective trauma, 1866-1871

In 1866, 1870 and 1871, Fenians invaded Canada from the United States as part of their campaign for an Irish independence.[15] Apart from a Fenian victory at Ridgeway in June 1866, Canadian troops were able to contain these incursions with relative ease. Most historians have embraced contemporary descriptions of the attack in 1866 as 'an ephemeral affair'.[16] Irish-American Catholics accepted this view largely because the Catholic Church was relieved of an awkward element within its own ranks. William D'Arcy's study of the Fenians fitted the invasion into an ideological space present in discussion of the abortive rebellion in Ireland in 1848: organisation was laughable, leadership was weak and this led to inevitable defeat.[17] This reflected how Irish nationalism was represented; emotionally superficial, fickle and shallow. Those Fenians involved in violence lacked all rationality and motivation but were the product of natural depravity. But this historiography is a caricature that condemns Irish nationalism, whether in Canada or the United States, as an inevitable failure: Fenianism failed because it had to fail.

Canadian historians have, with notable exceptions, regarded Fenianism as an external threat and have downplayed its importance as a powerful force within the Irish-Canadian community in the 1860s.[18] Irish-Canadian Catholic loyalism and the opposition of the Catholic Church precluded widespread support for the Fenians and as a result, the connection of Canadian Fenians to the American movement has been neglected.[19] It is easy to write off the Canadian

---

[15] For recent discussion of the Fenians in an Atlantic context see my *Famine, Fenians and Freedom, 1830-1882*, (Authoring History), 2071, and *Rebellion in Canada, 1837-1885, Volume 2: The Irish, the Fenians and the Métis*, (CreateSpace), 2012.

[16] See, for instance, Neidhardt, W. S., *Fenianism in North America*, (Pennsylvania State University Press), 1975, p. 81.

[17] D'Arcy, William, *The Fenian Movement in the United States: 1858-1886*, (Russell & Russell), 1947.

[18] This was certainly not the view of contemporaries. For instance, of the 17,000 letters in the Sir John A Macdonald Collection, 5,000 were concerned with the Fenians.

[19] Neidhardt, W. S., *Fenianism in North America*, (Pennsylvania State University Press), 1975, pp. 41-42, Senior, Hereward, *The Fenians and Canada*, (Macmillan of Canada), 1978, pp. 46-75, and Toner, Peter M., ''The Green Ghost': Canada's Fenians and the Raids', *Eire-Ireland*, Vol. 16, (4), (1981), pp. 27-47, provide accounts of Fenian development and activities.

Fenians in the 1860s as an irritant, but their actions during 1866 suggest that D'Arcy McGee was correct:

Canada and British America have never known an enemy so subtle, so irrational, so hard to trace, and, therefore, so difficult to combat.[20]

In the past twenty years there has been a significant reassessment of Fenianism and Canada that has looked beyond negative contemporary rhetoric to the nature and extent of Fenian organisation in Canada and how people reacted to what many saw as a threat to Canada's security. It is in this context that it is now possible to identify the traumatic effects of Fenianism on Canadian politics and society.

The striking difference with the rebellions in Lower Canada was that the collective trauma was short-lived and episodic. It existed in 1866 and 1868 and although fear of further Fenian invasion persisted into the 1880s, the collective trauma did not and was replaced by a collective amnesia about Ridgeway.[21] There was no commemoration of Ridgeway until the men who had fought successfully lobbied for recognition. Their campaign led to formal recognition in 1890 and a decade later federal and provincial governments finally issued medals and land grants. Over the next few decades Ridgeway gradually faded from memory. In the aftermath of the Boer War and with the enormity of casualties during the First World War, the battle was gradually forgotten. In 1931, Canada's Memorial Day was moved to 11 November and the few remaining veterans were not included. Ridgeway is not commemorated, its casualties are not recognised in National Books of Remembrance and their gravestones scattered across southern Ontario and in Toronto, do not have National War Grave status and are uncared for by the government.

A successful Fenian invasion of Canada was not a preposterous idea in 1866. The Toronto *Leader* said that the Fenians had crossed the border and ruthlessly devastating the countryside.[22] The Toronto *Globe* called on the American government to bring an end to the Fenians.[23] Rumour was widespread and there were Fenians 'panics'

---

[20] Cit, Wilson, David A., 'Swapping Canada for Ireland', p. 2 at http://www.irishcanadiansociety.net/Swapping_Canada_for_Ireland_Fenians.pdf

[21] Vronsky, Peter, *Ridgeway: The American Fenian Invasion and the 1866 Battle That Made Canada*, (Allen Lane Canada), 2011, pp. 262-295, examines the memory of Ridgeway since 1866.

[22] *Leader*, 9 March 1866.

[23] *Globe*, 15 March 1866.

in Prince Edward Island and Nova Scotia.[24] Amid reports of massive Fenian gatherings in New York City and Philadelphia, in Canada the *York Herald* noted:

>...it is beyond question that in numbers, ruffianism and recklessness, Fenianism is dangerous to life and property on the border. A sudden raid, made at an unguarded moment, would result in more outrage and plunder than we care to submit or ought to be exposed to.[25]

There were large numbers of unemployed ex-soldiers available for Fenian recruitment. Toleration of Fenian activities during the American Civil War when the Fenian Brotherhood had been allowed to construct its own military framework within that of the United States, its purchase of cheap war surplus weapons and the federal government's ambivalence toward their filibustering plans, all suggested that the Fenian Brotherhood had tacit government backing. Even under stable political conditions, widespread negative attitudes toward Britain and the weight of Irish ballots would have encouraged the American government to handle Fenians with care, but with Congress and the Executive at loggerheads over Reconstruction, the political importance of the Irish vote was greatly exaggerated. Finally, most Americans had a 'continentalist' vision and anticipated Canada's future annexation. It is not surprising that the Fenian invasion in June 1866, incursions in 1870 and 1871 and rumours of further raids in the 1870s had 1880s was a traumatic experience for many Canadians. A Welland County villager recalled sixty years later:

>It is said that in remote Irish settlements of Canada there were parties who were in sympathy with the Fenian movement and who were expected to acquire the property of their neighbours if the invasion was a success. In York County (Toronto) there were known to be at least two Fenian head-centres and much secrecy was observed in the movements of these people. Quantities of pikes were said to be stored in the houses of members of the organizations. Of this I am informed by a then Toronto citizen who has a distinct recollection of the Fenian Raid.[26]

---

[24] Macdonald, Edward, 'Who's Afraid of the Fenians?: The Fenian Scare on Prince Edward Island, 1865-1867', *Acadiensis*, Vol. 38, (1), (2009), pp. 3-33, and Cameron, James M., 'Fenian Times in Nova Scotia', *Nova Scotia Historical Society Collections*, Vol. 37, (1970), pp. 103-152.

[25] *York Herald*, 9 March 1866.

[26] Sherk, M. G., 'My Recollections of the Fenian Raid', *Welland County Historical Society Papers and Records*, Vol. 2, (1926), p. 63.

Initially, the Fenian attacks had a traumatic effect on Irish Canadians still distressed by the cataclysmic impact of the Famine. News of the raids in June 1866 came as a surprise to the Irish Catholic press in Toronto that had discounted the likelihood of any incursion.[27] The *Irish Canadian*'s first reaction, probably in self-defence, was to repeat its earlier comments that Fenian action in Canada would not win Ireland's freedom.[28] Its editor criticised the anti-Catholic reaction when even the daily Protestant papers were playing down the Irish Catholic response to the raid. In reply to a comment that the Irish Catholics of the city were disloyal and not to be trusted, the editor remarked that such comments were unwise for they offended a large portion of the populace at a time of great distress and excitement. The *Canadian Freeman*, which had discounted the danger from the Fenians the previous autumn,[29] expressed a clearer and more forceful opposition to the Fenian 'marauders'.[30] The feeling of disgust and indignation that spread throughout the province was equally shared by the Irish Catholics who were as ready as Protestants to affirm their duty of loyalty and allegiance to Canada.

Although exaggerated, the idea of Irish-Canadian support for the Fenians was widely reported in the press. This was reinforced by the discovery of arms caches, for instance, in Griffintown and wild rumours that the Fenians would be given a 'warm reception' on their arrival. The *London Free Press* twice reported that attempts had been made to cut the city's telegraph lines.[31] A letter found on 6 June made clear that the Fenian Brotherhood was relying on Canadian Fenians for small operations and to quarter Fenian troops during the Niagara Raid.[32] Five Grand Trunk railway workers arrested after Ridgeway had helped Fenian troops gain access to a local rail depot.[33] There was also a widespread belief that a significant proportion of the Irish in the British army were expected to either desert or join the Fenians. For Canada West's dominant Anglo-Protestant culture, the Fenian raids were a perfect opportunity to smear Irish-Canadians, especially Irish Catholics, with disloyalty. McGee recognised:

---

[27] For instance, *Canadian Freeman*, 9 November 1865, 16 November 1865, 1 February 1866 and 15 March 1866.
[28] *Irish Canadian*, 6 June 1866.
[29] 'Panic Writing', *Canadian Freeman*, 23 November 1865.
[30] *Canadian Freeman*, 7 June 1866.
[31] *London Free Press*, 2, 8 June 1866.
[32] Neidhardt, W. S., 'The Abortive Fenian Uprising in Canada West: A Document Study', *Ontario History*, Vol. 61, (2), (1969), pp. 74-76.
[33] *Sarnia Observer*, 15 June 1866.

Let not Irishmen in Canada deceive themselves; it is to the frenzy of some of our deluded countrymen that this stigma owes its origin.[34]

The challenge facing the government was how to isolate Canadian Fenians without alienating Irish Catholic Canadians in general.[35] This was difficult with the sympathies of Irish Catholics for an independent Ireland and the anti-Catholic backlash after the raids. The Ottawa Irish nationalist J. L. P. O'Hanly feared a 'sectarian war of extermination' against Catholics after McGee's assassination in 1868.[36] Moir suggested:

The extreme nationalism of the Fenian Brotherhood threatened to undermine the Catholic Church...as well as the peace of Canada. This double dimension of Irish Catholicism and Irish nationalism was in turn confronted by the national agenda of the older Orange Order that perpetuated a parallel Protestant political and religious faction.[37]

This occurred even though the Catholic Church censured Hibernians and Fenians as they became more extreme. In 1864, Toronto's Bishop Lynch and in early 1866 the archbishops of Dublin and New York condemned the Fenians[38] and it was reported that Fenians were denied Christian burials in Buffalo.[39] There were also some calls of moderation within the Canadian press with the *Brockville Recorder* reminding Canadians:

...there are thousands of Roman Catholics, true hearted and loyal men that would as strenuously oppose and as firmly resist the encroachments and designs of Fenianism as any Protestant in all the land.[40]

---

[34] McGee, Thomas D'Arcy, *An Account of the Attempts to Establish Fenianism in Montreal*, (Post Printing and Publishing), 1882, p. 30; it was originally published in three parts in the *Montreal Gazette* during August 1867.

[35] See, Rafferty, Oliver, 'Fenianism in North America in the 1860s: The Problems for Church and State', *History*, Vol. 84, (1999), pp. 257-277.

[36] O'Hanly, J. L. P., to Hearn, John, 4 May 1868, O'Hanly Papers, Library and Archives Canada, MG29, B11.

[37] Moir, John S., *Church and Society: Documents on the Religious and Social History of the Roman Catholic Archdiocese of Toronto*, (Archdiocese of Toronto), 1991, p. 91.

[38] *Globe*, 19 February 1866, 10 March 1866.

[39] O'Connor, John, *Letters of John O'Connor, M.P., on Fenianism*, (Hunter, Rose & Co.), 1870, pp. 8-9.

[40] *Brockville Recorder*, 14 June 1866.

Public perception of a Fenian-Catholic alliance was misplaced. The Fenians accepted support from all denominations. Irish Protestants held prominent positions in the Fenian Brotherhood, the main Fenian generals were all Protestant and the *Barrie Examiner* noted a quarter of imprisoned Fenians at Brantford were Protestants.[41] McGee drew a sharp line between Fenians and Irish Catholic Canadians but this proved difficult in an atmosphere of paranoia and where Canadian Fenians still posed a major threat to security.[42] However, some Canadians disagreed with this pessimistic analysis:

> A Montreal special says the rumors of a Fenian invasion create no excitement here; the people laugh at the reports, and look upon them as a very transparent attempt to hoax the Canadians and oh eat us out of the custom duties.[43]

Intelligence that the Fenians were planning to invade in June 1866 was ignored by the Canadian government largely because of the hollowness of previous rumours. As a result, when the invasion occurred on 1 June, it came as a surprise. Lord Monck responded to an invasion by 'a lawless band of Marauders' with a combative and congratulatory address to the Legislative Assembly in which he stated:

> The entire people have been thoroughly aroused by recent occurrences; and it must now be apparent to all, that the whole resources of the Country, both in men and means, will at any moment be cheerfully given in repelling any invasion of their home.[44]

The extent of the political trauma was reflected in the government's draconian response diverting attention from its misguided complacency. Canadian Fenians were still active a week after the invasion and this explains why *Habeas Corpus* was suspended for a year on 8 June.[45] This gave the government the right to detain

---

[41] *Barrie Examiner Extra*, 7 June 1866.

[42] See, *Canadian Freeman*, 20 September 1866.

[43] The *Deseret News*, 4 June 1867.

[44] *Journals of the Legislative Assembly of the Province of Canada from June 8 to August 15, 1866 ... in the twenty-ninth and thirtieth years of the reign of ... Queen Victoria: being the 5th session of the 8th Provincial Parliament of Canada*, (Hunter, Rose & Co.), 1866, pp. 3-4.

[45] *New York Times*, 14 June 1866, gives an American perspective on suspension. See also, ibid, *Journals of the Legislative Assembly of the Province of Canada from June 8 to August 15, 1866 ... in the twenty-ninth and thirtieth years of the reign of ... Queen Victoria: being the 5th session of*

anyone suspected as a threat to the public peace for one year without evidence or cause and was intended to contain the internal Fenian threat. Further legislation allowed a prisoner's right to trial by jury to be replaced by military court martial.[46] However, courts martial were not used largely because of opposition from London.[47] This may have been out of proportion to the number of active Fenians but it showed the level of defensive insecurity, trauma and uncertainty that pervaded provincial thinking.

Though there was some criticism in the press, suspending Habeas Corpus proved effective in dealing with the internal Fenian threat. The authorities used their new powers immediately with arrests of suspected Fenians in Montreal and elsewhere.[48] Some authorities were overzealous: 20 men singing Fenian-like songs on a train going through Hamilton were arrested on 13 June, but the authorities were embarrassed to find that they were all Union veterans singing old war songs.[49] The Canadian government was well aware of the existence of Canadian Fenians who, though small in number, were perceived to be able to tip the balance of Canada West's conflict with the Fenians. It was this defensive insecurity that prompted the draconian response from government.[50]

A military review was staged on Montreal's Champ de Mars to celebrate the successful defence of British North America, but the Fenian campaign had exposed fundamental weaknesses in the militia system. In Britain, *The Times* was particularly critical commenting in late 1866:

> What has become of the Canadian Militia, of which we have seen such imposing musters—on paper? What of the volunteers? Have they entirely collapsed since the great Booker battle? Can there not be collected from amongst three millions of loyal Canadians, a sufficient native force to scatter

---

the 8th Provincial Parliament of Canada, p. 2. See also the reports in *Le Canadien*, 10, 13 June 1866.

[46] This process was only allowed when foreign nationals committed crimes on Canadian soil that were punishable by death and the Fenian invasion fitted this definition, *Globe*, 5 June 1866.

[47] See, for instance, Earl of Carnarvon to Governor-General Monck, 7 July 1866, *Correspondence respecting the recent Fenian aggression upon Canada*, (Hunter, Rose & Company), 1869, p. 79.

[48] *London Free Press*, 9 June, 12 June 1866.

[49] *Globe*, 13 June 1866.

[50] Ibid, *Correspondence respecting the recent Fenian aggression upon Canada*, pp. 35-38, details the less than positive response to the Canadian government's legislation from the British government.

to the winds a handful of Fenian ragamuffins without dragging across the Atlantic those regiments which we can so ill spare...[51]

Local military defence was the responsibility of John A. Macdonald and the debacle threatened his confederation plans and his ambition to lead Dominion Canada's first government. A clique of politicians and militia officers covered up the disaster. Alfred Booker, who led the forces defeated at Ridgeway, was charged with mishandling his volunteers. The court of inquiry held at Hamilton on 3 July failed to assign blame while indicating Booker's personal courage.[52] The local press was critical of the inquiry's failure to ascertain the truth and judged the report a 'whitewash'. Lieutenant-Colonel Dennis was brought before a court of enquiry for cowardice and reckless conduct in exposing his men.[53] He was acquitted on six counts though George Taylor Denison, the president of the court privately felt Dennis culpable of disobeying orders and published a dissenting opinion questioning his judgment. The raids reinforced Canada's sense of military vulnerability, especially because Britain was seriously considering reducing its garrison, if not its outright withdrawal.[54] The latter stages of the Confederation debates were to some degree held in an atmosphere of military crisis and the greater military security that would be gained through combining colonial resources was one of the factors that weighed heavily in Confederation's favour.

In November 1867, John A Macdonald, in his role as Prime Minister and Minister of Justice announced that his government intended to renew the suspension of the Habeas Corpus. He argued that, as the international activities of the Fenians remained a continued danger, suspension should remain in force and be extended across the new Dominion.[55] Caution was, for Macdonald, essential. The events

---

[51] 'The Canadian Crisis', *The Times*, 22 October 1866.

[52] See, 'The Enquiry into Col. Booker's Conduct', *Ottawa Times*, 7 July 1866, p. 2.

[53] See the court of inquiry into Dennis' actions, printed in Macdonald, Capt. John A., *Troublous Times in Canada: A history of the Fenian raids of 1866 and 1870*, (W. S. Johnston & Co.), 1910, pp. 247-255.

[54] For the context of British attitudes to imperial defence, see Beeler, John Francis, (ed.), Schurman, Donald M., *Imperial Defence 1868-1887*, (Routledge), 2000, originally submitted as a Ph.D., thesis in 1955. For Canadian attitudes, see Morton, Desmond, *Ministers and generals: politics and the Canadian militia, 1868-1904*, (University of Toronto Press), 1970.

[55] See, Wilson, David A., 'The D'Arcy McGee Affair and the Suspension of Habeas Corpus', in Wright, Barry, and Binnie, Susan, (eds.), *Canadian State*

of 1866, far from undermining Fenianism, had become a source of inspiration for revolutionaries on both sides of the Atlantic. There was widespread anger within Fenian circles at the trials and sentences of Fenian prisoners, and it was largely British pressure that led to the Canadian government not executing any prisoners. The Fenian Brotherhood remained a formidable force recently responsible for violence in England, and was still powerful in Ireland.[56] Macdonald presented Fenianism as an external threat and the suspension bill consequently generated little opposition.[57] However, the Halifax *Morning Chronicle* condemned the measure as 'outrageous'[58] and the *Morning Freeman* was initially sceptical arguing that the government should wait until an actual emergency arose before suspending Habeas Corpus. In general, there was no public protest and it generated little debate in parliament.[59] This, as Macdonald knew, was only half the story and deliberately omitted the Canadian Fenians and their role in Fenian strategy.

How widespread collective trauma was in 1866 and 1868 is difficult to estimate. Intense after the invasions in June 1866 and McGee's assassination in April 1868 and compounded by fears of the loyalty of Irish-Canadians, its intensity quickly receded in part because of the prompt action by Macdonald's government in providing additional security. It remained a residual trace throughout the 1870s and 1880s in anti-Catholicism and re-emerged briefly during the invasions in 1870s and 1871. Memory of the Fenian movement soon faded and later generations of Irish Catholic Canadians emphasised their loyalty during the decades following Confederation. They increasingly became part of the English Canadian mainstream, what has been called the 'de-greening' of the Irish though this should not be exaggerated and republican Irish nationalism revived in the early-twentieth century.[60] Whether the Fenians invasions hastened Confederation is doubtful, since the process had already begun, but

Trials, Volume 3: Political Trials and Security Measures, 1840-1914, (University of Toronto Press), 2009, pp. 85-92.

[56] 'The Fenian Imbroglio', *Irish Canadian*, 1 January 1868.

[57] *St Catherines Constitutional*, 21 November 1867, reported the parliamentary debates on Tuesday 19 November.

[58] Halifax *Morning Chronicle*, 2 December 1867.

[59] Timothy Anglin had been critical of the initial suspension, see, *Morning Freeman*, 10 July 1866.

[60] McGowan, M. G., 'The de-greening of the Irish: Toronto's Irish Catholic press, imperialism, and the forging of a new identity, 1887-1914', Canadian Historical Association, *Historical Papers*, (1989), pp. 118-145.

they exerted a strong influence over its eventual outcome and in that respect:

Canadians have gained more in national character during the last six years than in the previous twenty, and... the outrageous proceedings of the Fenians...have been among the chief agencies.[61]

Riel, the Métis and collective trauma

This section will focus on the Métis rather than the First Nations though there are important parallels in their experience.[62] In Lower Canada, collective trauma relates to the continuing effects of the rebellions in 1837 and 1838 on French-Canadians. The rebellions took place over a relatively short timescale, a matter of weeks spread across a year, and in a confined geographical space. The traumatic effect of the Fenian invasions was short-lived and episodic. By contrast, among the Métis and the First Nations involved in the rebellions in 1885, the sense of collective trauma emerged over a longer time-scale and in more expansive public space. It was not the result of a single event but a gradual process of collective realisation that lasted for much of the nineteenth century and evolved through several stages.[63]

The Métis descended from the children of British and French-Canadian fur traders who married First Nations and Inuit women, mainly First Nations Cree, Ojibwa or Saulteaux and played a central role in the success of the western fur trade. The fur trade was dominated by two competing companies: the Hudson's Bay Company formed in London in 1670 and the North West Company formed a century later in Montreal. The NWC dominated the plains and forests from Upper Canada, even though the lands stretching eastward from

---

[61] *The Weekly Globe*, 1870, cit, ibid, Neidhardt, W. S., *Fenianism in North America*, p. 135.

[62] Waiser, Bill, and Stonechild, Blair, *Loyal Till Death: Indians and the North-West Rebellion*, (Fifth House Publishers), 1997, 2010, explodes the myth of a grand Métis-Indian alliance. See also, Tobias, John L., 'Canada's Subjugation of the Plains Cree', *Canadian Historical Review*, Vol. 64, (1983), pp. 519-548.

[63] Dr Maria Yellow Horse Braveheart, conceptualised historical trauma in the 1980s, as a way to develop stronger understanding of why life for many Native Americans is not fulfilling 'the American Dream'. Her work is particularly relevant to the Métis. See particularly her 'Wakiksuyapi: Carrying the historical trauma of the Lakota', *Disaster and Traumatic Stress: Research and Intervention, Tulane Studies in Social Welfare*, Vol. 21-22, (2000), pp. 21-22, 245-266.

the Rockies legally formed part of Rupert's Land owned by the HBC.[64]

The initial stage began in 1812 when the first Scottish settlers arrived at Red River, seen by the Métis as a threat to their dominance of the local economy. The process of change in Rupert's Land began in 1809 when Lord Selkirk bought financial control of the HBC, in order to found a new colony within its territories.[65] The War of 1812 and the hard winters of 1812-1813 and 1813-1814 led to restrictions on the export of pemmican and on running buffalo, a practice seen as driving herds out of the reach of the settlers. To the Métis, these were direct attacks on their way of life. In 1816, asserting what they saw as their rights, a group of Métis buffalo hunters led by Cuthbert Grant, of Scots and Cree descent, were involved in a prairie skirmish at Seven Oaks, where twenty settlers, their new governor, Robert Semple and one Métis were killed.[66] The killings appear not to have been planned but for the settlers and other Canadians Seven Oaks was a 'massacre'. This justified the subjugation of the Métis and confirmed their image as a barbaric and savage people. This view of the Métis as less than civilised was then reinforced by generations of historians that allowed the rebellions in 1869 and 1885 to be seen as inevitable clashes between civilised and primitive societies.

Red River settlers acted as a catalyst sharpening Métis awareness of their distinctive culture and way of life. The Métis participated with growing confidence in two worlds: one Indian and pre-capitalist, the other European and capitalist.[67] Ens maintains that Métis identity was defined less by biology or blood but by the economic and social niche they carved out for themselves within the fur trade. They adapted quickly to the changed economic conditions of the 1840s and influenced change by opening new markets especially in the buffalo

---

[64] Bumsted, John M., *Trials and Tribulations: The Emergence of Manitoba 1821-1870*, (Great Plains Publications), 2003, set the context for events in the late 1860s. See also, Morton, W. L., *Manitoba: A History*, (University of Toronto Press), 1957, second edition, (University of Toronto Press), 1967.

[65] Gray, J. M., *Lord Selkirk of Red River*, (Macmillan), 1964, remains useful but has been largely superseded by Bumsted, J. M., *Lord Selkirk: A Life*, (University of Manitoba Press), 2008, see especially pp. 181-218, on the establishment of Red River.

[66] Ibid, Bumsted, J. M., *Lord Selkirk*, pp. 303-316. See also, Bakewell, Lawrence J., *The Battle of Seven Oaks: A Métis Perspective*, (Louis Riel Institute), 2010. On Grant see, Woodcock, George, 'Cuthbert Grant', *DCB*, Vol. 8, pp. 341-344.

[67] Ens, Gerhard J., *Homeland to Hinterland: The Changing Worlds of the Red River Métis in the Nineteenth Century*, (University of Toronto Press), 1996, provides an overview of change for the Red River Métis.

robe trade. Nonetheless, pressures on the Métis way of life were increasing and rising industrial demand for buffalo hides resulted in overhunting.[68] Also native belief that the free gifts of nature were to be shared was being challenged by an increasing number of settlers, whose agricultural and industrial way of life was based on a more restricted access to the land and its resources.

The second phase in the developing collective trauma for the Métis corresponded to the growing economic competition from largely Protestant settlers after 1850 and the destruction of the buffalo, the core of their physical and spiritual well-being. Once politicians in Ontario recognised that the western interior was a potential location for settler expansion, there was increasing pressure on the Métis way of life. Rising land prices in Ontario and the explosion in railway construction that eventually led to the building of Canadian Pacific Railway created visions of commercial wealth that could only be accomplished by western expansion.[69] From the early-1860s, large numbers of Anglophone Protestants settlers arrived from Ontario, who were generally insensitive to Métis culture, hostile to Roman Catholicism and many were advocates of Canadian expansionism. Morton concluded that the Métis' chief fear was not immigration but the settlers' language and Protestant religion.[70] At the same time, many Americans migrated there, some of whom favoured annexation of the territory by the United States. These perceptions of race, class and religion reinforced social divisions in Red River even among the Métis. The English-speaking Métis saw themselves as part of a 'European or agricultural party' and closer to civilisation than the French-speaking Métis who continued to hunt or take part in trading expeditions and who seemed to be veering towards 'the native or aboriginal party'.[71] Against this backdrop of religious, nationalist and racial tensions, political uncertainty was high and was now handled with monumental

---

[68] Foster, John, 'The Métis and the End of the Plains Buffalo in Alberta', in Foster, John, Harrison, Dick, and MacLaren, I. S., (eds.), *Buffalo*, (University of Alberta Press), 1992, pp. 61-78.

[69] Warner, Donald F., *The Idea of Continental Union: Agitation for the Annexation of Canada to the United States 1849-1893*, (University of Kentucky Press), 1960, pp. 99-127, considers the annexationist issues in relation to the Red River Settlement.

[70] Morton, W. L., (ed.), *Alexander Begg's Red River journal; and other papers relative to the Red River resistance of 1869-1870*, (Champlain Society), 1956, p. 2.

[71] Friesen, Gerald, *The Canadian Prairies: A History*, (University of Toronto Press), 1987, pp. 92-97.

ineptness leading to resistance in 1869 and 1870 and to the North-West rebellion in 1885.[72]

The third phase in the evolving collective trauma among the Métis occurred between 1869 and 1885 culminating in their military defeat. Although the 1871 census counted 9,800 Métis, of whom 5,720 were French compared with about 4,000 English speakers and less than 1,000 Canadian settlers, population growth was increasingly the result of Ontarian immigration.[73] The mishandled transfer of political authority for Rupert's Land from the HBC to the new Dominion precipitated Riel's resistance in 1869-1870. The Manitoba Act 1870 resolved the constitutional impasse and contained most of the rights demanded by the Métis including guarantees of land title. The rapid alienation of Métis land after 1870 has been blamed on the large numbers of Ontarian settlers arriving in Manitoba, the 'thriftless' and 'improvident' character of the Métis and land speculators who took advantage of the unwitting Métis. Some of the Métis could not cope with changing economic conditions and this pushed them further into the interior. The tragedy was that Riel was absent during the crucial period of land distribution between 1870 and 1885 and the Métis nation began to disintegrate. This view was challenged in the 1970s and 1980s by historians who concluded that the Métis were not simply nomadic people but 'persistent settlers'. Some Métis adapted well to their new economic realities and became successful farmers, merchants and professionals and that, far from being pushed out of Red River, they were attracted by economic opportunities to move into the Western interior. The rapid alienation of land was the result, not of Ontarian settlers or speculators, but of the failure of the federal government to allow the bulk of land grants to pass into Métis hands. Whatever the government' culpability, the Métis acquired only a fraction of the land to which they were entitled and as a result, many Red River Métis left Manitoba. For Sprague, the 1885 Rebellion was a direct result of these policies.[74]

For those involved in North-West Rebellion in 1885 the results were disastrous. Riel was unable to construct a coalition of the oppressed as he had in Manitoba and his support among the Métis

---

[72] For discussion of the Red River Resistance, 1869-1870 and the rebellion in 1885, see Brown, Richard, *Rebellion in Canada, 1837-1885, Volume 2: The Irish, the Fenians and the Métis*, (CreateSpace), 2012, pp. 305-345, 354-421.

[73] *Census of Canada, 1870-71*, (I. B. Taylor), 1876, Vol. 4, pp. 380-387.

[74] Sprague, D. N., *Canada and the Métis, 1869-1885*, (Wilfrid Laurier University Press), 1988, and ibid, Friesen, G., *The Canadian Prairies: A History*, pp. 197-199.

was significantly weaker. Sir John Macdonald was not prepared to negotiate as he had done in 1870 and the Canadian Pacific Railway facilitated the rapid deployment of troops to put down the rebellion. Within three months, federal control of Saskatchewan was re-established and Riel, who had proved a flawed political and military leader and led his people to defeat, was imprisoned awaiting trial and execution. The Canadian government reinforced its authority in Saskatchewan trying members of the First Nations it believed were guilty of treason.[75] The Rebellion also helped to placate settler frustration towards eastern Canada. Instead of focussing their anger at federal government, they now directed their anger at the Métis. The increasing alienation felt by western settler communities was replaced by a movement of Canadian nationalism based on the perceived common 'threat' of Métis and Indian armed insurgency.

The final stage in the collective trauma of the Métis was their systematic marginalisation within prairie society. Race became central to how those living in Saskatchewan were treated. Macdonald declared that his government would deal with the Métis either as Indians or as Whites but not as a distinct people, a policy of non-recognition that culminated in the Métis being taken out of the census as a distinct people in 1941. English Canadians dealt with a restive minority nationality by defining it out of existence. Canadians settlers, both English and French speaking, were soon privileged over Aboriginal peoples in Saskatchewan. In addition, their property and homes were protected while Métis homes and property were destroyed by military and volunteers following their defeat. Many Métis in Saskatchewan dispersed and those who stayed and who were decided by the government to be non-participants in the conflict were given 'scrip', land or monetary allotments valued at $160 to $240. This proved a systemic failure. Many Métis never received their scrip and other Métis families did not have the money to invest in the farming equipment needed to make use of land and sold their scrip.

Métis scrip was often sold to corrupt capitalists who, after following the Treaty No. 8 Half-Breed Commission to northern Saskatchewan, offered payment of between $70 and $130. Nine-tenths of scrip issued to Métis ended up in the hands of bankers, lawyers, speculators and financial institutions. Great wealth was generated from the dispossession of Métis from their lands. This dispossession

---

[75] There were 84 trials: 71 for treason-felony, 12 for murder and Riel's trial for high treason. Of the 81 Indians jailed, 44 were convicted and 8 hanged for murder. Of the 46 Métis taken into custody, 19 were convicted, 7 conditionally discharged and Riel was hanged; the rest were either unconditionally discharged or not brought to trial.

continued after the scrip fiasco, with many Métis forced to become squatters or residents on land called 'road allowance'. As more displaced Métis joined together on the side of these roads, small shanty communities built of discarded lumber or logs begun to spring up, creating the term 'The Road Allowance People'. From 1885 to 1945, the landless Métis moved from locale to locale, often forcibly, in order to make a living and live among themselves. During these decades, colonialism also began to take away the Métis' individual and collective identity as they were deprived of their land because of systemic racism, scrip speculation and government policies such as the Prairie Farm Rehabilitation Act 1935 that gave the state the power to remove the Métis forcibly from their homes.

As more settlers flooded into the prairies, the Métis' social marginalisation increased. Because they were not taxpayers or landowners, their children were denied basic access to public schools. Some Métis children managed to enter reserve schools or were accepted into separate Catholic institutions but they were a small minority. Those Métis children who attended these schools often encountered discrimination from other children, teachers, priests and nuns. The Michif language, their customs and even their poverty were ridiculed. Without a basic education, there was little chance for social improvement and until the 1930s and 1940s provincial and federal governments failed to address their social, economic and political marginalisation.

The creation of Alberta and Saskatchewan as provinces in 1905 further complicated matters as the Métis were now divided under different provincial governments making a coordinated approach to their problems more difficult and also making it difficult for them to speak with a single voice. While the cultural dispossession of their collective and individual identity was testing, the loss of their land was in many respects more traumatic because it took away the economic levers of survival from large sections of the Métis community. Their dream of living free and independent lives was abruptly taken away from them. Métis communities were largely self-governed on a local basis but subject to persecution by Canadian officials. They encountered a settler society that did little to ensure that their cultural, educational and land rights would be protected. Despite local involvement, the Métis people received little national recognition or political rights until 1982, when they were named one of Canada's three Aboriginal people. The following year, the Métis National Council was created bringing together Métis organisations in each province to represent the Métis nation on the national and international stage.

At an end?

The ways in which we remember the past and the ways in which its histories are constructed play a significant role in determining how we see our places in society today and how we perceive our possible futures. The ways in which minority rights are protected and the extent to which those minorities have cultural or political autonomy within their localities raises questions about how the interests of minorities are reconciled within majoritarian democracies. Within the Canadian system of government, this question is mediated in the relationship between provincial and federal governments and through key judicial decisions on constitutional principles. This is, however, a process that took a century to establish and the experience of the nineteenth century suggests that 'Canada First' was the *raison d'être* of much political thinking and practice and where attempts were made to subsume minorities within an anglicised state.

The persistence of rebellion against colonial and then federal executive government between 1837 and 1885 shows that the idea of 'Canada First' was not without vehement critics among those minorities who felt, not without justification, that their existence as distinctive ethnic groups was threatened by the broader continental interests of capitalist oriented economic and political interests. Those communities called for ethnic recognition and political autonomy or separation, something that was incompatible with the long-term objectives of the governing political elite for a centralised, executive dominated Protestant state.

We cannot measure the traumatic effect of the Rebellions of 1837-1838 without considering its background and aftermath. The rebels represented the single attempted seizure of power by the French-Canadian community and marked the beginnings of greater collective awareness and calls for greater political responsibility. The failure of the rebellions in 1837 and 1838 was followed by the Durham *Report* in which French-Canadian society was judged harshly.[76] Instead, he found 'two nations warring in the bosom of a single state...a

---

[76] Martin, Ged, *The Durham Report and British Policy: a critical essay*, (Cambridge University Press), 1972, republished 2008, provides a useful critique of the *Report* and 'Attacking the Durham myth: seventeen years on', *Journal of Canadian Studies/Revue d'Études Canadiennes*, Vol. 25, (1990), pp. 39-59, provide a further critical thrust. Ajzenstat, Janet, *The Political Thought of Lord Durham*, (McGill-Queen's University Press), 1988, provides a revisionist approach. Ducharme, Michel, 'L'État selon Lord Durham: liberté et nationalité dans l'empire britannique', *Cahiers d'Histoire*, Vol. 18, (1998), pp. 39-64, is a challenging contribution.

struggle, not of principles, but of races' and a 'deadly animosity that now separates the inhabitants of Lower Canada into the hostile divisions of French and English'.[77] By contrast, he found the British minority forward-looking, concerned to advance the material development of the province and frustrated by French-Canadian opposition to any progressive measures.[78] Durham concluded that French-Canadian society was not viable and unable to establish a suitable national identity and that French-Canadians were 'a people without history and without literature'.

The intention behind his words is even more devastating since he was not entirely wrong. Unlike other peoples who rose up against monarchies and empire, French-Canadians were neither numerous nor rich and did not have a long history or remarkable cultural heritage. The descendants of French settlers distinguished themselves from French officials who came to and then left New France, but French-Canadians were never recognised as a separate cultural group by the French authorities and this tradition continued under British rule after 1760. What distinguished French-Canadians was their language and their Catholicism, both regarded as central to their heritage, which they sought to protect from assimilation into a British, Protestant polity. Weinmann suggests that the rejection of England to whom French-Canadians transferred their allegiance after being abandoned by France in 1760 was far more traumatic than the political violence itself.[79] Conscious of their weakness, French-Canadians had little regard for either England or France and only wished to preserve their language and their religious faith. For some this was achieved by working within the system of government introduced in 1841, while others sought solace in the revived Roman Catholic Church. But in the decades after 1840 there was a steady stream of French-Canadian immigrants to the northern United States though, for many, this was as much an economic as a political decision.

Durham maintained that individual rights should be preserved and that the operation of a democratic political system would provide

---

[77] Lucas, C. P., (ed.), *Lord Durham's Report on the Affairs of British North America*, 3 Vols. (Oxford University Press), 1912, reprinted, (Augustus Kelley), 1970, Vol. 2, p. 16.

[78] Ibid, Lucas, C. P., (ed.), *Lord Durham's Report on the Affairs of British North America*, pp. 34-37.

[79] Weinmann, Heinz, *Du Canada au Québec, Généalogie d'une histoire*, (Hexagone), 1987.

the means for their 'natural' demise and assimilation.[80] Repression in 1837 and 1838 was swift and civic freedoms quickly restored largely because the revolutionaries of 1837-1838 never recovered from their defeat. This has generally been interpreted as evidence that a revolutionary spirit had never been a real option for French-Canadians. In fact, many of the key reformers after 1837 such as LaFontaine had been Patriotes but that after their defeat:

> Nous sommes des Réformistes, nous cessons d'être des Révolutionnaires.

The Reformers tended to define themselves as liberals, but their liberalism, Bédard acknowledges:

> ...is not a quest for freedom for the individual...it is a struggle for the recognition of a distinct nationality that felt marginalised.[81]

Progressive in economic and social matters, the Reformers were politically conservative, because they feared the 'potentially dangerous effects of democracy on the cohesion of the French-Canadian nation.'[82] The fear of democracy highlighted the tense relationship that politicians had with reformist politics and that being:

> ...scared of division, [was] probably typical of minority nations who fear for their survival.[83]

Traumatised by the division of political forces in 1837, for which they were largely responsible, reformers developed a 'fear of reflection' especially about their pasts as well as an obsession with cohesion, harmony and unity, an obsession that led to a purely cultural definition of French-Canadian nation.[84]

The initial perceptions of Union in 1841 among French-Canadians were overwhelmingly negative and for some, such as

---

[80] Ajzenstat, Janet, 'Liberalism and assimilation: Lord Durham reconsidered', in Brooks, Stephen, (ed.), *Political Thought in Canada: Contemporary Perspectives*, (Irwin Pub.), 1984, pp. 239-257.

[81] Bédard, Éric, *Les Réformistes: Une génération canadienne-française au milieu du XIXe siècle*, (Boréal), 2009, p. 95.

[82] Ibid, Bédard, Éric, *Les Réformistes: Une génération canadienne-française au milieu du XIXe siècle*, p. 110.

[83] Ibid, Bédard, Éric, *Les Réformistes: Une génération canadienne-française au milieu du XIXe siècle*, pp. 125-127.

[84] Ibid, Bédard, Éric, *Les Réformistes: Une génération canadienne-française au milieu du XIXe siècle*, p. 100.

Papineau, this remained the case. However, many of the initial concerns about the legislation proved short-lived largely because of the political manoeuvring of LaFontaine and his Reform Party in Canada East and the revival of the role of the Roman Catholic Church. By the late 1840s, responsible government had been accepted in London and the representative equality between the two parts of the United Province worked to the French-Canadian advantage when they lost their demographic dominance by the early 1850s. Union was perhaps less of a disaster for French-Canadians than many initially thought.

The Reformers of the 1840s and 1850s were once regarded as among the 'great Canadians' and Hippolyte LaFontaine ranged in the same pantheon in the history of Quebec as Jacques Cartier, Samuel de Champlain and Dollard des Ormeaux. Then came the Quiet Revolution debunking this history and replacing its heroes with magnificent losers. The Patriotes and the Rouges became the focus of interest while the Reformers were seen as opportunists, collaborators or even traitors though there appears to have recently been some rehabilitation of their status.[85] The problem with any approach to history that seeks to better understand an uncertain present and tries to understand that present through interrogating the symptoms and symbols of the past is that, in seeking to produce a grand narrative, it generally distorts the past and frequently fails to illuminate the present.[86]

The result of the incompatibility of the aims of minority groups and the needs of the colonial and then federal state has been different types of collective trauma and remembrance for the communities involved. For French-Canadians, that trauma persists despite the successful, if fraught, defence of minority rights in Quebec since 1841 and the devolved nature of provincial rule in today's Quebec. It is reflected in the historiographical shift from a focus on the reformist politicians of the 1840s and 1850s and the playing out of the political consequences of responsible government and later Confederation to the heroic and revolutionary actions of the radical Patriotes. That this is reflected in contemporary political thinking in the tensions between

---

[85] See, for example, Kelly, Stephane, *La petite loterie: Comment la couronne a obtenu la collaboration du Canada français apres 1837*, (Boréal), 1999.
[86] For instance, in *Le Fleurdelisé*, Spring 2013 celebrating the tenth Journée nationale des Patriotes on 20 May, Gilles Laporte suggests that patriotes were responsible for the birth of the free press in Canada in 1806 as well as responsible government in 1849. There may be some tangential justification for this using 'patriotes' but certainly not Patriotes since neither Bédard in 1806 or LaFontaine in 1849 were Patriotes in the sense that that term was used between the mid-1820s and 1839.

sovereignty or separation shows that the collective trauma evident in the aftermath of the rebellions is still unresolved. Can French-Canadians retain their cultural and religious heritage within a multicultural federal state and is a devolved system of government allow this to occur?

By contrast, the Fenian rebellions had a traumatic effect that was short-lived and episodic in character. Although the Fenian threat to Canada in support of Irish independence persisted from the mid-1860s to the 1880s, it was in the immediate aftermath of the invasions in 1866 and the assassination of D'Arcy McGee in 1868 that its traumatic effect was at its most intense. Politicians such as Sir John Macdonald were adept in portraying the Fenians as an external rather than internal threat and this helped to limit the trauma. This is reflected in the lack of immediate commemoration of those Canadians who died during the Fenian campaigns in 1866 and in the failure of historians until recently to consider the extent of Fenianism in Canada. The collective trauma caused by the threats from Fenianism was simply forgotten and became part of Canada's hidden history.

While French-Canadians were able to protect their heritage against attack even though they had risen in rebellion, the Métis of the North-West could not. Increasingly a minority in what they considered their own lands, their resistance in 1869-1870 and especially the rebellion in 1885 were represented by their opponents as evidence of a primitive culture that needed to be replaced by the more progressive, expansionist values of Ontarian Canada. Their way of life disintegrated because of the destruction of the buffalo herds and the questionable approach to their land rights by provincial and federal government. This initiated decades of collective trauma when the Métis' economic, social and cultural traditions were dismantled and their very existence was erased from the 1941 National Census. Some Métis adapted to the new conditions, while others succeeded by denying their heritage by claiming to be French-Canadian but most did not drift into economic dependence. Most of today's Métis live in cities and towns, send their children to public or separate schools and are self-supporting with the same rights and aspirations of other Canadian citizens. Yet of the experiences considered in this chapter, theirs has been the most traumatic and long-lasting. It took over a century for the Métis to obtain constitutional recognition and their rights remain under judicial consideration. In January 2013, the Federal Court ruled in *Daniels* that 200,000 Métis and 400,000 non-status Indians in Canada are indeed 'Indians' under the Constitution Act 1867 and fall under federal jurisdiction. This resolved the complaint among non-status or Métis people that for years they have been told they were a provincial responsibility, only to have the provinces tell them they were the purview of the federal government, something that had left them in a jurisdictional limbo.[87] *Daniels* is not about Métis rights such as land, harvesting or self-government: land rights, for instance the Supreme Court in March 2013 ruled in *Manitoba Métis Federation v. Canada* that 'the Federal Crown failed to implement the land grant provision set out in s. 31 of the Manitoba Act, 1870 in accordance with the honour of the Crown'. It simply answers the constitutional question of whether the federal government had legislative jurisdiction for Métis.

The position of French-Canadians and the Métis in modern Canadian society remains contested and their collective trauma links their experiences in the past with their experiences today. The American economist Thomas Sowell uses the term 'cosmic justice' to identify injustices that may have occurred decades before but whose effects have been felt over generations by minority groups.[88] Governments may make symbolic concessions, but the cost of compensating minority groups will be borne by other living Canadians. One of the paradoxes of cosmic justice is that those who may have committed wrongs and those who may have been wronged are long dead but this does not prevent peoples pursuing justice in our own time and for society as a whole carrying the costs. Winston Churchill once said, when Britain was in its greatest peril and experiencing an intense collective trauma, 'it is not the end, it is not the beginning of the end, but it is the end of the beginning'. It is a sentiment that could equally be applied to those groups in Canada that have in their past experienced collective trauma.

---

[87] The federal government appealed the decision to the Federal Court of Appeal on 6 February 2013. The next appeal level after that would be the Supreme Court of Canada. It is highly likely these appeals will take several years. It is expected that the federal government will not move forward on implementing *Daniels* while the case is under appeal. It will likely take the position that the 'matter is before the courts' in order to avoid discussions and negotiations with the Métis Nation on the potential implications from *Daniels*.
[88] Sowell, Thomas, *The Quest for Cosmic Justice*, (The Free Press), 1999, pp. 1-48,

8 Conclusions

From the mid-sixteenth until the mid-twentieth century, the Protestant-Catholic divide was the primary religious, political and social fracture in the European, North American and Australasian worlds. During the nineteenth century Canada witnessed 'wars of religion' that had many of the same characteristics as the 'wars' that occurred in Europe: a 'war of words', sectarian violence and civil and community conflict. This is not to suggest that religion was the only reason for these conflicts but that as a cause of conflict in Canadian politics, religion has not been accorded the import it held for contemporaries. Although this should not be overdrawn, there were similarities between nineteenth century Canada and Ireland with widespread anti-Catholic feeling, a powerful Orange Order and a French-Canadian Catholic population in Quebec alienated from the English-speaking Protestant majority in the rest of the country. Unlike Ireland, by 1900, the country adopted a path in which religious conflict, though tensions still existed, was contained within an increasingly secularised society.

As the colonial and federal state sought to enhance its authority and establish political stability, religion especially in its populist form acted as a source of conflict and instability. Sectarian violence predated Famine immigration but was intensified by it. In the Maritime Provinces and in Ontario, conflict over employment, the development of the Orange Order and its aggressive marching and Irish defence of their communities resulted in running street battles especially during the late 1840s, 1850s and 1860s. What led to their decline was not a reduction in tensions between Orange and Green, confrontations continue after 1870, but the opposition of political liberals to crude populist sectarian displays and the success of conservative constitutionalism in containing and controlling public disorder.

In each of the rebellions there was an underlying tension between Roman Catholicism and Protestantism that, in many respects represented Canada's 'wars of religion'. French-Canadians, many Irish-Americans and Irish-Canadians and French Métis were united in their Catholicism while their opponents in the loyalist colonial and federal states found unity in their Protestantism. Although there were clear doctrinal differences between Catholicism and Protestantism, the issue was less one of belief itself than of the collective identity that came from having particular beliefs and of their social, political and cultural expression. Perhaps dealing with ideas is easier than dealing with people but the result is an editing out of the humanity but editing in the inhumanity of the rebellions by removing the people who played a role in the events or at least those who acted out of humanity. The French-Canadians, the Fenians and the Métis had to lose not because they were Catholic but because of the cultural values that their Catholicism inculcated contradicted the modernising, expansionist 'manifest destiny' of the Canadian state.

Central to the ending of the 'wars of religion' was the recognition and acceptance of pluralism in religion and the increasingly secular nature of Canadian society.[1] This is not to negate the importance of individual religious belief, and the degree to which this was a matter of private rather than societal significance was not decided in favour of the former until the mid-twentieth century. Religion observance was gradually regarded as one among many demands on the individual's time, interests and beliefs and became less significant in defining and situating one's place in the community. The impact of secularisation for Protestants and Catholics was substantially different, was contested and, often grudgingly, eventually accepted at different times and in different ways by different communities.

The 1840s marked the beginnings of a devotional revolution in Catholicism that saw a revitalisation of religious life and the strengthening of the church's role in education and social welfare. Unlike in Protestantism, secularisation was a twentieth not a nineteenth century occurrence. In Quebec, fears of assimilation resulted in the Catholic Church being transformed into the aggressive defender of French-Canadian heritage, culture and nationalist aspirations. The central place of the Catholic Church in education, health services and welfare continued into the twentieth century. Despite a history of anti-clericalism and radical demands, evident among Patriotes and the Rouges for a separation of church and state, secularisation did not develop as a major force in Quebeçois society until the Quiet Revolution and the Second Vatican Council. Although the devotional revolution impacted on English-speaking Catholic communities, those communities existed in less homogenous societies than French-speaking Quebec. For instance, in the diverse and more pluralistic society of Ontario, something that may explain its more extreme sectarian violence, the Catholic Irish were under greater pressure to conform to the values of English-speaking Canada. Although resisted by local churches, this led to accommodations between Protestants and Catholics that, in the case of the significant number inter-faith marriages in Toronto compromised Catholic

---

[1] Marshall, David B., 'Canadian Historians, Secularization and the Problem of the Nineteenth Century', Canadian Catholic Historical Association, *Historical Studies*, Vol. 60, (1993-1994), pp. 57-81, is a valuable historiographical survey of the issue.

religious beliefs as the children of these marriages were not always brought up in the Catholic faith. This indicates the potency of secularisation in pluralistic societies.

The forces of secularisation within Protestant culture were more powerful. In Protestant Canada, the 1840s marked the beginnings of the separation of church and state, a contentious political issue that acknowledged the realities of pluralism and dissent within Protestantism. The persistence of religious pluralism forced those who believed in an established church, though the Anglican Church never came close to achieving this in the Canadian provinces, designed to uphold one 'true' faith reluctantly to abandon any claim to have a religious monopoly. Protestant denominations now were subjected to the vagaries of the religious market and had to compete for the souls of the people in order to maintain adequate support. Conviction that an established faith was essential for religious progress was replaced by the 'voluntary principle', the belief that the state should not support the churches or clergy. Instead, an increasing number of evangelicals thought that support should be based on voluntary contributions made solely by church members and supporters. Only in this way, voluntarists argued, would true religion flourish as it would have to make no compromises with the state. A certain level of toleration was a necessary response to the diversity of religious beliefs and practices that was firmly rooted in the fabric of Canadian society by the 1850s, but it had limits. Populist rivalry and bigotry persisted between the main Protestant denominations and there were limitations to the toleration offered to religious groups beyond the Protestant mainstream. Protestant-Catholic bigotry also was a persistent theme throughout the nineteenth century often focussing on divisive issues such as provincial schools questions or the role of religious parades rather than on how church members interacted at local levels. [2]

Secularisation generally occurs when people are confronted with fundamental changes in their lives. Advances in technology, the development of an individualistic capitalist economy, a growing emphasis on consumerism and leisure, urbanisation and changing patterns of thought undermined the personal and social significance of the traditional church-dominated Sunday. In Canada as in Britain, this predated the rise of evolutionary thought and biblical criticism of the late-nineteenth century and calls into question the timing of the 'crisis of faith' with which they are generally associated. This did not mean that religion was suddenly and dramatically moved to the margins. It

---

[2] McGowan, Mark, 'Rethinking Catholic-Protestant Relations in Canada: The Episcopal Reports of 1900-1901', Canadian Catholic Historical Association, *Historical Studies*, Vol. 59, (1992), pp. 11-35.

remained a vibrant force within society, church growth continued and there was extensive revivalist activity. The church remained a powerful force but competition for support from a host of social forces and institutions began to move the church away from the core of society and culture to one in which it had to share its traditional status as being integral to society and people's lives. The pluralistic character of Canada meant that no one institution, activity, set of beliefs or moral code could dominate.

The nineteenth century saw a redrawing of the boundaries between religious and secular across the Atlantic world, a process that had its origins in the medieval dichotomy between the transcendental Civitas Dei and the immanent Civitas hominis. In fact, the gradual process of secularisation in the nineteenth century only makes sense as a response and reaction to the medieval Christian classification of reality into 'spiritual' and 'temporal'. During the nineteenth century, especially after 1860, for Canadian Protestants, there was a blurring of the boundaries of the religious and the secular while Roman Catholics were able to maintain clear boundaries and there was a strong antagonistic dynamic between lay and clerical. This distinction was also evident in their attitudes to modern capitalism and the state. For Protestants, there was 'collusion' between the religious and the secular with little evidence of tensions between Canadian Protestantism and capitalism. By contrast, Canadian Roman Catholicism often found itself on a collision course with secular institutions whether economic or political because of their Protestant nature. This was evident in the changing relationships between religion, violence and state building.

Index

About the Author

Richard Brown is a Fellow of both the Royal Historical Society and the Historical Association. He was, until he retired, Head of History and Citizenship at Manshead School in Dunstable, and has published sixty-three print and Kindle books, over 50 articles and papers on nineteenth century history and countless reviews. He is the author of a successful blog, The History Zone, which has a wide audience among pupils, students and researchers.

Recent publications

The Woman Question: Sex, Work and Politics 1780-1945, (Authoring History), 2020. Also available in a Kindle edition.
Radicalism and Chartism 1790-1860, (*Reconsidering Chartism*, Authoring History), 2018. Also available in a Kindle edition.
Britain 1780-1945: Society under Pressure, (Authoring History), 2018. Also available in a Kindle version.
People and Places: Britain 1780-1950, (Authoring History), 2017. Also available in a Kindle version.
Disrupting the British World, 1600-1980, 2nd ed., (*Rebellion Quartet*, Authoring History), 2017. Also available in a Kindle version.
Famine, Fenians and Freedom, 1830-1882, 2nd ed., (*Rebellion Quartet*, Authoring History), 2017. Also available in a Kindle version.
Britain 1780-1850: A Simple Guide, (Authoring History), 2017.
Three Rebellions: Canada, South Wales and Australia, (*Rebellion Quartet*, Authoring History), 2nd ed., 2016. Also available in a Kindle version.
Roger of Sicily: Portrait of a Ruler, (Authoring History), 2016. Also available in a Kindle version.
Robert Guiscard: Portrait of a Warlord, (Authoring History), 2016. Also available in a Kindle version.
Abbot Suger, The Life of Louis VI 'the Fat', (Authoring History), 2016. Also available in a Kindle version.
Chartism: A Global History and other essays, (*Reconsidering Chartism*, Authoring History), 2016. Also available in a Kindle version.
The Chartists, Regions and Economies, (*Reconsidering Chartism*, Authoring History), 2016. Also available in a Kindle version.
Chartism: Localities, Spaces and Places, The North, Scotland, Wales and Ireland, (*Reconsidering Chartism*, Authoring History), 2015. Also available in a Kindle version.

Chartism: Localities, Spaces and Places, The Midlands and the South, (*Reconsidering Chartism*, Authoring History), 2015. Also available in a Kindle version.

Chartism: Rise and Demise, (*Reconsidering Chartism,* Authoring History), 2014

Before Chartism: Exclusion and Resistance, (*Reconsidering Chartism,* Authoring History), 2014.

Printed in Great Britain
by Amazon

50397426R00102